Market-Driven
Strategies
in Health Care

Dean C. Coddington
Keith D. Moore

Foreword by Robert H. Waterman, Jr.

Market-Driven Strategies in Health Care

Jossey-Bass Publishers

San Francisco • London • 1988

MARKET-DRIVEN STRATEGIES IN HEALTH CARE
by Dean C. Coddington and Keith D. Moore

Copyright © 1987 by: Jossey-Bass Inc., Publishers
350 Sansome Street
San Francisco, California 94104

&

Jossey-Bass Limited
28 Banner Street
London EC1Y 8QE

Library of Congress Cataloging-in-Publication Data

Coddington, Dean C.
  Market-driven strategies in health care.

  A Joint publication in the Jossey-Bass health series
and the Jossey-Bass management series.
  Bibliography: p.
  Includes index.
  1. Hospitals—Marketing. 2. Strategic planning.
I. Moore, Keith D. II. Title. III. Series: Jossey-Bass
health series. IV. Series: Jossey-Bass management series.
[DNLM: 1. Delivery of Health Care—economics—United
States. 2. Marketing of Health Services—trends—United
States. W 74 C669m]
RA965.5.C59   1987   362.1′068′8   86-46330
ISBN 1-55542-045-1 (alk. paper)

Manufactured in the United States of America

The paper in this book meets the guidelines for
permanence and durability of the Committee on
Production Guidelines for Book Longevity of the
Council on Library Resources.

JACKET DESIGN BY WILLI BAUM

FIRST EDITION
    First printing: May 1987
    Second printing: August 1988

Code 8718

A joint publication in
The Jossey-Bass Health Series
and
The Jossey-Bass Management Series

Contents

Contents

Foreword

In one way or another, each of us is affected by the health care establishment in this country. Whether we must undergo a long hospital stay or do what we can to remain healthy on a day-to-day basis, the quality and cost of health care are of concern to us all. This thoughtful, carefully researched book discusses the sound and fury that has surrounded dramatic changes in the health care field in comprehensible terms. It creates synthesis out of seeming discontinuity, applies reason to apparent chaos, and treats each issue with the calm conviction that it can and probably will be sensibly resolved. With over $400 billion being spent annually by Americans on health care, there never was a time with more at stake.

This book starts where change usually begins—the marketplace. It identifies the forces affecting the three main market segments in health care: employers, physicians, and consumers. The most fundamental of these forces, I believe, is cost. The rising cost of health care, coupled with the difficulty of evaluating quality and effectiveness, is now an overriding issue for many employers. They want to know what they are getting for their money; they have lost patience with the inefficient, cost-plus approach health care organizations often take to doing business. This book examines the employer's cost/quality problem in depth. It then concludes that despite the fact that employers face very real cost pressures, they are not inclined to sacrifice quality care to expense considerations.

Although I do not doubt the accuracy of this conclusion, and although many health care providers may find it reassuring, I believe that none of us can overlook the fact that America's health delivery system continues to be outrageously inefficient and riddled with quality problems. Steps are being taken to correct these deficiencies, but they constitute a slow and modest beginning compared with the steps American industry has taken to reduce costs and improve quality in response to foreign competition.

Physicians are the second and most important market segment because they remain in a position of power as the industry changes. It is still the physician who usually decides which hospitals will be used and which treatments will be prescribed. These decisions set in motion a train of events that determine total costs, quality, and service. Physicians occupy the driver's seat and exert a dual influence as both customers of the system and power figures within it. This book analyzes physicians' roles as agents of change from both perspectives.

More than anyone else, physicians occupy a natural leadership position for spearheading change from within. Unfortunately, although physicians in this country have awesome technical competence, I believe their record as implementors of change is dismal. Regrettably, several factors argue that doctors will not rise to the challenge of initiating effective change. First of all, they treasure their independence too much to work effectively as a united group. Physicians have about as many societies, associations, and special task forces as other professionals. But because these groups are notoriously political and seem to have an interest in maintaining the status quo, they have stimulated little change over the years. A second force is the dramatic growth in the number of physicians. We already have too many, and in the near future we will have many too many. As in any other business, this oversupply will force their price down and dilute their collective power. New physicians will be only too glad to become salaried employees of profit-making hospital chains, health maintenance organizations, and other centers that provide health care outside the normal hospital. This will create an interesting situation: on the one hand, physicians will maintain their natural power base; on the other hand, there is every indication that they will not use it effectively.

The third market segment is, of course, the patient—the person who is both the focus of the system and at the mercy of it. This book suggests that consumers have dramatically changed their approach to health care, and therefore are serving as powerful catalysts for change throughout the entire industry. Consumers are becoming better educated, more discriminating, less accepting of poor quality products and services, more sensitive to cost and quality tradeoffs, more discriminating with regard to advertising, and less willing to be pushed around by the business establishment.

Only recently has the consumer's newly found sense of health care power been manifest. Traditionally, a seriously ill or badly hurt patient had no power; he or she was only too glad to receive whatever ministrations the doctor and hospital saw fit to dole out. But that is changing. Americans feel more responsible for their own health. Not only are they taking better care of themselves, and thus needing less medical care, but when they do need care, they are less prone to overlook inefficiencies in the system. A year ago, a good friend of mine had a serious accident. Within two days after the accident she had been x-rayed three times. The first time the x rays were overexposed, and the second time they were exposed correctly but the hospital lost them. Twenty years ago this sloppiness might have seemed a small price to pay for the care she was given at a time of crisis. But now she was outraged. Not without cause, she reasoned, "If this is happening with x rays, what other mistakes are being made that I will never learn about?"

This is an action-oriented book, dealing primarily with potential changes in response to competition within the health care system. It outlines strategies and presents approaches for tailoring the strategies to specific circumstances at hand. This relates to one of the major deficiencies that I see in the health care delivery system: teamwork. With the patient as the focal point, the team itself should consist of the doctors, nurses, hospital staff, and related parties who are organized to return the patient to health. But my observation is that this group of people acts like anything but a team. Doctors rarely talk to each other, and they all treat nurses like members of a lower-level caste. Nurses fill out reports that doctors never read. Different nursing shifts do not make the transfer of responsibility in a coordinated, cooperative way. Hospital administration is often treated as a necessary evil rather than as another means to benefit the patient. The emergency room is often disconnected from the rest of the hospital. Hospitals and health systems have the makings of a natural team, but what often results is a stunning lack of teamwork. It is up to the patient or the family members to try to coordinate these often recalcitrant team members. But the patient is often incapable of performing this role, and the family may be too timid to do it well. Until health care practitioners can work more effectively as a team, the cost of health care will always be higher, and the quality lower, than it needs to be.

Health care is in the midst of a period of destabilization; such dramatic change can provoke either a chaotic or a constructive response. It is in everyone's interest that the response be constructive and that the system be improved. This book is written for people in supervisory, administrative, governing, and managerial positions in health care organizations. It gives them both the factual ammunition and the strategic direction to improve the health care delivery system during this time of transition. It makes a vital contribution to the health care industry and is of more than passing interest to any of us who are affected by the quality of America's health care.

San Francisco, California
March 1987

Robert H. Waterman, Jr.
President,
Waterman & Company, Inc.
Coauthor, In Search of
Excellence

Preface

This book has its origin in 1981 when we each began serving as trustees of hospitals: Dean Coddington at Swedish Medical Center in Englewood, Colorado, and Keith Moore at Spalding Rehabilitation Hospital in Denver.

The two of us viewed our jobs as hospital trustees as opportunities for community service. Neither of us saw any relationship between the types of decisions we were participating in as volunteers at the two hospitals and our occupations as consultants for competitive industries like telecommunications, banking and finance, and high-technology manufacturing. Our clients included a television network, cable system operators, cellular telephone start-ups, banks, venture capital firms, medical equipment manufacturers, and the like. We dealt with decisions regarding new start-ups, market segmentation, business feasibility models, diversification, and product line management. We expected our hospital board experience to be refreshingly devoid of these terms. We thought we were embarking on something similar to church service, school board membership, or the Boy Scouts.

We were soon to learn otherwise. Forward-looking chief executive officers of hospitals were already conditioning their trustees to look for a dramatic shift toward competition among health care providers. As we struggled to master the rules and incentives of a health care reimbursement system that could often not be reconciled with our sense of effective cost management, we began to hear rumblings of changes. We heard that the payment system of the future might involve the use of vouchers, or something called "capitation," or—an even vaguer term— prospective payment.

The forecasts proved to be mostly correct. The biggest changes began occurring in early 1983. Hospital occupancy plummeted. Although hospital admissions remained constant, the average length of stay dropped dramatically. We were surprised at the timing of the changes; the diagnoses-related group payment system that was supposed to trigger reduced hospital utilization was not scheduled to go into effect until early 1984.

In retrospect, it is evident that a combination of factors came together in early 1983. Physicians began paying more attention to how much time their patients were spending in hospitals. Partially stimulated by poor economic conditions, employers' interest in health care cost containment accelerated. Larger firms began to modify their benefits programs to include increased deductibles and copayments, second opinions on surgery, and increased coverage of outpatient procedures and to eliminate the first dollar coverage that encouraged the use of medical specialists and hospitalizations. Health maintenance organizations (HMOs) began to gain members; the Minneapolis story of high HMO market penetration and severe competition among health care providers attracted increasing national attention. As a result of these and other factors, the face of the U.S. health care industry changed significantly, and there was little chance of reverting to the good old days when nearly everything was reimbursed regardless of cost.

Both as trustees and as consultants, we began to explore strategies that a hospital or health care system might use to survive and prosper. The strategies we examined are familiar—finding ways to differentiate product lines, diversifying, reducing costs, increasing emphasis on marketing, merging, or selling out. Coddington, along with Lowell Palmquist, chief executive officer of Swedish Health Systems, and Bill Trollinger, another Swedish Medical Center trustee, developed these concepts into an article, "Strategies for Survival in the Hospital Industry," published in the *Harvard Business Review* (May-June, 1985). This article, and our desire to analyze the currently available options in more depth, led to this book.

As the health care industry shifted into a substantially more competitive stance, the need to more carefully allocate financial resources became evident to management and governing boards. Our firm began to receive requests to perform marketing research, economic analysis, and strategic planning for organizations in the industry (hospitals, multihospital systems, HMOs and other health plans, entrepreneurs marketing health care products, and group practice physicians). Initially we found that our most valued attribute was the ability to bring experience from other competitive industries to bear on the problems and opportunities of the health care industry. We soon learned, however, that implementing health care strategies often required more than a direct transfer from other industries. Health care organizations have special characteristics because of the values they reflect and the community roles they play. Hospitals are unique in their division of responsibilities and decision making among physicians, staff, management, and governing boards.

The first wave of change in health care is history. There is enough operating experience available to begin to evaluate industry watchers' forecasts of patient-days, HMO penetration, hospital finances, and the like. We also have enough experience to begin to critically evaluate the effectiveness of the industry's first wave of competitive responses—preferred provider organizations (PPOs), urgent care centers, outpatient surgery, aggressive advertising, and the like. And we have begun to experience on a day-to-day basis the growing tension between alternative levels of service and the financial bottom line.

Now it is time to take stock and rechart our course. We still face any number of uncertainties, and there is every reason to believe that the course of most health care systems will change again. However, we know much more than we did in 1984.

Charting a future course for hospitals and health care systems is the subject of this book.

This book is intended for top managers and trustees of health care organizations, including local health care systems and hospitals, for physicians and other professionals serving the industry, and for academicians interested in the dynamics of an industry undergoing tremendous change in a very short period of time. A local health care system usually includes one or more acute care hospitals and a variety of other entities such as specialty hospitals, urgent care centers, and ambulatory care centers. Over the past decade, several hundred U.S. hospitals have reorganized themselves into local health care systems with the acute care hospital as one of several subsidiaries under a parent corporation.

This book deals with various strategic initiatives on a broad basis. It is not intended as a substitute for effective strategic planning at the local level; it is designed to stimulate thinking and action and to set the stage for a strategic approach tailored to the specific circumstances of a given health care system.

Our goal is to help hospitals, health care systems, and other health care providers survive and prosper in the changing marketplace. This book is not designed to influence U.S. health care policy, nor is this a historical study of how the health care industry got to where it is today. However, as numbers-oriented consultants, we frequently refer to industry trends and key indicators (past trends and projections to 1990 and 1995 of hospital admissions, patient-days, HMO/PPO penetration, number of physicians per 1,000 citizens, and others). These health care industry indicators are provided in Appendix A.

Overview of the Contents

Part One describes the three major health care market segments—physicians, employers, and consumers—in some detail, in order to set the stage for the identification of appropriate strategies. This first part also reviews several external factors influencing the health care marketplace, now and in the future, including federal and state government policies, economic conditions, and medical technology.

Part Two describes ten different strategies in depth, including examples and an analysis of the strategic implications of each strategy. Part Three, on charting the right course, discusses important elements, or building blocks, for achieving an improved competitive position (choosing and integrating the broad strategies, developing a strategic plan, funding strategic initiatives, and making the hard choices in the decision-making process) and concludes with our vision of what the health care industry will be like in the next three to five years. A more detailed discussion of each chapter appears in the introduction to each part.

Throughout the book we have paid special attention to key elements of health care: quality of care (both hospital and physician), alternative delivery systems (HMOs and PPOs) and their probable effects, and the relationships between hospitals and physicians. To address the latter concern, we have included several suggestions that may be helpful to physicians as they also find it necessary to compete in a drastically changing market characterized by a surplus of doctors, severe price discounts for HMOs and PPOs, and many new forms of competition (urgent care centers, closed-panel HMOs, interspecialty rivalries).

Acknowledgments

Several individuals and organizations made substantial contributions to this book. We especially thank our associates at Browne, Bortz & Coddington, Inc., for allowing us the time to prepare this work, and for their wholehearted support and encouragement. Suzanne Stenmark White assisted in many aspects of the book, especially in the chapters on physician bonding and physicians as a market segment. Arthur Steiker assisted in the appendix on economic analysis and modeling. Matt Bixler performed much of the research and analysis on the strategy of downsizing, and Ann Bortz organized much of the research on consumer behavior. Susan Velsir and Richard Argys conducted the statistical research and prepared most of Appendix A. Robyn Marschner conducted several computerized searches of the literature and prepared the references and bibliography; her efforts are especially appreciated. Susan Johnson prepared the graphics. And, our excellent staff of word processor operators—Julie Spaeth, Mary Helen Friesen, Debra Hash, and Kelly Owens—were productive and patient through the many drafts of this book.

We have already mentioned Lowell Palmquist, chief executive officer of Swedish Health Systems. Lowell, more than any other person, is responsible for whatever success we have had in our efforts to serve the health care industry. John Oswald, administrator of Swedish Medical Center, also made numerous contributions, especially to the chapters on product line management (centers of excellence), becoming a low-cost provider, and downsizing. Richard Clarke, president of the Healthcare Financial Management Association, was especially helpful in the development of our ideas on diversification, access to capital, and the appropriate use of health care management resources. John Hershberger, chief executive officer of Spalding Rehabilitation Hospital, helped develop our concepts regarding physician relations.

Over the past two years we have had the opportunity to work with Voluntary Hospitals of America, a system of more than 600 nonprofit hospitals. This experience has broadened our perspective on health care industry trends and competition and has given us insights into the role of large multihospital alliances. Robert Kitzman and Robert Vernon have been especially supportive, and we very much appreciate their confidence.

Among investment bankers, Chris McCarthy and Deborah Buresh at Goldman Sachs, and Lee White and Jack O'Connor at Smith Barney were most helpful in providing data and insights relative to access to capital.

The book contains insights shared by numerous other practicing health care managers. A partial list includes Glenn Mitchell, chief executive officer, and Michael Keating, vice-president, Alternative Delivery Systems, Alliance Health Systems, Norfolk, Virginia; Bruce Allen, former vice-president for marketing, Community Hospitals in Fresno; Robert Smith, vice-president, National Medical Enterprises; and Gary Strack, chief executive officer, Orlando Regional Medical Center. This list could be extended, and we gratefully acknowledge the insights gained.

Several individuals reviewed drafts of the manuscript and offered many helpful comments. We especially appreciate the efforts of David O'Neill, western regional vice-president for Voluntary Hospitals of America; Robert Hernandez, associate professor, the University of Alabama at Birmingham; and Darrell Thorpe, M.D., formerly with Partners National Health Plans and now with the Tucson Medical Center. (Darrell was also editor of *Health Care Strategic Management.*) Robert Alexander, Larry Griffin, and Brian Peterson, all of Swedish Health Systems, reviewed various chapters and offered many valuable suggestions. Leigh Truitt, M.D., Anne Moore, M.D., and James Freeman all reviewed early drafts and provided useful comments.

Denver, Colorado   Dean C. Coddington
March 1987   Keith D. Moore

In memoriam
JOHN S. GILMORE
colleague, mentor,
and friend

The Authors

Dean C. Coddington is managing director of Browne, Bortz & Coddington, Inc. (BBC), an applied marketing and economic research firm located in Denver, Colorado. He is also chairman of the board of trustees of Swedish Medical Center, a 328-bed acute care hospital in Englewood, a southern suburb of Denver.

Coddington helped found BBC in 1970. Prior to that he worked as a research economist at the University of Denver's Research Institute for eleven years. While at the University of Denver, he taught graduate-level courses in management, entrepreneurship, and engineering economics. Coddington has his M.B.A. degree (1959) from Harvard Business School and his B.S. degree (1954) in civil engineering from South Dakota State University.

During his twenty-seven years in consulting and market research, Coddington has prepared more than 300 reports and has appeared as an expert witness on more than 100 occasions. Much of his work has been in banking, economic development, and new product marketing. During the past two years, he has shifted into full-time research and consulting for the health care industry.

Coddington has written numerous articles, including four in the *Harvard Business Review*. The latest, in the May-June 1985 issue, was entitled "Strategies for Survival in the Hospital Industry." Other recent articles have appeared in *Trustee* magazine (July 1986), *Healthcare Forum* (September 1986), and *Healthcare Financial Management* (December 1984).

Keith D. Moore is a director of BBC and has been with the firm since 1982. He currently serves as a director and chairman of the finance committee for Spalding Rehabilitation Hospital in Denver. Spalding is an 80-bed facility specializing in stroke, orthopedic, and pain rehabilitation. From 1975 to 1981, he was head of the Industrial Economics and Management Division of the University of Denver's Research Institute, where he was responsible for $3 million per year in applied research in technology transfer, research and development management, corporate planning, energy and resource economics, and governmental management strategies. From 1969 to 1975, Moore was a senior economist with a Denver-based consulting firm, teaching assistant at Harvard University, and a U.S. Marine platoon commander in Vietnam. Moore has a masters degree in city planning (1973) from Harvard University and a B.A. degree in economics (1968) from the University of Texas.

Moore's thirteen years' consulting experience has focused on strategy development for corporations, new business start-ups, and public sector agencies. Current clients include a bank, a venture capital firm, two state housing finance authorities, a television network, and two hospitals. He has twice managed new start-ups for the American Broadcasting Company.

Market-Driven Strategies in Health Care

Part One

Today's Health Care Marketplace

"What do you mean, 'Look ahead three years?'" the CEO of a multihospital system recently asked us. "I can't look ahead three *weeks.*"

Add health care to the list of American industries undergoing rapid, fundamental changes. In fact, perhaps health care belongs at the top of the list. Few industries have had to deal simultaneously with a 180-degree change in the way hospitals are paid, a precipitous drop in demand, major shifts in the way new business is acquired, and a change in the traditional role of their key constituencies—in this case, physicians and patients.

A Period of Destabilization

Numerous changes have occurred in health care in recent years, yet they have begun to hit home for most health organizations only since 1983. Consider, for example, the following four areas.

1

Prospective Payment: DRGs. Read the health care literature of the early 1980s and you will not see the term *DRG* (diagnoses-related group) or *ADS* (alternative delivery systems). Attend a health care conference today and these will be two of the most talked about subjects.

The concept of prospective payment, of which the DRG system is one example, has changed the incentive system for hospitals. It focuses on the need to keep costs to a minimum for each type of illness, or "product line," with the hospital retaining any savings if patient costs are below standard and being penalized if costs are above the Medicare-specified maximums. Hospitals now view themselves in terms of the product lines they produce, and many hospital administrators and physicians are finding out, for the first time, how efficient or inefficient they are in producing these product lines. The days of charging on a "cost-plus" basis are gone, probably forever, and the risk of high costs has been shifted from the purchaser (or third-party payer) to hospitals and physicians.

There is little doubt that prospective payment will spread to all hospital patients, not just those covered by Medicare. Blue Cross/Blue Shield and many other health insurance companies are moving in this direction in several states, and physicians may soon be subject to a similar fixed-price system for their fees.

Excess Capacity. After years of growth and high occupancy levels, the hospital industry has experienced a downturn. In the case of one of the acute care hospitals we work with, Swedish Medical Center, the curve broke in April 1983. In that regard, Swedish is typical of a large number of hospitals in the United States.

When the downturn first occurred, many hospital administrators and trustees thought it was a temporary "blip." As time has passed, however, it has become increasingly evident that a much more significant, long-term change has taken place. Sophisticated forecasts now indicate a gradual decline, or at best a leveling off at substantially lower levels of utilization.

What caused the downturn? There are many opinions, but it is safe to say that a number of factors contributed to it:

- The economic recession of 1980–1982, which forced industry, especially large unionized employers, to carefully assess their health care benefit packages and take several cost-containment actions, including increased use of deductibles and copayment provisions in employee health insurance programs.
- More market penetration by HMOs and PPOs, with their greater emphasis on keeping patients out of hospitals and controlling the length of stay for those admitted.
- Increased competition from large group-practice clinics and outpatient diagnostic and surgery centers.
- Changes in the way doctors practice medicine. Physicians are becoming more cost-conscious and are doing a more efficient job of controlling patient admissions and length of stay.
- More emphasis on diet, exercise, and wellness.

It is presently estimated by a variety of knowledgeable health care industry observers that the U.S. hospital industry has at least 25 to 30 percent too many beds. Joseph Califano (1986), in his book *America's Health Care Revolution: Who Lives? Who Dies? Who Pays?* says that the number of hospital beds may be reduced 30 percent by 1990 and another 20 percent by 1995 (p. 204). There are about one million hospital beds in use today. Even in areas of rapid population growth—for example, the southwestern U.S.—the need for hospital beds is significantly less than in 1980.

Other segments of the health care industry are also suffering from excess capacity. In many large metropolitan areas (San Diego, Portland, and Boston, for example), there are too many physicians. Most forecasts are for a large (70,000 or more) nationwide physician surplus by 1990.

Competition. Previously friendly hospitals are engaging in a variety of aggressively competitive actions—recruiting physicians from each others' staffs, claiming quality differences in advertising campaigns, and cutting prices for such selected services as normal deliveries.

As if competition between acute care hospitals were not sufficient, many free-standing urgent care facilities, outpatient surgery facilities, and diagnostic centers have been established to compete for the same patients. It is estimated, for example, that there were over 3,000 urgent care centers in late 1985, compared with 180 in 1980—an increase of over 500 per year. Outpatient surgery centers are likewise more prevalent. It is estimated that less than 10 percent of all surgery was performed outside hospitals in 1980; by 1985, the proportion approached 30 percent, and many experts believe that 40 to 50 percent of all surgery will be performed away from the hospital by 1990.

Outpatient birthing centers are also being promoted, particularly in larger markets where competition is more severe. It may be possible for these birthing centers to capture as much as 40 percent of the market traditionally controlled by hospitals. This assumes, of course, that these centers and the obstetricians who use them can solve their malpractice insurance premium problems.

HMOs (health maintenance organizations) are a rapidly growing part of the health care industry. The number of subscribers was nine million in 1980, twenty-one million in 1986; many industry observers project that the number will approach fifty million by 1990. Since HMOs emphasize preventive medicine, practice careful screening before subscribers are admitted to a hospital, and carry out close monitoring of patients while they are hospitalized, the overall impact of HMOs is a reduction in hospital usage.

PPOs (preferred provider organizations) are a more recent mechanism, designed to provide low-cost medical services for employees of larger firms. Big organizations are using their leverage to make special financial deals with physicians, clinics, and hospitals, usually negotiating across-the-board discounts for services and implementing utilization review and other cost-containment strategies.

Medical Staff–Hospital Relations. Physicians continue to control the level of hospital usage. They admit the patient, prescribe treatment, and decide when to discharge the patient. But they are subject to pressures never felt before. Many physicians' practices are experiencing lower demand, pressure to discount fees, and more and more reviews of and constraints on decision making. Physicians are now competing more intensively with one another.

Young primary care physicians, the gateway to future admissions growth, are being hardest hit.

Hospitals are now trying, much more aggressively than in the past, to find ways to establish stronger bonds with their medical staff, and physicians are also more interested in closer relationships with their hospital. Construction of medical office buildings adjacent to hospitals has been a popular way to bond physicians to hospitals, largely by offering convenience (and sometimes below-market rentals) to physicians. The newest trend in the industry is the "joint venture" between physicians and a hospital. Hospital–physician joint ventures normally involve the commitment of financial resources by both parties and typically include outpatient surgery centers, radiology (imaging) centers, laboratories, and partnerships to contract with HMOs and PPOs.

Writing in the *New England Journal of Medicine*, Eli Ginzberg (1986) argues that the health care industry is undergoing not just rapid change but a period of destabilization. The seeds of destabilization were sown over a fifteen-year period—as hospital boards and administrators were lulled into a bureaucratic cost-plus pricing mentality, as cross-subsidization of the elderly and poor became commonplace, and as medical schools began producing what is now an apparent oversupply of physicians. The seeds of destabilization were harvested with the introduction of a highly competitive, cost-conscious, market-driven environment. Ginzberg asks, "Will the forces of destabilization overwhelm the points of resistance that have begun to emerge? . . . Continued destabilization must be slowed and then reversed if we are not to undermine what has proved to be a highly satisfactory and effective system of care for most Americans" (p. 757).

Social systems seldom remain destabilized for long periods of time. Markets and organizations adjust to changes, and a new set of standard practices, strategies, and assumptions becomes commonplace. However, in this process, competitive advantage often shifts from one type of organization to another.

Making a Midcourse Correction

This book is about learning from the recent period of health care industry destabilization; it is about understanding change, adapting to it, and getting on with the work of positioning local health care systems for the future.

The first challenge of today's health care organization is to navigate carefully through the remaining period of destabilization. This cannot be successfully accomplished without acting decisively, often making decisions on less than perfect information. As in any rapidly changing environment, mistakes will be made. These will have to be identified quickly and corrected without excessive embarrassment or apology.

The second challenge is to anticipate what "business as usual" will be like in the future and, on that basis, to establish the health care organization's future competitive strategies. In looking to the future, it is no longer necessary to rely solely on intuition or on industry futurists' crystal balls to understand what the health care business will be like when it reestablishes itself. Most health care organizations have had three to four years operating experience in the new competitive environment. What has worked and has not worked in the market-driven health care economy can be observed. Patterns of adjustment among employers, consumers, and physicians are beginning to emerge. It is also possible to draw analogies from what has happened in other rapidly changing industries—airlines, telecommunications, and banking—that have gone through similar competitive adjustments. Now is the time to assess what has been learned and to make the appropriate adjustments.

Beginning with the Marketplace

How does a health care organization chart a midcourse correction that makes sense? In our view, the task begins with a solid assessment of the marketplace. It is clear that the health care business environment of the future will be market-driven; therefore, it is important to begin with an understanding of who is making today's health care decisions, how these decisions are being made, and what consumers, employers, and physicians expect and want from health care providers.

Our first four chapters, Part One, provide an overview of the marketplace. They attempt to set the stage for the key elements of this book, the analyses of what can be learned from the successful and unsuccessful application of the ten competitive strategies described in Part Two.

In health care, there has been much discussion about who the market is. Is it the medical staff? After all, they are the ones who attract patients and admit them to hospitals. Or is it employers and the health insurance plans they buy for their employees? And how about the consumer? Is the consumer's role in the physician and hospital selection process increasing or decreasing? Recent surveys, one in *Hospital* magazine and the other in *Modern Healthcare,* came to opposite conclusions on the influence consumers exert in hospital selection. The *Modern Healthcare* survey concluded that consumers are becoming more active in the process; the research we have conducted supports this position. Clearly, hospital staff, employers, and consumers are all factors in the market, and all three market segments are in transition now as they respond to changing pressures and opportunities.

But even to view the health care market as three segments is an oversimplification. Among employers, for example, larger firms behave much differently in their health care cost-containment and health plan strategies than do smaller organizations, and unionized firms are far different than nonunion businesses. Among consumers, women behave differently in terms of health care decision making than do men. In addition, there are major differences in health care behavior by age, income, education, and marital status. Physicians in practice ten years or less exhibit substantially differing attitudes from those in the last decade of their practice, and primary care doctors have needs and perspectives that are far different from those of surgeons.

The first three chapters, addressing each of the three major market segments described above, are based on a combination of numerous recent studies, as well as our own survey and focus group research. Chapter Four addresses other key external trends, such as economic conditions and medical technology, facing the health care industry.

1

The Employer Market

The battle for market control in health care is most intense at the
level of large employers—corporations, state and local government, not-for-profit organizations, and labor unions. Most large
employers have already instituted a variety of health care cost-
containment strategies and are leaders in self-insurance and the
formation of preferred provider organizations (PPOs). The
tremendous competition among alternative delivery system
providers (of which both HMOs and PPOs are examples) is aimed
primarily at employers as the purchasers of health plans for their
employees.

Excluding not-for-profit organizations, there are over
600,000 U.S. firms with twenty or more employees (U.S. Bureau of
the Census, 1985a). Current estimates of these U.S. employers, by
size, are shown in Table 1.

According to *Time* magazine, U.S. companies spend about
$91 billion each year to provide health insurance to more than 130
million workers and family members (Castro, Delaney, and Dolan,
1986, p. 64). Their insurance providers account for approximately
$59 billion in payments for hospital services, or 35 percent of the
nation's total hospital expenditures (see Table A.1, Appendix A).

Table 1. U.S. Employers, by Size.

Number of Employees	Number of Firms
20–49	389,000
50–99	132,000
100–249	69,000
250–499	19,000
500–999	7,600
1,000 or more	4,600
Total	621,200

Employers with twenty or more employees represent about 70 percent of these totals.

This chapter describes the results of recent research into employer health plan decision making. How do employers differ in their current and likely future health care cost-containment strategies? How do employers make decisions about the wide array of competing plans? What role do benefits consultants and brokers play in the health plan decision-making process?

Employer Health Benefits Strategies

Employers have varying objectives for their health benefits programs. Some seek cost containment; a few see a possibility of substantial cost reductions. Some seek streamlined, hassle-free administration; others try actively to influence the well-being and productivity of their employees.

Several recent studies of employer health plans have yielded often confusing and sometimes contradictory results. We believe, however, that most differences in employer health plan actions can be explained on the basis of three variables: the size of the organization, the type of labor market involved, and the organization's overall human resources strategy. Very large firms (over 500 employees) have generally been more aggressive in cost-containment efforts. Firms in oversupplied blue-collar labor markets have generally taken a tougher stance on cost containment. Many of these labor markets are also heavily unionized.

Firms with strong management convictions on human resources issues tend to be more interventionist, not only in "pure" cost containment but in such related issues as wellness and flex plans. Thus we see more new health plan initiatives in, for example, natural resource industries and construction ("Medical Benefits Costs . . . ," 1985, p. 10).

We also believe that the health care industry has suffered from too many generalizations based on a single type of organization: the large organization, operating in a buyer's market for blue-collar employees, with an interventionist attitude toward human resources. Examples such as Joseph Califano's and Lee Iacocca's efforts at Chrysler, or even surveys of *Fortune* 500 firms' activities, provide a picture of the cutting edge in cost containment. However, they are not representative of the vast majority of firms, which are not focusing on limiting health care costs. Instead, these firms are simply trying to be informed buyers, weighing health plan costs against the value received.

Employer Options. Today's employers confront a wide variety of options in the health plan marketplace. They can choose among traditional cost-containment approaches that police "inappropriate use"—providing second opinions on surgery and other forms of utilization review. They can place more of the cost and/or policing burden on the employee by using flex plans and increased copayments and deductibles. They can attempt to circumvent insurance industry problems by self-insuring. Or they can choose among new alternatives available as a consequence of health care provider competition—primarily HMOs and PPOs. There is also an array of options spawned by the combination of the above factors with wellness programs, health care utilization data bases, industry coalitions, and incentives to reduce double insurance coverage within households.

The most popular employer cost-containment strategies are second opinions on surgery and coverage of outpatient procedures. Roughly half of all employers have implemented these cost-containment measures. The use of these two measures varies by size of firm, with very large organizations (500 employees or more) about twice as likely to have implemented them as smaller organizations (20 to 100 employees).

Nearly 40 percent of all firms are self-insured, although this proportion varies from region to region. The highest percentage of self-insured companies is in the Southeast (64 percent) and the West (55 percent) (Coopers & Lybrand, 1983). Size also plays a role; the proportion of firms with self-insurance exceeds 70 percent for larger organizations.

As many large and midsized employers have moved into self-insurance, the role of the third-party administrator has increased. As of 1984, this group had 22 percent of the group health plan market. Third-party administrators typically handle claims processing, actuarial services, and other activities on behalf of clients. With the expected growth of PPOs, however, "we may be seeing the beginning of a shakeout as the consolidation of third party administrators increases through merger and acquisition activity. Given the maturing market, third party administrators must now compete with each other as well as with these new competitors for market share" (Temple, Barker, & Sloane, Inc., 1985).

Alternative delivery systems continue to grow in market share. Of employees covered by an ADS, we estimate that 10 percent are members of HMOs and 3 to 4 percent are members of PPOs. These market shares are likely to increase dramatically. We estimate that by 1990, 30 to 35 percent of employees and their families will be covered by HMOs or PPOs, with the larger number in PPOs. Others place this figure much higher.

The preceding cost-containment measures are most likely to be found in very large organizations. Other popular cost-containment measures—preadmission certification, health care utilization data bases, wellness programs, and increases in employee deductibles and copayments—are still more heavily concentrated among larger employers.

Actions by Very Large Employers. The nation's largest organizations have been the most active in cost containment; however, the jury is still out as to how successful these efforts will be. Like other firms, very large firms have tended most often to initiate second opinions and other forms of utilization review. As one recent example, General Motors enlisted leaders of the United Auto Workers, along with Blue Cross/Blue Shield and Metropolitan Life Insurance, in an accord aimed at cutting GM's $2.34 billion medical bill for its two million employees and dependents. According to *Time* magazine, "The insurance companies agreed to help reduce GM's medical costs by $234 million over three years. In turn, the U.A.W. consented to accept some changes in GM benefits, including a requirement that workers get second opinions before surgery. Now, according to the California-based Health Research Institute, a nonprofit firm, some 35 percent of major U.S. corporations are trying to hammer out similar agreements with their unions" (Castro, Delaney, and Dolan, 1986, p. 64).

The most comprehensive review of health care cost-containment strategies of very large firms (*Fortune* 500 companies and top nonindustrial organizations) was prepared by Regina Herzlinger and Jeffrey Schwartz (1985) and reported in the *Harvard Business Review*. Under the category "limiting inappropriate use," the authors covered four initiatives often used by large firms—second surgical opinions, retrospective reviews, concurrent utilization reviews, and preadmission certification. The study showed mixed reaction to second opinions and their contribution to decreased hospital utilization. (One large employer found that second opinions induced more surgery than they prevented.) Retrospective review of provider bills was proven to be cost-effective in terms of reducing health care costs; and large employers claimed to have had some success with concurrent utilization reviews, which take place while the patient is hospitalized (the key appears to be how well concurrent reviews are administered). Preadmission certification by a nurse practitioner is a technique used by many large companies, the survey found, but its cost-effectiveness has yet to be determined. Based on Herzlinger and Schwartz's results, it appears that the effectiveness of very large employers' efforts to limit inappropriate use is still indeterminate.

As a group, very large organizations have not made significant changes in shifting costs to employees. Within the firms surveyed in the above study, 97 percent of all employees were covered by health plans, and 90 percent of the firms paid 75 percent or more of their employees' health insurance premiums. More than 90 percent of the firms said that employee copayments were 20 percent or less. Over half of the large companies protected their employees from health care costs exceeding $1,000 per year.

In general, larger firms are positive about HMOs and their ability to control health care costs. Employees like HMOs because such health plans usually have very low copayments and deductibles, but they dislike limitations in the choice of doctors and hospitals. Employers surveyed expressed several concerns about HMOs, however: they worried about potential for adverse selection by less healthy employees, poor management and questions of financial strength, and unproven ability to contract with lower-cost doctors and hospitals. Nevertheless, 60 percent of the comments from larger companies about HMOs were positive, according to Herzlinger.

On the use of outpatient facilities, a second phase of the study, conducted by Herzlinger alone (1985), again presented a picture of mixed results. Many larger firms offered benefits for outpatient procedures (diagnostic testing, same-day surgery); about half reported that ambulatory surgery and preadmission testing were cost-effective—but only one of five outpatient programs was well regarded by employees. Herzlinger noted that hospital-based facilities tend to be older and less costly than the newer ambulatory centers, which have to include start-up costs in their prices; as a consequence, hospitals have been able to compete successfully with the new free-standing ambulatory facilities. Hence employers have not been able to achieve significant savings by stressing care outside the hospital.

Herzlinger asked larger firms about their likelihood of using a number of different health care cost-containment strategies if they had to reduce their health care costs by 10 percent. The strategy most chosen—34 percent said there was a "high" probability of taking such action—was to become involved in a business coalition, a voluntary association of businesses, usually in a metropolitan area, to deal with what they perceive as high or uncontrolled health care costs. Business coalitions tend to emphasize data collection and improved understanding of health care. Herzlinger concluded, however, that "in general, coalition membership is very time consuming and yields uncertain benefits."

Another study, sponsored by the Equitable Life Assurance Society Company in 1983, found that 64 percent of the 250 large companies interviewed had experience with business coalitions aimed at health care cost-containment (Louis Harris and Associates, 1985, p. 56). Business coalitions were rated second out of eighteen cost-containment programs; only "requiring employees to pay a part of their health insurance premiums" was more popular (65 percent). In terms of effectiveness, however, fewer than half of the firms involved in business coalitions rated them as "very effective" in reducing health care costs.

In a third phase of her health care review, Herzlinger and coauthor David Calkins (1986) focused on how large companies promote wellness. Of 219 companies with wellness programs, 65 percent provided physical exams, 47 percent had drug and alcohol abuse programs, 36 percent promoted smoking cessation, 29 percent had stress management programs, 28 percent emphasized fitness, and several had a combination of these programs. Herzlinger and Calkins are optimistic about the positive impact of wellness activities and their longer-term potential for reducing health care costs, if properly planned and carried out.

Actions by Other Types of Firms. We cannot report comparable research on the experiences of smaller firms—for example, primarily white-collar firms with between 20 and 200 employees, which represent the fastest growing segment of the U.S. economy. Such research exists, but it has been conducted for national health care systems and alternative delivery system providers and the results are generally proprietary. Most of the findings discussed below are based on focus group interviews conducted around the country with employer representatives (personnel and benefits managers, controllers, and CEOs). The focus group discussions usually involved ten or twelve people spending one-and-a-half to two hours discussing their firms' efforts to control health care costs.

Smaller and midsized firms do not appear to be as concerned, on an overall basis, with their health care costs as are larger firms. Our focus group experience indicates that managers of smaller firms tend to look at health insurance benefits more from the point of view of an employee. We have talked with only one or two firms that were planning to reduce their health care costs; nearly all small firms want as comprehensive a plan as possible within the limits of what they are now spending (and adjusted for reasonable price increases).

Most smaller and midsized employers say that they depend on their health plan as their primary source of health care cost-containment initiatives. Most firms with fewer than 500 employees are not self-insured. They concentrate on finding the most cost-effective plan for their employees. In terms of the cost-containment initiatives used by larger firms—second opinions, coverage of outpatient procedures, tightening up deductibles and copayments—smaller and midsized firms see these being incorporated into their indemnity insurance. The personnel manager of a construction firm employing 250 persons said, "In a year or two all health plans will provide managed care in the form of second opinions, concurrent review, and preadmission certification; such plans will be commonplace rather than unusual."

HMO offerings and HMO enrollment in smaller and midsized firms vary substantially based on industry and the labor market. For example, HMO salespeople report considerable success with high-tech firms and employees, universities, and state and local governments. They report poor success with natural resource, construction, and real estate firms. Enrollment levels also vary substantially based on informal, word-of-mouth communication within firms. For the employer considering the HMO, however, the key factors are the perceived service level and value received per dollar, not the potential cost savings.

PPOs have not become a significant factor for the smaller and midsized firm. There is talk in chambers of commerce and other business groups in competitive, leading-edge areas, however, of combining forces to match the buying clout of large employers.

Very few smaller firms have formal wellness programs, although many recognize the value of behavior modification and wellness activities. Wellness efforts in smaller firms tend to be

informal (or at least not connected to a health plan) and often
begin by example (company executives who take up running, lose
weight, or stop smoking). This does not mean that smaller
employers place less value on wellness; just the opposite appears to
be true. Our research results indicate that smaller firms tend to
place more value on happy, healthy, and productive employees.

Health Plan Decision Making

In selecting health plans for their employees, what do
employers consider? How important is cost, both to the firm and
to employees in the form of out-of-pocket expenses? Freedom of
choice? Geographic coverage by physicians and hospitals? Is a
plan offering national or regional coverage preferable to one with
local coverage? How about benefits design features and service?
And what about the reputation for quality of physicians and
hospitals available through specific plans?

Based on our focus group research with employers, and our
efforts to model the employer decision-making process, we have
concluded that the price of a proposed health plan is usually not
the most important consideration. The nature of benefits, some
freedom of choice, geographic coverage of the provider network,
and service are more important than price. Perceptions of
physician and hospital quality are also important, especially in
considering HMOs and PPOs, in which employees are given
financial incentives to use certain providers. The price of a health
plan must be in the competitive range in order to be considered,
but it is usually not necessary to offer the lowest-cost plan to
successfully sell a plan to employers.

As of the mid-1980s, most employers were either self-insured
or had purchased traditional, fee-for-service indemnity plans.
There has been a movement toward inclusion of cost-containment
provisions in these plans (for example, increased deductibles and
copayments, second surgical opinions, coverage of outpatient
procedures, preadmission certification), with employees retaining
their freedom of choice of physicians and hospitals. Most employers with these types of "managed care" plans are relatively

satisfied; it will not be an easy marketing job to get them to substitute a PPO or to allow additional HMOs into the firm.

Employers typically review their health plans once a year. If the existing plan has provided good service (usually defined as causing few, if any, employee complaints) and the proposed price increase for the coming year is reasonable (up to or slightly in excess of the inflation rate), the chance of a new plan being able to oust the existing health plan is small. Employers are reluctant to change health plans, because of the potential for disruption and dissatisfaction among employees. So if the existing plan is viewed as satisfactory, new plans face tough sledding.

Nevertheless, employers usually compare what is available in the insurance marketplace with their present plan or plans. Most have a systematic evaluation of alternatives; the analysis is conducted by staff or by benefits consultants and brokers.

The key word in health evaluation is *cost-effectiveness.* What are we getting for our money? The problem is that most employers, especially those with fewer than 500 employees, do not know how to evaluate effectiveness. Quality of care is especially difficult for employers to evaluate; they tend to rely upon employee feedback and the reputation of various physicians or physician groups and hospitals.

A number of national firms are betting that health plans providing regional or national coverage will fare well against local competitors. Partners National Health Plans (a cooperative venture of Aetna and Voluntary Hospitals of America), for example, is targeting large national firms with employees distributed throughout the United States. Our research indicates that for certain types of employers, a statewide, regional, or national delivery system will provide a competitive advantage.

Eric Schlesinger of the Boston Consulting Group says that employee acceptance of health plans is a function of two major variables: freedom of choice and cost. Freedom of choice includes the ability to select a geographic location for care, select a doctor and hospital, and maintain existing provider (physician, hospital) relationships. He develops the following continuum of health care options, working from high freedom of choice, at the top, down to low freedom of choice.

- Unmanaged fee-for-service
- Fee-for-service with cost-containment provisions
- Broad-panel PPO
- Broad-panel HMO
- Narrow-panel PPO (limited number of physicians and hospitals)
- Narrow-panel HMO
- Group/staff HMO (such as Kaiser)

Schlesinger defines *cost* as total out-of-pocket expenditures (copayment, deductibles, others), and says that employees are sensitive to relatively small differences in out-of-pocket costs ($50 to $100 per year). "Each consumer will select the insurance plan that offers what he or she sees as the right mix of cost and freedom of choice" (Schlesinger, 1985, p. 4).

To answer the questions posed at the beginning of this discussion of employer health plan decision making, we believe that the two most important factors employers consider are the benefits design and freedom of choice, with cost being less important. For an HMO or PPO using some type of preferred provider network, geographic coverage and the quality of physicians and hospitals in the plan are very important. A step below these considerations is service (claims processing, a minimum of hassle for the employer, and lack of employee complaints). Health plan prices to employers must be competitive but not necessarily the lowest in the area. Costs to employees, which are viewed as part of benefits design, are very important.

Benefits Consultants and Brokers

Our research among small and midsized employers reveals that a very high proportion rely on benefits consultants and brokers. We have found such consultants to be heavily involved in analysis of health plans and influential in their recommendations. Herzlinger and Schwartz noted similar results in their study of very large employers: "More than 65 percent of the respondents use consultants to analyze benefit packages used by competitors, to redesign benefit packages, and to furnish cost-containment ideas.

Consultants have also proved useful in designing the means of introducing changes in benefit packages to employees and in negotiating with insurers" (1985, p. 78).

The benefits consultant and broker industry is not well defined, primarily because many of the leading firms practice in a variety of insurance fields besides health care. Major firms in this industry, and the ones with the largest networks of offices, are listed in Table 2 (Geisel, 1985, p.3):

Table 2. Major U.S. Benefits Consultants/Brokers.

Name of Firm	Number of U.S. Offices
Johnson & Higgins	41
William M. Mercer-Meidinger, Inc.	42
Towers, Perin, Forster & Crosby	24
Frank B. Hall	40
The Wyatt Co.	28
Hewitt Associates	21
Human Resource Management Group	40

Indemnity carriers have traditionally worked closely with brokers and consultants and paid them commissions for their services. Commissions typically run from 2 percent of monthly premiums for larger employers, to 6 percent for employers with fewer than ten employees. (Despite the term *benefits consultants,* most members of this group receive commissions on premiums.) In reality, there is not a great deal of difference between brokers and benefits consultants; both act as intermediaries between employers and health plans, or between employers and third-party claims administrators for self-insured firms.

HMOs have traditionally bypassed the intermediary and marketed directly to employers. They usually develop their own direct sales force and concentrate on larger employers and their employees. As a result, there has been substantial friction between benefits consultants and brokers and HMOs, and it is rare for benefits consultants and brokers to include HMOs in their analysis and recommendations. As the major indemnity insurers who have traditionally used consultants and brokers join with providers to market HMOs and PPOs, we believe that this historical rift will be reduced. Brokers and benefits consultants will increasingly include HMOs and PPOs in the plans they evaluate, and they will receive normal commissions for their services.

Having interviewed a number of benefits consultants and brokers, both in focus group settings and on a one-on-one basis, we are impressed with the key role they play in employer health plan decision making. Their perceptions of HMOs, PPOs, and other health plans mirror the interests of their clients. For example, those representing larger firms (500 employees or more) emphasize the cost-containment features of new health plans and are especially interested in utilization review procedures. Benefits consultants and brokers working with larger employers also tend to be more data-oriented; they want to be able to analyze physician and hospital charges on the basis of case mix and intensity of service.

Benefits consultants and brokers working with smaller firms tend to favor health plans that are not radically different from existing indemnity plans. They say that benefits design and freedom of choice are more important than low cost; as noted earlier, employer costs are a consideration, but are not as important as other factors to smaller employers. In assessing PPOs, few favor large disincentives for using physicians and hospitals not on the preferred list.

The benefits consultants and brokers we have interviewed believe that HMO and PPO market penetration will increase steadily between now and 1990, with ADS penetration among employees and dependents likely to be in the 35 to 50 percent range by that year. Many benefits consultants and brokers also expect the differences between HMOs and PPOs to diminish over the next few years; they expect greater use of capitation (fixed monthly payments to providers on a per-capita basis), heavy incentives to use preferred providers, and better utilization review.

Benefits consultants and brokers see little value in the discounts provided by hospitals and physicians. One broker said, "They [discounts] are a mirage. Physicians just increase the number of visits to regain lost revenues. Hospitals do more tests or otherwise recoup their discounts. What will really pay off is tough utilization review and a good data base."

Brokers and consultants tend to favor national health insurance firms, ones with well-known brand names, over smaller, local HMOs or PPOs. They are more comfortable in recommending larger firms to their clients; they have confidence that such insurance companies and their health plans will be around for a few years. In addition, it is easier to sell employers and employees on plans with names they recognize (Aetna, Prudential, Blue Cross/Blue Shield, Humana).

The health insurance industry, including consultants and brokers, is bullish about "triple-option plans"—plans that offer an HMO, a PPO, and a traditional indemnity plan, all available from one company. CIGNA and Blue Cross offer such a combination of plans in certain markets, and Partners National Health Plans appears to be moving in that direction. The objective is to provide a full range of products that can satisfy all of the customers' health insurance needs, thereby challenging not only traditional insurance products but also HMOs (Fox and Anderson, 1986, p. 24).

According to most brokers and benefits consultants, there will be a shakeout in health plans in coming years. They see most locally owned plans, many with poor management and limited financial resources, being absorbed by larger organizations.

Even with their expertise in health plans, some brokers and benefits consultants confess to being confused by the large number of new health plans, each with different features, prices, and provider networks. "I can't keep up with it," said one consultant. "I try to pick a few plans, study them thoroughly, and recommend them to my clients. PRUCARE looks interesting, and I've analyzed it in detail using a matrix to explain it to my clients. But I can't do this for all of the plans; I just don't have the time."

Most brokers and consultants are not concerned about maintaining their fees and commissions, even given the increase in ADS. They believe their services are even more valuable today, due to the complexity of the health plan market.

When asked about the characteristics of a PPO that they would feel comfortable recommending to their clients, answers tended to vary somewhat, depending on the size of the clients' work force:

Larger Clients	*Smaller Clients*
• Reputation of plan	• Reputation of plan
• Utilization review procedures	• Benefits design
• Other cost-containment measures	• Provider network (freedom of choice)
• Data base	• Service
• Benefits design	• Price
• Price	
• Extent and quality of provider network	

When asked about groups that are attempting to assemble networks of cost-effective physicians, most of the benefits consultants and brokers expressed skepticism. "How can you tell who's cost-effective?" was a common response. Most seem to agree that the only way to control physician costs is with strong utilization review and other cost-containment strategies, not by preselecting physicians thought to be cost-effective in the way they practice medicine.

Benefits consultants and brokers play a key role in helping educate employees about health plans. "This is the key to success in putting in a PPO with strong incentives and disincentives," said one broker. "Employees have to understand the plan; there is so much bad information out there in the marketplace that it is easy to become confused."

Future Trends and Implications

The importance of market segmentation is one of several themes running throughout this book. We expect the health plan objectives of different segments of the employer market to diverge, not converge, between now and the early 1990s.

Many firms in major industries in the United States have little choice but to pursue a broad range of cost-reduction policies, including those affecting health care. They are faced with intense foreign competition, shrinking domestic markets, and often an oversupply of labor.

Large employers have a deal to strike with health plan and health care providers. They need price breaks; in return, they can offer a high volume of business. The key question is how far larger employers will be able and willing to go to deliver their side of the deal. Will they be able to deliver high volume to a single hospital? The evidence to date suggests that only a limited number of firms have been able to do so. Those large employers with employees dispersed throughout the country may have only modest volumes to offer any single hospital. They will have a strong incentive to deal with national systems of hospitals so that they can take advantage of their strongest bargaining position. Additionally, many large firms are located in tight labor markets, and they will be seeking better, more productive labor relations. Often these firms will choose not to rock the boat by limiting their employees' choice of health care providers.

Nonetheless, deal making between the large industrial employer and health care insurers and providers is occurring at a rapid rate; this is one reason why PPO enrollment is more than doubling each year. However, these large employers do not represent either the largest or the fastest growing segment of business. The key challenge to health care insurers and providers today is how best to meet the needs of the large number of smaller employers.

Small and midsized employers differ substantially in their approach to health care cost containment and in health plan decision making. However, the vast majority see themselves as value shoppers, not bargain hunters. These firms can be expected to take advantage of the buyer's market in health care, but they are likely to demand more choices among health plans, more flexibility, and a more unified, simplified system for processing of the claims, all at reasonable costs.

This readiness to ''shop'' on the part of employers presents substantial marketing opportunities for the health plan brokerage, administration, and insurance industries. Never has the health plan market share been more up for grabs. It also imposes increases in operating overhead on all health care intermediaries. These added expenses are likely to be reflected in reduced payments to health care providers, not higher prices to employers.

2

The Physician Market

"I see the changes, and I'm competing," said a middle-aged family practice physician. "We're open more hours. I've joined every HMO and PPO in the community. And every time I look up and see someone go into the hospital's urgent care center across the street, I send the CEO a note telling him I've referred another patient to a specialist who practices across town."

The more than 500,000 physicians in the United States are both a key part of the health care provider network and an important market segment for hospitals, pharmaceutical companies, equipment manufacturers, and others seeking to serve their needs. In most cases, they continue to be the most important market segment for hospitals. Not only do doctors control much of the patient flow to hospitals, but their decisions and actions have a tremendous impact on the hospital industry's financial viability, particularly under prospective payment systems such as DRGs.

Physicians, meanwhile, must contend with changes in their own marketplace. What are these changes in the market for physician services? What are the resulting changes in physician practice patterns and attitudes toward the future? And what about changes in physicians' interest in relationships with hospitals and health care systems?

Physician Supply and Demand

The number of physicians in this country more than doubled between 1960 and 1985—from 259,000 to 541,000. The number is projected to increase to 707,000 by the year 2000.

Until recently, the physician surplus was a phenomenon that health care industry observers read about and built into models projecting likely future industry conditions. Now, however, the impact of the surplus is being felt acutely by physicians themselves, as well as by hospitals and consumers. In 1963, there were 143 physicians per 100,000 population in the United States. By 1980, there were 202 physicians per 100,000 population, and by 1985 the ratio was 227 per 100,000. The U.S. Department of Health and Human Services projects that the number of physicians per 100,000 population will increase to 235 in 1990 and to 260 by the year 2000 (Califano, 1986).

The projected supply far exceeds anticipated needs under current practice patterns. The Graduate Medical Education National Advisory Committee (GMENAC) asserts in their analysis of the supply of doctors that only between 188 and 190 physicians per 100,000 population are needed under the current U.S. health care system. When an HMO model is used as the basis for their projections, even fewer doctors are needed—106 for each 100,000 people enrolled. Moreover, by 1990 even fewer HMO doctors than calculated by GMENAC will be needed to meet the national primary care needs—20 percent fewer primary care physicians for children, and 50 percent fewer primary care physicians for adults (Steinwachs and others, 1986). Meanwhile, physicians also find themselves competing increasingly with nonphysician providers— podiatrists, chiropractors, optometrists, nurse practitioners.

Standard economic theory gives us an idea of what to expect in a buyer's market for physician services: more services available in less desirable geographic areas, more intense competition between physicians in attractive living areas (and overall), and lower physician fees. These changes have occurred as expected. For example:

- There has been an increase in physicians practicing in rural areas. Many specialties (anesthesiology, child psychiatry, and diagnostic radiology, for example) are growing much faster in rural areas than in urban areas (Reynolds, 1985).
- Physicians in urban areas are competing with one another in numerous ways. Primary care physicians and specialists are competing to retain patients by extending the types of services they offer; specialists provide primary care services to patients originally in for specialty services, and primary care physicians perform procedures that historically would have been referred to a specialist.
- After more than doubling (from $52,000 to $108,400) between 1974 and 1984, physician incomes are now increasing at around 2 percent per year.
- Fee discounting is common as physicians join new HMOs and PPOs. Discounts of 20 percent or more are common, and they run substantially higher in specialties such as general surgery.
- Physician incomes are as much as 40 percent higher in fast-growing Sun Belt states than in established areas such as New England (Reynolds, 1985).

Physician Perceptions of Changes

Physicians face increasing uncertainty as they consider the future of their medical practices. Almost daily, physicians hear or read about a new development in the delivery of and reimbursement for their services. Realizing that it is critical to understand physicians' immediate and long-term concerns before attempting to predict their responses to change, we have assisted several hospitals in identifying such concerns through focus group interviews with physicians.

Many factors continually influence the practice of medicine. From the physicians' perspective, however, the factors are becoming more numerous, more invasive in terms of their practice, and more threatening to their economic security. Although technology has been a revolutionary factor in the practice of medicine, in our recent discussions with physicians, technology was seldom mentioned as an influence; the factors discussed below were of a greater concern.

   Increased Competition. From the physicians' perspective, increased competition comes from a variety of sources. The most commonly mentioned categories of competition are:

• *Hospitals.* Aggressive actions by competitor hospitals result in the erosion of the individual physician's market share as well as the erosion of the medical staff's and associated hospital's market share.
• *ADS growth.* Of particular concern are closed-panel HMOs such as Kaiser, which take patients away from physicians.
• *Other physicians.* The developing physician surplus makes it extremely difficult for new physicians to establish a practice and for established doctors to retain the patient base they have developed. In addition, the surplus creates increasing competition between and within medical specialties—for example, orthopedic surgeons purchasing x-ray equipment and OB/GYN physicians serving a higher proportion of their patients' primary care needs.

   Many physicians view the surplus as "diluting their practice." There are now more physicians in each specialty area, and physicians are extending the scope of their practice. Specific comments from our focus groups include:

Surgeon: My practice is becoming diluted with all the specialists.

OB/GYN: I think family practitioners will be doing more in the way of specialty work. . . . There are more and more doctors out there. . . . I'm not as busy as I would like to be.

Internist: There is a dilution of my practice . . . by the tremendous number of internists.

Internist: I think the number of physicians has outstripped patient demand. . . . When I started I was the only one [in my subspecialty]. . . . Now there are large numbers of highly trained internists—family practitioners who can handle a lot of subspecialties.

Two of the areas of competition, ADS growth and the physician surplus, are structural changes and thus perceived by physicians as beyond their control. Hospital actions, however, receive considerable attention from physicians, in large part because hospital initiatives are within their sphere of influence. It appears that almost any action taken by a hospital that extends beyond direct inpatient care and serving as a tool for physicians will be perceived by at least some physicians as competition.

Other less frequently mentioned sources of competition include the development of independent free-standing clinics, urgent care centers, minor emergency rooms, doc-in-the-box chains, and diagnostic centers.

Changes in Payment Mechanisms. Changes and modifications of payment mechanisms concern almost all physicians. Most doctors believe that any changes to the current traditional, fee-for-service system will hurt their practice. Areas of concern include:

- *Impact of ADS on fees and paperwork.* Physicians feel pressure to join HMOs and PPOs to maintain or increase patient volume but are then forced to accept negotiated fees that are lower than their customary charges. In addition, their paperwork is increased.
- *Increased business involvement in health care delivery.* Increased involvement will lead to changes in benefits and coverage, providing incentives or disincentives for use of services, direct negotiations with providers for lower or capitated fees, and increased patient "shopping" based on insurance coverage.
- *Prospective payment or the possibility of capitation.* Both these possibilities present a large threat to physicians. However, the majority of physicians believe radical payment changes are inevitable. It appears that most individual physicians feel powerless to reduce the momentum in this direction (although

the AMA is actively participating in such discussions of this subject).

Physicians do not want to consider giving up their traditional payment system, especially at a time when incomes have leveled off or are dropping.

Lack of Control of Their Destiny. In addition to changes in payer mechanisms (Kaiser, other HMOs, PPOs, and prospective payment), many physicians participating in our focus group sessions expressed a feeling of helplessness about other events and changes that seem to be threatening their practice and their existence as fee-for-service physicians. Their greatest fear is that they will become employees of the hospital, the federal government, or large corporations and that they will thereby lose their independence and power. Some doctors believe that economic factors (higher costs, increased competition, pressure to lower fees) will squeeze many physicians out of business.

Physicians read, hear, sense, and anticipate changes, but they are usually unable to identify those points of intervention that would serve their interests. As mentioned earlier, hospital actions that potentially affect physicians' practices are the most susceptible to intervention, although many physicians are skeptical about their hospital's willingness to listen and accommodate them.

In many interview sessions, physicians made the comment that "practicing medicine isn't fun anymore." This comment relates to several of the factors discussed in previous paragraphs, but especially to the loss of control and consequent frustrations.

Other Factors. Several other factors influencing their practice of medicine were mentioned by doctors, but less frequently. However, when the concerns *were* expressed, it was with conviction:

- Increases in malpractice insurance premiums.
- Diversions from the practice of medicine or the actual delivery of care to meetings and marketing and business matters.
- Increases in the number of nonpaying patients.

- Public acceptance of lower-quality medical care.
- Less willingness on the part of hospitals to provide new technology.
- Emphasis on health promotion and the subsequent reduction in need for medical care. (This concern was not meant to be critical of health-promotion activities, but rather was a recognition of a factor impacting many doctors' practices.)
- "Industrialization" of medicine.
- Emphasis on medicine as a market-driven business.

Physician Optimism About the Future. Despite the numerous concerns discussed above, our research indicates that the majority of physicians are optimistic about the future of their medical practice. Younger doctors are most optimistic; those in the declining years of practice are usually less concerned about what happens. Those with the greatest concerns are in their forties and fifties, yet, as a group, even these physicians are generally optimistic.

Why do medical professionals have so much optimism when there are so many external factors threatening their traditional ways of practicing medicine, being paid for their services, and interrelating with their peers? We do not have the answer, but we can speculate. We have noticed in interviewing hundreds of small-business owners over the past twenty years that, regardless of the circumstances (poor economic conditions, new competitors opening next door, higher costs, and lower prices), the majority are optimistic. They think they can outperform their competitors; they have confidence in themselves. Being small-business owners themselves, physicians may have many of the same characteristics. They are self-confident and intelligent, and they have highly technical and specialized skills. It seems to us that they are bullish about their ability to find ways to accommodate their practices to the new competitive, price-sensitive marketplace.

Physician Market Segments

Physicians have responded with anything but a single voice to changes in their profession. In most hospitals today, "the opinion of the medical staff" is an outdated concept. There is a growing body of published surveys on the changing attitudes and actions of physicians. In addition, we have used a combination of one-on-one interviews and focus groups with physicians to explore opinions and actions in greater depth for numerous hospitals and insurer clients. Our review of the available data convinces us that, depending on the issue involved, the best way to predict physician receptivity to a concept is first to identify market segments based on specialty, years in practice or value systems, and then to analyze the concept from the perspective of each segment.

Physician Segmentation on the Basis of Specialty. The need for separate consideration of primary care physicians and specialists is obvious for many decisions. To begin with, patient acquisition strategies differ. Primary care physicians receive the vast majority of their patients through the patient's self-referral. The patient chooses the doctor, based on recommendations of family or friends, on the basis of insurance coverage, and so on (see Chapter Three). The typical specialist, on the other hand, relies on referrals from other physicians for 30 to 50 percent of his or her business. Neurologists and neurosurgeons receive almost 70 percent of their patients through physician referrals.

Physicians in different specialties also differ in the closeness of their association with hospitals. Family practice physicians, allergists, and dermatologists, for example, conduct the vast majority of their business in their offices. Others—internal medicine, general surgery, nephrology—see large numbers of inpatients. Still others—neurosurgery, cardiology, radiology—are often heavily dependent on large capital investments by hospitals and health systems.

Physicians also differ in time spent with patients. General practitioners, family practice physicians, and pediatricians spend an average of eleven to twelve minutes per encounter with a patient. Neurologists, cardiologists, endocrinologists, and gastroenterologists spend twenty to twenty-four minutes. Psychiatrists spend the longest, an average of thirty-eight minutes (*Medical Practice in the United States*, 1981).

Physician Segmentation on the Basis of Years in Practice. Wotruba, Haas, and Hartman, in "Targeting a Hospital's Marketing Efforts to Physicians' Needs" (1982), describe different phases in a physician's career that relate to age and to the number of years a physician has been in practice. They note that, not unlike attitudes in other professions, physicians' concerns and attitudes about their practices, goals, lifestyles, and incomes can be related to particular stages or experiences in the profession. The changing environment—particularly competition with other physicians, hospitals, and purchasers—is disrupting the traditional career cycle of physicians. Physicians near the end of their working years, for example, are not always in the comfortable and satisfied position they had expected by this point in their career. Confronted with the rapidly changing health care environment, many of these physicians simply choose to retire rather than "fight the system."

Practitioners in the middle phase of their career also tend to view the changes as a disruption of the traditional cycle. This is the point in their career at which their practice should be busy, their income increasing, and—at the later end of this period—they should be enjoying more leisure time. Unfortunately, this cycle is not materializing for many physicians in this category. They are opening satellite offices to cover two or more locations, extending office hours, participating in ADS, and providing services at a discounted rate. Physicians in highly competitive markets do not have the patient load they would like and are not generating increased net incomes.

Finally, younger physicians are in the most difficult position; with older physicians and hospitals in a patient acquisition mode, it is extremely difficult for young physicians to gain access to patients. Many younger doctors are attempting to deal with these difficulties by participating in physician referral services and ADS and by joining group practices.

Physician Segmentation on the Basis of Personality Groups. In our research, we have found that market segmentation by either specialty or years in practice does not account for a number of the current differences in physician attitudes and actions. To be sure, responses on many issues related to specific hospital services can still be best analyzed on the basis of specialty. For example, one can go a long way toward understanding a physician's attitude toward a highly specialized low back program by understanding whether he or she is a neurosurgeon, orthopedic surgeon, or physiatrist. It is also possible to predict attitudes toward paying for a referral service, knowing whether the physician is new or has an established practice.

Many of the newer threats to "business as usual" in medical practice, however, are more diffused. They depend on the physician's personal response to broad-based change. We have become increasingly convinced that many of today's issues can best be analyzed on the basis of four major personality groups among physicians:

- *Early innovators.* These physicians aggressively embrace new technologies, approaches, and financial concepts. They are less security-conscious than their peers, and generally highly optimistic about their practice. They tend to be younger, but some have been in practice for a long time. They are similar to "early adapters," who play a key role in new product innovation in consumer electronics and other industries. In today's medical environment, they are seen constantly suggesting or trying new joint ventures, office arrangements, and comarketing agreements.

- *Joiners.* Unlike early innovators, joiners are generally pessimistic about their medical practice. Joiners see the changes coming, and they believe they will be hurt. They are trying to cut their losses by trying everything—joining more than one medical staff, joining every possible PPO.

- *Traditionalists.* Traditionalists have a clear idea of how to practice medicine. They are most often disturbed by the changes. Traditionalists may oppose many efforts by medical staffs or hospitals to compete; they urge holding the line.

- *Pure practitioners.* The pure practitioner says, "I learned how to be a doctor, not a small-business owner." In rapidly increasing numbers, this segment of the medical community is eschewing private practice, even an already well-established practice, and joining staff model HMOs or taking paid positions on hospital-based staffs.

The Quality Segment of the Future. "Our troubles are just beginning," said the head of a six-month-old IPA (independent practice association)–based HMO. "We just got our first quality assurance data, and they show that the head of the IPA is ordering and being reimbursed for three times as many tests as anyone else." In the future, we believe an additional critical segmentation of physicians will be based on their methods of practice, cost-effectiveness, and (to the extent it can be measured) quality of care. While there exist groups, such as peer review organizations, that are currently involved in monitoring the quality and appropriateness of care and in identifying aberrant patterns in physicians' practices, these organizations fail to provide clinically based normative standards that can be used to monitor physicians' practices. Systems to better describe, monitor, and evaluate physician quality in terms of outcome, though in the process of being developed, are as yet a few years away. However, once such standardized criteria are developed, there will be high demand, especially by such large purchasers as ADS and employers, for documentation of doctors' quality and efficiency before purchasing physician services.

Future Trends and Implications

We have heard a few hospital administrators express the following sentiment: "Given a few years, we'll have them [the physicians] eating out of our hands." We do not believe this will happen. Physicians are experiencing wholesale changes. By and large, however, they are not on the defensive, and we do not expect that they will be. As will be discussed in more detail in Chapter Ten, it is better to work with physicians, respecting their positions of strength and recognizing them as a group that will continue to bring substantial resources to the table as new physician-hospital partnerships are hammered out.

We expect physicians, as business people, to become more hard-nosed, cost-conscious, market-oriented, and open to new ventures or other financial arrangements. The easy flow of referrals among physicians in different specialties is also likely to undergo change as doctors more actively direct their marketing efforts toward each other.

As time progresses, we expect an increasingly higher proportion of the remaining private practice physicians in competitive urban markets to be either early innovators or joiners, with fewer traditionalists choosing to practice in these markets and more pure practitioners choosing something other than private practice. The young, primary care early innovator deserves special attention in today's marketplace—attention that presents special problems for those hospitals in which the organized medical staff is dominated by older, specialist traditionalists.

We expect private practice physicians to adopt many of the currently evolving aspects of other competitive service businesses. These include organized marketing programs, larger group practices, and performance-based incentives. The basis of future coordinated marketing efforts will be the practice-building activities already carried out by many physicians today:

- Joining HMOs or PPOs
- Using advertising and public relations
- Training staff in patient relations
- Extending hours
- Joining physician referral services
- Becoming more active on the medical staff of one or more hospitals (to increase referrals)
- Generating referrals through professional activities (papers, meetings)
- Joining group practices
- Joining independent practice associations (IPAs)

With the physician surplus gaining momentum, we expect doctors, especially those just starting into the practice of medicine, to become much more marketing-oriented. New primary care doctors, for example, will not be able to wait for word-of-mouth advertising to attract patients; they will find it necessary to reach out for patients or to join a group practice that already has an established base. Physician compensation will increasingly be a function of the ability to attract patients, with the top generators of business reaping the rewards, as is now true in other professions (law, accounting, architecture, management consulting). In fact, an "up or out" approach may develop; successfully attract patients, and in increasing numbers, or leave.

Referral and admission practices within the private practice medical community will be based more frequently on financial incentives. Larger group practices will allow physicians who are high-volume referral sources to participate more often in the profits resulting from their referrals. These large-group practices will also negotiate aggressively with the hospitals to which they admit most of their patients.

3

The Consumer Market

"I know our hospital's census is dropping, but if you look ahead three to five years, the proportion of people in our market area over sixty-five will increase by half again. When that happens, there will be a shortage of beds in our area." We have heard this scenario on more than one occasion. Is it wishful thinking or a realistic projection of what will happen?

Consumers are the ultimate market for health care services; they are the patients. What will be the future consumer demand for health care services? How, for example, does the aging of the population, and the corresponding impact on demand for health care services, relate to overall improvements in health due to our emphasis on diet, exercise, and the desirability of not smoking? How will consumers' concerns be reflected in the marketplace? For example, what is the consumer's role in selecting physicians, health plans, and hospitals, and how is it likely to change over the next few years? Finally, what are the most useful ways to segment and approach the consumer market?

Factors Influencing Consumer Health Care Demand

Technically speaking, demand determines the quantity of goods or services that will be purchased at a specified price. Using this definition, the demand for health care is influenced by several factors, including the general health of consumers, the payment mechanisms for health care, the ability to pay on the part of those footing the bill, and the priority placed on purchasing health care versus other types of goods or services.

   Shifting Demographics and the Need for Health Care Services. There are 239 million people living in the United States. Figure 1 shows the number in each major age and sex cohort for 1985, as well as projected numbers for 1995 (U.S. Bureau of the Census, 1985b, p. 25). The projections clearly show that the older groups, those persons aged forty-five to sixty-four, and sixty-five and over, will increase very substantially. In 1985, these two groups represented 30.7 percent of the U.S. population; by 1995 they will represent 33.6 percent.

   How will these shifts affect the number of visits to physicians' offices, number of surgical procedures, number of admissions, and patient-days?

   An older population is certainly a factor in favor of higher usage of medical services. In 1984, United States consumers aged sixty-five and over had an average of 350 hospital discharges per 1,000 residents; this compares to 132 per 1,000 consumers aged fifteen to forty-four (Richter, 1986, p. 16). Counterbalancing this trend, however, we are riding the crest of a strong "wellness wave," which most observers expect has further potential to reduce inpatient visits. Still other factors relate to medical practice itself—for example, the utilization rates that result from an HMO-based medical practice as opposed to a cost-reimbursement-based medical practice, and the continuing growth of outpatient surgery. The combined effect of all of these factors on future health care utilization has been the subject of numerous analyses, leading to a wide range of projections (discussed in greater detail in Appendix A).

   Our forecasts of the effects of these factors on three indicators of the quantity of health care services are shown in Table 3. These data and projections indicate that despite the aging of the population, the overall health care market, as measured in number of total transactions (visits, admissions, procedures) will continue

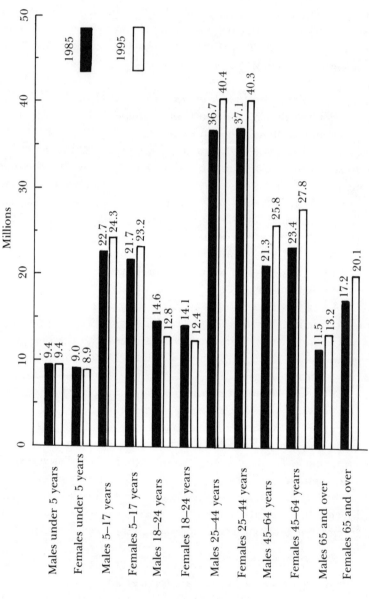

Figure 1. Age Cohorts by Sex in 1985 and 1995.

Millions

1985 ■   1995 □

Cohort	1985	1995
Males under 5 years	9.4	9.4
Females under 5 years	9.0	8.9
Males 5–17 years	22.7	24.3
Females 5–17 years	21.7	23.2
Males 18–24 years	14.6	12.8
Females 18–24 years	14.1	12.4
Males 25–44 years	36.7	40.4
Females 25–44 years	37.1	40.3
Males 45–64 years	21.3	25.8
Females 45–64 years	23.4	27.8
Males 65 and over	11.5	13.2
Females 65 and over	17.2	20.1

Source: U.S. Bureau of the Census, 1985b, p.25.

Table 3. Projected Health Care Market Indicators.

Key Indicator	1985	1995
Number of visits to physicians' offices (per person)	5.2	5.1
Hospital inpatient admissions (millions)	33.4	31.0
Hospital inpatient days (millions)	237.1	198.4

to decrease between now and 1995. Perhaps more important, we can expect still further shifts in health care payment. These are discussed below.

Shifts in Payment Mechanisms. Payment mechanisms used by consumers have shifted dramatically before, and they are about to shift again. Eli Ginzberg (1986) points out that the health care industry experienced numerous repercussions when third-party reimbursements increased from 77 percent to 91 percent of total costs (p. 758). Now we prepare for a reduction in those reimbursements from 65 percent currently to 15 percent in 1995, in terms of proportion of the work force covered by commercial indemnity insurance.

This loss of commercial indemnity coverage will result from the combined effects of demographic shifts of a large segment of the population into Medicare eligibility, and growth in the ADS market share. (The competitive factors within the health care insurance industry are discussed in more detail in Chapter Six.) The anticipated shift between 1985 and 1995 is summarized in Table 4.

The overall implications of this shift, addressed throughout the book, are massive. The first implication for consumer demand is that commercial indemnity insurers, the typical third-party payers of "usual and customary fees," will drop from 65 percent to 15 percent of the total consumer market.

Consumers' Willingness and Ability to Pay. As discussed in Chapter One, the typical working consumer is likely to be given more and more flexibility and choice in health plans. How, then,

Table 4. Shifts in Payment Mechanisms.

Health Plan Coverage	Percent of Population	
	1985	1995
Commercial Indemnity Insurance	65%	15%
HMOs and PPOs	10	60
Medicare (Includes Medicare HMOs)	12	14
Other Public Sources (Department of Defense, Veterans Administration, Other)	3	3
No Insurance, Indigents	10	8
Total	100%	100%

Source: Data extracted from Public Relations Division, Health Insurance Association of America, 1985, pp. 4, 11; projections to 1995 are the authors'.

will consumers respond to these options? What will be their ability and willingness to pay for basic and supplemental health services?

Our consumer focus group research for hospitals and HMOs has led us to believe that most consumers in households earning more than $35,000 per year are willing to pay out of pocket (over and above their health plan costs) for additional services. If they perceive an opportunity to receive a better room, more personalized services, or less waiting time to receive a medical remedy, they will often be willing to pay for it.

The income distribution of U.S. households in 1985 is shown in Table 5. These data indicate that in 1985, 28 percent of U.S. households earned $35,000 or more. Projections suggest that by 1995, about one-third of all households will be in this income group (expressed in 1985 dollars—that is, inflation eliminated from the comparison), indicating that the proportion of U.S. households able to pay for quality health care is large and growing. The percentages translate into 86 million persons in households earning $35,000 or more by 1995.

Consumer Choice in Health Care

Not surprisingly, the health care literature has begun to highlight the issue of consumer decision making. This tends to

Table 5. U.S. Income Distribution, 1985.

Household Income	Percent of Population
Under $15,000	33.3%
$15,000–$24,999	21.8
$25,000–$34,999	16.9
$35,000–$49,999	15.3
$50,000 and over	12.8
Total	100.0%

Source: U.S. Bureau of the Census, 1985b, p. 445.

happen in any industry that becomes competitive. There is growing evidence that the consumer has begun to play an increasingly large role in all aspects of health care decision making. If our view of likely employer actions in the future is correct, consumers will be offered even more choices than they have today. What can we learn, then, from what the consumer has chosen thus far?

Choice of Physicians. A number of different national surveys, several of which were performed by National Research Corporation (NRC) and have recently appeared in *Modern Healthcare,* have shown that about 80 percent of all U.S. consumers twenty-five and over have a personal physician. The proportion of consumers with personal physicians varies from 76 percent for those in the twenty-five to thirty-four age group, to 84 percent for those sixty-five and over. There are only slight variations by income; that is, those in the higher income categories are just above the average in terms of having a personal physician.

Given the expected large-scale shifts toward HMO and PPO coverage, where it is frequently necessary to have a primary care doctor as a "gatekeeper," we expect a slight increase in the proportion of consumers with a personal physician. However, that proportion is unlikely to exceed 85 percent.

How do consumers select a primary care physician? According to a number of different surveys, about 50 percent of all consumers select their doctor on the recommendation of friends and family. Approximately 10 percent go to the same physician they have been going to for years and do not remember how they initially chose that doctor; 10 percent are referred to their physician by a hospital or another doctor; 3 percent select their physician because of HMO requirements; 4 percent go to their doctor because they know him or her personally; 2 percent use the telephone book to find a doctor; and 22 percent either do not know how they chose their doctor or identify other methods for selecting a particular physician (Jackson and Jensen, 1984).

If today's consumer research correctly predicts tomorrow's consumer behavior, referral services will become a part of the selection mode for many consumers. In recent surveys, 15 percent of consumers indicated use of physician referral services, and approximately 60 percent said they would make use of them if available (Jensen, 1986).

The selection process varies, depending on the degree of physician specialization required. Primary care physicians receive over 90 percent of their patients through some form of direct decision making by the consumer, while many specialists receive over half their patients through a referral by another physician (see Chapter Two).

The physician selection process differs for men and women. Women select the physician for their household 53 percent of the time, while men do so only 28 percent of the time. Women express a "willingness to seek a physician with whom they feel comfortable even if they must shop around." Most women and men are satisfied with their current choices of physicians. However, perhaps related to their greater role in choosing physicians, a higher proportion of women are satisfied (81 percent) than men (71 percent) (Jensen, 1986, p. 66).

Choice of Health Plans. To date, many consumers' choice of health plans has been confined to deciding whether to enroll in the single commercial indemnity plan or the single HMO offered by employers. However, an increasing number of households have begun to do comparison shopping between alternative commercial indemnity plans, or alternative HMOs and perhaps PPOs. Many come from two-income households, with alternative plans available from both the husband's and wife's employers.

Based on our focus group research, the health plan selection process differs substantially from physician selection. Although household decision making on health plans is usually done together, men are more likely than women to play the more active role. Thus far, neither advice from physicians nor advice from friends and relatives plays a key role. (We believe the physician's role will change, however, as physicians come to recognize the fundamental importance of this decision.) The consumer's fellow employees, employer, and/or union are the key sources of health plan advice.

Consumer comparisons of health plans focus on several issues—whether or not the current family physician is on the physician panel, out-of-pocket costs, coverage limitations, hospital availability, and general freedom of choice of providers. Most research shows that the physician is the key to consumers' health plan choice: accessibility and quality top the list.

Current research into consumer health plan behavior reveals a substantial amount of inertia. Most consumers with commercial indemnity coverage are satisfied with the present fee-for-service system. Their few complaints relate to the relatively minor efforts by most plans at cost containment—for example, having to go through a primary care gatekeeper, use of preadmission certification, and second opinions on surgery. The least difficult part of the HMO marketing job has been accomplished—attracting younger, middle-income consumers who are less likely to have established ties to physicians, hospitals, or other health care providers. From here on out, it will be harder. The consumer transition to ADS will be relatively easy if there are no major differences in the plan from the consumer's point of view. However, ADS plans that limit the consumers' choice of physicians may meet heavy resistance. As indicated in Chapter One, we do not see most employees having either the incentive or the commitment needed to overcome this resistance.

Choice of Hospitals. Ninety percent of all adult women and 75 percent of all adult men have had at least one experience as a patient in a hospital. About one-quarter of the U.S. population has been hospitalized in the past three years; only 13 percent of adults twenty-five and over have never been hospitalized. Looking ahead, these overall percentages are likely to decrease as more diagnostic and surgical procedures are performed on an outpatient basis. Therefore, from a marketing viewpoint, the number of consumers having a firsthand basis for evaluating hospitals will decrease slightly over the next few years.

Until recently, conventional wisdom has been that the consumer selects the physician, and the physician selects the hospital. When we first surveyed consumers on their hospital selection patterns in 1985, we could not believe our data: a high percentage of consumers hospitalized in the past three years say that they (that is, the consumers) selected the hospital, or that the decision was a joint one with their physician.

Recent interviews with physicians support the notion that a change has occurred; consumers *are* becoming more active participants in hospital selection. Physicians are tending to look more and more at the decision as a joint one with the patient.

For consumers, the factors most often considered in hospital selection are convenience (proximity to home), presence of their physician on the hospital's medical staff, reputation for quality of care, good past experience, and presence of specialized services (Inguanzo and Harju, 1985b, pp. 90–94). The relative importance of these factors varies by age, with younger patients emphasizing convenience slightly more than persons in other age categories.

What about the future? How will the major changes in health plan coverage affect the consumer's role in the hospital selection process? We believe that these changes will have a major impact. First, consumers will be offered financial incentives to use hospitals designated as preferred providers in the company health plan; selection of a hospital not in the plan will normally require a substantial extra payment (disincentive) out of the consumers' pocket. (As noted earlier, if consumers perceive significant quality differences among hospitals, many will be willing to pay extra.) Second, it is likely, at least in the next few years, that physicians will seek privileges in multiple hospitals in order to be available on their patients' various health plans. This means that consumers may be able to use their regular physician at two or more hospitals, broadening their choice.

As discussed in Chapter Five, it is critically important that hospitals attempt to differentiate themselves (on the basis of, for example, quality of care, convenience, equipment/technology, reputation, cleanliness) in order to attract increasingly knowledgeable consumers. There are large dollars at stake in this issue, and for many hospitals, it is a matter of survival.

Consumer Market Segments

In an era of consumer choice, market segmentation becomes critical. Marketing approaches can be made far more efficient if they are tailored to specific types of consumers. Products and services can yield higher consumer satisfaction if they are tailored to meet specific needs. At this point, there are several commonly used market segments—women (aged twenty-five to sixty-five), seniors (sixty-five and over), working men, and children (newborns to age eighteen). Examples of more refined consumer market splits include working women with children, women under forty with a college education (by far the most interested and knowledgeable consumer group when it comes to health care), single women, and seniors seventy-five and over (frail). There is no single best approach to consumer market segmentation; it depends on the marketing approach for any new program or service being considered. As mentioned in Chapter Seven, a hospital considering a comprehensive breast diagnostic center would target high-risk women (aged forty and over). A new service for people with serious back problems would target the relatively small group of people with such problems. For a new congregate care facility, the population seventy-five and over in a specific geographic area would be the relevant market segment.

Providers' immediate interest in the health care markets of women and the elderly is well founded in terms of the size of these two market segments. Specialized services for women are often the most profitable part of a hospital's activities, while the over-sixty-five age group makes the most intensive use of health care services. It follows that as the ranks of the elderly continue to swell well past the turn of the century, seniors will continue to represent the largest market segment, in terms of dollars, for doctors and hospitals. These two segments—women and seniors—are described in more detail in the paragraphs that follow.

Women's Market. There are seventy-four million women in the United States between the ages of eighteen and sixty-four. They represent 31 percent of the population, but approximately 61 percent of all surgeries. In financial terms, women's health is approximately a $280 billion market.

A survey of hospital trustees indicates that about one-quarter of all hospitals are already involved in a specialized women's health program or a women's facility. Another 11 percent say that their hospital is planning to develop a women's health program, while 16 percent say that their hospital is considering such a move. This trend reflects current interest in the women's health market.

Our research indicates that a substantial proportion of all women prefer a hospital that specializes in women's health services, with younger women especially interested. Given the increased emphasis on women's health, and the advertising and public relations efforts being expended on behalf of women's health centers, it is our prediction that the market will increasingly favor specialized women's services.

Sally Rynne, an authority on the women's health market, points out that the key is breadth of services. "Any women's health program that is oriented only towards the reproductive system is missing the mark" (1985). Women's health programs at acute care hospitals often include several of the following: OB/GYN, mammography/breast screening, nutrition and weight control (education), stress management, osteoporosis, mental health, chemical and alcohol dependency, fitness, PMS, parenting, cosmetic surgery, and oncology. Yet our focus group research has shown that most women do not know what a hospital offers when it promotes a women's health program. Women tend to think in terms of OB/GYN services and are generally confused as to what else may be included. Most women's health centers associated with acute care hospitals have not yet successfully communicated with women in the age, income, and educational groups most likely to be interested in a comprehensive women's health program.

Seniors' Market. As noted earlier in this chapter, the seniors' market is growing: there are 28.7 million persons aged sixty-five and over in this country, with that number expected to increase to 34.0 million by 1995. According to the latest data on the subject, persons sixty-five and over comprise 12 percent of the population but account for 33 percent of all hospital beds occupied (Dychtwald, 1985, p. 66).

Seniors' health care concerns are varied, with Medicare and insurance coverage at the top of the list. Other concerns are quality physicians, good hospital care, availability of specialists, and illness prevention. Despite the fact that nearly all persons over age sixty-five have Medicare, Medicare supplemental insurance (called Medigap insurance), and continued coverage from their company insurance, a high percentage still worry about their ability to pay in the event of catastrophic illness or injury.

Because mortality is decreasing, fewer of the elderly are dying from acute conditions, while more of this age group are acquiring chronic illnesses or disabling conditions. This, plus society's high general level of mobility, has prompted high interest in a spectrum of arrangements that combine housing and medical care.

This spectrum ranges from recreation-oriented retirement communities to condominiums, cooperative housing (similar to condominiums, but with cooperative ownership), congregate living (including housing, meals, and personal services—usually for persons aged seventy-five and over), assisted living, and skilled nursing homes. About one million persons live in the approximately 2,300 U.S. retirement communities, and this number will undoubtedly grow as the over-sixty-five segment of the population continues to expand well past the turn of the century. According to the president of Gerontological Planning Associates, "Hospitals must enter the continuing care market to survive and retirement communities are high on the list of services hospitals must begin offering. . . . Continuing care communities will serve as feeders to other hospital services such as acute care, home care, hospice care and counseling . . ." (Wallace, 1985, p. 79).

The most pressing, relevant need within this spectrum is for nursing homes. Between 1978 and 2003, according to the U.S. Department of Health and Human Services, the number of nursing home residents should increase by 57 percent. In order to keep up with this growth, 320 100-bed nursing homes would have to be built each year until 2003.

Although the need for long-term nursing home care is rapidly increasing, the cost of such care is not covered by Medicare or by any other type of health insurance. With the cost of care running as high as $25,000 annually, seniors' anxiety about their ability to pay their medical bills is well founded. The little coverage that Medicare does offer is limited to skilled nursing facilities. "Although Medicare covers up to 100 days of nursing home care, on the average it only pays for 28 days . . . because it is designed to cover post-hospital care. To qualify, patients must have been in a hospital, need skilled nursing care and have a potential for rehabilitation" (Riche, 1985, p. 36). Medicare supplemental insurance does not normally cover the cost of nursing homes; such policies typically pay only the difference between the Medicare benefits and the nursing home charges for the days that Medicare covers for short term care.

This suggests an unmet need for further health insurance coverage in the area of long-term care. One group recognizing this need is the American Association of Retired People (AARP); with Prudential, they are in the process of developing such a plan. Not only would the envisioned policy cover long-term nursing home costs, but it would also provide such services as visits by a home health care aide or physical therapist so that those persons preferring custodial care in their own home would be able to make that choice.

Future Trends and Implications

We began this book with a discussion of the destabilization of the health care industry. Now add a new factor for the future: fragmentation. We are witnessing increasing consumer choice relative to health plans and health care services, an increasing divergence in services sought by different segments of the consumer market, an increasing likelihood that employers and insurers will be tailoring programs and shopping for high value received for each dollar of expenditure.

Market and provider fragmentation has several implications for the health care industry. First, it means more flexibility in the provision of services, more options for consumers. This market flexibility creates a need for more entrepreneurship and a greater customer orientation at all levels of the health care system. Fragmentation also necessitates better coordination, more communication, and somewhat higher costs for providing more specialized services tailored to the needs of very specific market segments.

Perhaps more important, fragmentation means that for many providers, the economics of each service or program will have to stand on its own. In the future, it will not be as easy to cross-subsidize indigent care with profits from a strong women's health program. Instead, it will be necessary to invest in new women's health services in order to retain market share for that part of the market.

4

Government, Economic, and Technological Trends

In addition to the three major market segments just discussed—employers, physicians, and consumers—there are a number of additional external factors, usually beyond the control of local health care systems, that are critical in assessing the relevance of the future strategic options described in Part Two. These factors include government policies (for example, Medicare reimbursement levels, certificates of need, and malpractice insurance rates and the availability of this type of coverage), national and local economic conditions, and expected changes in medical technology.

The brief discussion that follows can be supplemented by referring to the projections contained in Appendix A. We contend that the major changes of the past four years, and the countervailing forces that are emerging, suggest a more orderly health care environment over the next three to five years. Although considerable uncertainty remains in the health care environment, we believe the period of greatest destabilization is gradually coming to a close.

Government Policies and Business Regulation

Medicare. At the federal level, Medicare can be expected to continue to use prospective payment as a basis for reimbursement, with DRGs as the payment unit for the near term. Some allowance for capital recovery may be included, but overall the amounts paid for DRGs will continue to be tightly controlled. Federal deficit problems almost assure increasing financial pressure on the Medicare program. Price increases for DRGs will be substantially less than the Consumer Price Index.

Medicare will probably refine its DRG system to allow for "severity of illness" (described in more detail in Chapter Thirteen). This will help tertiary care hospitals (many are teaching and research facilities) but work against smaller hospitals and those that handle less complex cases.

Physicians' fees are likely to be converted to a prospective payment basis for Medicare patients, and federal policy will continue to encourage Medicare beneficiaries to enroll in HMOs. By the mid-1990s, Medicare (and many other insurers) is likely to reimburse physicians and hospitals on a capitation basis.

Peer review, especially for Medicare, will be more thorough: "The care rendered by hospitals will undergo increased review and evaluation. . . . The sophistication and agressiveness of these organizations [peer review organizations] will greatly increase. . . . Increasingly review organizations will be focusing on the question of identifying the best hospitals to be treating specific kinds of patients" (Averill and Kalison, 1986, p. 52).

CON. At the state level, certificate of need (CON) laws will be virtually nonexistent by 1990. This is not to imply that CON laws have not been effective in curtailing huge outlays for medical equipment and bricks and mortar; we believe persuasive evidence exists that they have been effective. The existence of such laws has also helped health care systems access the capital markets; potential investors in hospital tax-exempt bonds have had more confidence knowing there were controls on the construction of new hospital capacity, that to qualify for CON approval a project had gone through a rigorous review process. But the fact remains that CON laws are inconsistent with a free market, and the health care industry has become a highly competitive market.

In efforts to gain competitive advantage, even more acute and specialty care hospital capacity is likely to be built. This flies in the face of dire predictions of massive hospital closures because of excess capacity and declining demand, but it is consistent with what is happening in other U.S. industries: office buildings, shopping centers, and banking offices are also experiencing substantial excess capacity.

Overall Health Policy. Demographic shifts will cause a significantly higher portion of the population to be eligible for Medicare. Market fragmentation will place pressures on health care insurers and providers to provide customized, high-value products for each market segment. Together, these factors will mean fewer and fewer dollars available to cross-subsidize either the Medicare or the indigent population.

Our crystal ball with respect to overall indigent and Medicare financing problems is no better than those of other industry watchers. Regardless of the overall financing outcome, however, there will be more and more economic pressures for multitiered health care services. The economic forces are clear; more consumer market segments, including more affluent elderly patients, will demand and be willing to pay for a higher level of service than that which will be reimbursed by the federal government. Ethical considerations may not be able to override economic pressures in providing service differences affecting medical outcomes. Market pressures to provide a "first cabin" hospital experience will be strong.

Malpractice Insurance. Rapidly escalating premiums for malpractice insurance are having a substantial impact on the way physicians practice medicine and how hospitals compete for physicians' business. The birthing center movement, for example, may never get off the ground because of obstetricians' perceived higher risks at these facilities. This physician group is under intense financial pressure because of escalating malpractice rates (a premium of $30,000 per year is not uncommon). By 1990, we believe that most states will have moved to place a cap on medical malpractice awards. This action will be especially important to smaller hospitals and those in rural areas, and to physicians in high-risk specialties (for example, obstetricians and neurosurgeons). In the meantime, hospital and medical staff strategic initiatives will be increasingly influenced by the perceived threats of lawsuits and the potential impacts of these legal actions on malpractice premiums.

National and Local Economic Conditions

Since 1983, when the health care environment entered its period of greatest destabilization, economic conditions in the United States have been relatively stable, with inflation and interest rates generally declining. Local economic conditions have varied tremendously, from boomlike growth in parts of Florida to severe depression in areas dependent on mining or heavy manufacturing. What the future brings, in terms of national and local economic conditions, will obviously have important implications for many health care systems, hospitals, and physicians.

Forced into making a short-term forecast of the U.S. economy, we see slow growth, no significant increase in the Consumer Price Index, relatively low interest rates, and continuing federal budget deficits in the $150 billion to $250 billion range. The U.S. economy has tremendous excess productive capacity in virtually all sectors; therefore, new growth will be hard to come by. On the other hand, the overhang of productive capacity should restrain inflation. On the latter point, future inflation rates, the price of oil is an imponderable.

In preparing a local health care environmental assessment, future economic trends in the market area are critically important. How many new jobs will be created each year? Conversely, will there be a decline in employment and an outmigration of population? Will local employers tighten up on employee benefits, especially health plans? The present employer inertia in changing health plans described in Chapter One could change if economic conditions deteriorate, and the problem of uncompensated care could worsen. Local economic forecasts are available in most areas of the United States, and these studies should be reviewed and incorporated into the strategic planning process.

Likely Changes in Medical Technology

Medical technology has played and will continue to play an important role in the health care environment. Rapid advances in medical technology and an equally rapid diffusion of technology have had a strong impact on the quality of care (both treatment and outcome) as well as on the costs of treatment and overall U.S. health care expenditures.

A Look Back. Historically, there has been a strong link between new technology and the hospital. As improvements in technology occurred, hospitals generally adopted the new technology to satisfy their medical staff, for prestige, and to attract patients. Although new technologies typically led to additional costs, such technologies have historically conferred benefits that outweighed the costs: improved processing speed and elimination of invasive, costly, and more risky procedures (for example, the CAT scan replacing exploratory brain surgery, or the drug cimitedine replacing ulcer surgery). Rapid market adoption has been predicated on two key factors—government validation of the safety and efficacy of new technologies and acceptance by insurers for reimbursement.

Future Trends. In the future, acquisition of medical technologies by hospitals will be influenced by several factors:

- Decline in volume of services
- Increased use of out-of-hospital technologies
- Increased specialization and regionalization of capital-intensive services

In an attempt to identify significant health care technologies that will appear in the next five to fifteen years, the Congressional Office of Technology Assessment (OTA), the government of the Netherlands, and the World Health Organization conducted a survey to identify those technologies. The large majority of survey respondents were academic researchers, both M.D.'s and Ph.D.'s; other respondents included representatives from industry and such U.S. agencies as the Food and Drug Administration, the National Institutes of Health, and the Center for Disease Control. Approximately 100 responses were received.

The responses fell into fourteen categories covering almost all aspects of clinical medicine, as well as computer and information technology, biologies and pharmaceuticals, basic sciences, and organizational and analytical technologies (see Table 6). The survey results published to date do not identify the predicted order and speed of development of the technologies.

From a very different perspective, the investment banking firm L. F. Rothschild, Unterberg, Towbin identified developing medical technologies that will continue to replace inpatient services (Vignola, 1984):

Service	*Site*
Parenteral nutrition	Home
Chymopapain	No surgery
Ophthalmic laser surgery	Outpatient
Arthroscopy	Outpatient
Continuous ambulatory peritoneal dialysis	Home
Inhalation therapy	Home
Immunodiagnostics	Home

In the same analysis, technologies expected to play an important role in the future were identified:

Service/Product	*Site*
Bone marrow transplant	Inpatient
Laser surgery	Outpatient/inpatient
Balloon angioplasty	Inpatient
Artificial organs	Inpatient
Hormonal research	Outpatient/inpatient
Magnetic resonance	Outpatient/inpatient

Table 6. Future Health Care Technologies.

I.   Artificial and Transplanted Organs and Tissues

Advances in immunosuppressive drugs and increased knowledge of the immune system will encourage tissue and organ transplants in existing and new areas. Transportation of artificial tissues and organs is expected to improve with implants and improved materials. Prosthetics will become more sophisticated.

II.   Biotechnology-Related

Biotechnology advances, such as monoclonal antibodies and DNA probes, will enhance diagnostic and therapeutic practices. Home diagnostic testing will be dramatically improved, as will vaccines and human gene therapy.

III.   Medical Imaging and Other Diagnostic Technologies

Existing and emerging imaging technologies will continue to evolve rapidly. Additionally, new imaging technologies will become available, such as imaging using nonlinear acoustic parameters of tissues and organs or using the kirilian effect.

IV.   Computer and Information Technology

Computer and information technology will be improved to assist in clinical medicine—diagnostic and therapeutic protocols, medical decision making, and patient monitoring. In addition, improvements in access to medical records and tying clinical and administrative data together will improve management in the health care system.

V.   Mental Health, Behavior, Psychiatry

The several fields applicable to behavior, such as neurochemistry, neurobiology, psychopharmacology, and behavioral science may be the setting for great advances in the coming decade.

VI.   Biologies and Pharmaceuticals

Advances in vaccines are highly dependent on advances in biotechnology. The potential exists for safer and more effective versions of current vaccines, but also for new vaccines against infectious diseases and against diseases that were formerly or are currently considered candidates for prevention through immunization.

VII.   Reproduction; Fetal and Child Health

New approaches to infertility and contraception will be developed, and improvements in fetal and child health will be seen.

VIII.   Surgical Advances

A full range of surgery-related advances was identified, ranging from operating room instrumentation and anesthesia develop-

Table 6. Future Health Care Technologies, Cont'd.

ments to improvements in wound healing. Surgery will be dramatically affected by laser transplants and implant technologies.

IX. Laser Technology

Laser applications in medicine are likely to increase in the future. Uses will include surgical applications (cutting, excisions, mending), medical applications (for example, photocoagulation or antitumor activity), stimulation or activation applications (for example, inert drugs within the body), and other possible applications.

X. Blood Banking

Blood banking technology is changing rapidly. Recombinant DNA technologies are being applied to the production of plasma proteins, and other technologies are under development for the production of the cellular components of blood. With advanced pheresis technologies, the role of blood banking institutions may broaden.

XI. Miscellaneous Therapies

Several types of therapies were identified. The large percentage of responses identified technologies relative to two leading causes of death—heart disease and cancer.

XII. Social and Rehabilitation

Very few responses fell into this category. Two general responses identified were in geriatric rehabilitation and centralized rehabilitation ADP (automated data processing) systems.

XIII. Organizational, Administrative, Analytical

Advances in this category do not involve specific clinical medicine technologies, but are the "process" technologies or technological applications that serve to support or organize the delivery of health care. Several specific responses were related to increased uses of computers and statistical analysis in the delivery of health care and technologies related to nonhospital treatment of patients.

XIV. Basic Sciences, Physics, Chemistry, Materials

Specific responses included several regarding implants as well as cyclotron advances and synthetic membrane technology.

Source: Adapted from Office of Technology Assessment, U.S. Congress, 1985.

Funding for research and development into new technologies is not likely to be as readily available as it has been in the past. Additionally, many hospitals' ability to acquire technology will be more restricted because of their inability to tap funding sources (see Chapter Seventeen). Both factors will slow the diffusion of new technologies.

Overall Trends in Utilization of Health Care Services

Patient-Day Trends. Although most industry observers believe that health care demand, especially for inpatient services, will continue to decrease, there is wide disagreement as to the magnitude and duration of the decline. Todd Richter of Morgan Stanley is one of the most pessimistic; he projects that by 1995 hospital patient-days will be half of what they were in 1986. Bernstein Research believes that with the recent drop in patient-days the hospital industry currently has 30 percent too many beds. Other industry observers believe that following the precipitous drop in patient-days from 271 million in 1980 to 237 million in 1985, demand has begun to level off. This leveling off scenario assumes that most of the fat has been taken out of the health care system, that the aging of the population will gradually lead to increased demand, and that most of the surgical procedures that can safely be performed on an outpatient basis are already being done that way, leaving only limited potential for further growth in the outpatient market.

In our opinion, overall U.S. demand for inpatient services will continue to decline for at least the next five years, but at a more gradual rate than experienced since 1983. There are a large number of forces influencing this trend; several were mentioned earlier. The increasing role of ADS, better-developed home health care services, and more emphasis on nutrition, exercise, and overall wellness will come together to influence the number of inpatient-days. Physician practice patterns in some parts of the United States, where there appear to be unwarranted numbers of surgeries for hysterectomies and other diagnoses, are likely to come into line with national norms. On the other hand, there is increasing evidence that hospitals and physicians may not be able to reduce length of stay much further, especially for Medicare patients. The typically low hospitalization rates for HMO members cannot, in our opinion, be extrapolated for the additional large number of new members expected in such plans; studies have shown that most HMO members are younger and tend to be healthier than the population as a whole.

Variations in Local Utilization. Given an overall national decline in demand for inpatient-days, how does this translate into impacts on a specific market area? We believe that there will be a wide range of local demand situations, ranging from substantial increases in patient-days to very drastic reductions in the use of hospitals. Why the great variations? Because of the large differences in physician practice patterns in some parts of the country, and changing demographics, especially in popular retirement areas such as Florida, Arizona, and southern California. In some Florida communities, for example, hospital inpatient demand increased 10 percent between 1985 and 1986.

Future Trends and Implications

These are the key characteristics that we see emerging as the health care system restabilizes:

- Customization within health plans, with a focus on higher value received per health plan dollar.
- A continuing growth in ADS, providing a focus on discounts from physicians and hospitals but with increasing emphasis on utilization review.
- Increased competition among physicians, with fewer solo practices, lower net incomes, and more intrusion of economic factors in referral patterns.
- A breakdown of consensus-based decision making within hospital medical staffs.
- Consumer market fragmentation, with more tailoring of services to specific market groups.
- More differentiation among local health care markets.

This last point is particularly important. Regardless of national trends, local markets are likely to differ far more than in the past. Some markets will have more or less competition among physicians or among hospitals. Some markets will be the focus of intense competition between health plans. Some will be dominated by large, cost-conscious employers.

Each health care decision maker must understand his or her market and then choose the best approach. Part Two builds a basis for choosing the right approach by examining the strategies used in different market situations.

Part Two

Strategies for Gaining
and Sustaining
Competitive Advantage

"The only way to describe my professional life is 'a deal a day,'"
said the chief financial officer of one hospital. Fortunately for
some administrators, and unfortunately for others, the destabilized
health care environment of the past four years has provided
hundreds of experiments in developing new strategies. Like any set
of experiments, only a small number have yielded positive results.
However, the lessons learned from a close look at this period can
be valuable in charting a course for the future.

Part Two of this book discusses ten possible broad strategies
for gaining and sustaining competitive advantage in today's health
care market. They range from attempting to differentiate from the
competition on the basis of quality, to emphasizing new alternative delivery systems, to diversifying into other related businesses.
Together, these ten broad strategies encompass most of the
competitive actions currently being taken by hospitals and health
care systems. None of the strategies is mutually exclusive; however,

few health care systems will find it desirable to pursue all ten. In essence, they are the building blocks for developing an organization's overall response to change.

Michael Porter, in his book *Competitive Advantage: Creating and Sustaining Superior Performance,* says that "competitive advantage grows fundamentally out of value a firm is able to create for its buyers that exceeds the firm's cost of creating it. . . . There are two basic types of competitive advantage: cost leadership and differentiation" (1985, p. 3). He goes on to say that "differentiation can be based on the product itself, the delivery system by which it is sold, the marketing approach, and a broad range of other factors" (p. 14).

Six of the ten broad health care strategies described in Part Two fall into Porter's category of differentiation:

- Quality of care—identifying quality attributes and communicating these to the various market segments.
- Centers of excellence—deliberately seeking to build strong centers of excellence (women's health, open heart surgery, and so on) or capitalizing on existing strong product lines.
- Aggressive marketing—investing money and effort in seeking to increase market share through aggressive marketing.
- Alternative delivery systems—attempting to gain more control over the payers and thus assure a flow of patients into the hospital or health care system.
- Vertical integration—controlling the availability of services through the continuum of care (primary care physicians and urgent care centers to inpatient services to long-term and home health care).
- Physician bonding—tying physicians into a specific health care system.

Three of the strategies clearly fall under Porter's broad category of cost leadership—being a low-cost provider, downsizing, and networking. Most of the competitive advantages realized thus far from networking—that is, being part of an alliance or multihospital system—have come from volume purchasing and other activities designed to reduce costs. Downsizing is usually carried out to gain economic advantage in terms of lowering costs more than revenues are reduced.

The strategy of diversification, currently popular with many health care systems, can have several objectives, from increased revenues and profits from sources other than inpatient services to spreading the risk by investing in a variety of ventures (usually within the context of the health care industry).

The ten health care strategies discussed in Part Two can be thought of as specific applications of Porter's basic strategies. However, the ten need not be thought of as mutually exclusive. The typical health care system will want to pursue four or five of the ten strategies and integrate them with one another in pursuing its primary goals.

An Overview of Ten Strategies

Our understanding of the various generic strategies available to health care systems has evolved over the past three years as we have monitored the health care literature and been involved in strategic planning for health care organizations and a variety of other businesses. The recent destabilization period, 1983 through 1986, has provided the health care industry with an opportunity to test such various approaches as ADS, vertical integration, and diversification. We believe the lessons learned during this period of rapid change can be valuable in assessing the various strategic options available.

1. Differentiation on the Basis of Quality. Differentiating health care on the basis of quality falls within Porter's second basic strategy; it means attempting to be a local industry leader in terms of image and service. In our experience, almost every organization states this as a goal, but only a few can realistically expect to accomplish this as their primary strategy. Still, it is important for hospitals and health care systems to attempt to differentiate themselves on the basis of one or a combination of factors. Hospitals, in particular, will have to differentiate themselves from their competitors or face the alternative of being viewed as generic health care providers. As providers of a generic (or commodity) product, such organizations will be increasingly subjected to price competition. Chapter Five discusses the implications of differentiating health care services in substantially more detail.

2. Aggressive Pursuit of Alternative Delivery System Contracts. The term *alternative delivery systems* (ADS) usually refers to HMOs and PPOs. Hospitals all over the United States are scrambling to sign contracts with HMOs and PPOs in order to gain access to more patients.

As of 1986, roughly one-quarter of all employers with thirty or more employees offered one or more HMOs. PPO activity is concentrated among firms with 500 or more employees, with a rapid decline in the usage of PPOs as the size of firm decreases.

A hospital—or any health care provider, for that matter—can decide whether or not to play the ADS game. The downside risk is that all ADS providers negotiate (usually successfully) for substantial discounts in return for providing patients.

Chapter Six discusses this important marketing and survival strategy in considerable detail, with projections of the financial implications to hospitals that are successful in attracting ADS business.

3. Diversification. A diversification strategy can be used to assist in cost leadership by taking pressure off the financial bottom line, or to assist in differentiating a health care system from its competitors by providing unique supplementary products or services. This strategy is not in conflict with the specialization or low-cost provider strategies discussed later in this chapter; in fact, it may complement them. Diversification by local health care systems and hospitals is not new, but it is accelerating because of deregulation, lower inpatient use, the need for additional revenues, and competition from other providers of medical services.

Hospitals that are serious about diversifying, broadening their revenue base, face several issues:

- How should diversification opportunities be identified, screened, and evaluated?

- What types of new ventures should be pursued? How far afield should they be from present activities?
- What are reasonable expectations in terms of the proportion of revenues (and contribution to the bottom line) from diversification activities?
- What can a hospital do to increase its chances of diversification success?

The first question for potential diversifiers is whether the hospital should take an active or passive approach to identifying opportunities for new ventures. Many hospitals have been besieged with so many proposals that they are in a reactive mode; simply responding to requests often takes all available staff resources.

Yet it is well worth the effort for hospital management to identify and assess opportunities for new ventures systematically. In effect, a strategic framework should be developed within which new diversification opportunities, both those developed internally and those coming from outside sources, can be properly evaluated.

What type of new ventures? In developing a diversification strategy, a hospital should first decide how far afield it wants to go. For an acute care hospital, for example, a medical office building adjacent to the main campus or a minor emergency center in a nearby shopping center are closely akin to the hospital's main line of business. How about home health care or a hospice? Or how about starting an HMO? This would get the hospital into the insurance business and into a field requiring a high level of marketing and sales savvy. How about developing and selling health care–related computer software? Or setting up a subsidiary to sell consulting services to others in the health care field?

One caution: the experience of firms in many other industries has repeatedly shown that the farther away an organization strays from its primary business, the greater the probabilities that problems will occur. Peters and Waterman, in their book *In Search of Excellence* (1982, pp. 292–305), repeatedly stress this point with their admonition that organizations should "stick to their knitting."

What are reasonable expectations from diversifying? The key word is *reasonable*. Initial expectations are often too high, and diversifying health care systems in general fail to anticipate the time it takes to develop a successful new business, or to integrate an acquisition into the present organization.

In the venture capital business, less than one-fourth of all initial investments succeed. Venture capitalists manage to channel over half of their funds into those firms that succeed. However, this requires quickly identifying the unsuccessful efforts and cutting them off. Most failures are identified within three years; most successes can be identified only after five to seven years.

There are a number of activities and attitudes that will increase the chances for successful hospital diversification initiatives. First, most studies of diversification and its success or failure have shown that commitment of top management is the key ingredient.

A well-thought-out strategic plan is the second critical element. This plan should be followed by detailed economic feasibility analysis and development of realistic business plans for each new venture (as discussed in detail in Chapter Sixteen).

Sufficient financial commitment is the third crucial element. It is rare for a new venture in health care or any other field to anticipate the capital needed to provide for an adequate start-up. A health care system will need to face the issue of coming up with additional capital; this is likely to be an unpleasant experience. Broadening a health system's staff to include managers with marketing and new business experience will enhance the probabilities of success.

Finally, hospitals should expect some ventures to fail; a diversification strategy should be judged as a whole rather than on the few failures that will undoubtedly occur.

4. Vertical Integration. The strategy of vertical integration involves gaining a measure of control over several related links in the health care delivery chain and influencing the patients' choice of providers in the later links. This is another way a health care system can differentiate itself from its competitors. The objective is to control patient access via the health plan, control care by physicians and hospitals, and even control patients after hospitalization by providing a continuum of care (through home care or long-term care facilities for the elderly). There are a variety of approaches, but most involve a health plan (usually a PPO or a family of health insurance products), one or more acute care hospitals, and a convenience-oriented feeder network.

All four large investor-owned chains are using this approach, although each has a different game plan for accomplishing vertical integration. Humana, for example, is emphasizing its health insurance product, Humana Care Plus, and extended-hours clinics (Humana MedFirst) in areas surrounding its acute care hospitals. National Medical Enterprises (NME), on the other hand, is emphasizing comprehensive services built around an acute care hospital in a campus-type setting.

Vertical integration differs from diversification in that diversification is usually a risk-spreading strategy, whereas vertical integration is an effort to dominate or control a market, or at least to maintain market share. However, the two strategies can be interrelated and work for the benefit of a health care system, hospital, or physician group.

5. Aggressive Marketing. Aggressive marketing can be used either to support an effort to establish a health care system as a marketplace leader in terms of quality or to differentiate its services within specific market segments. This is the strategy being pursued by a large number of health care systems, hospitals, and physicians, and is one of four strategies recommended by Jeff Goldsmith in "The Health Care Market" (1980). The major elements of this type of strategy are:

- Increasing direct marketing efforts to consumers. In most metropolitan areas, consumers are now hearing radio and television advertisements, or reading newspaper ads, promoting the services of specific hospitals.
- Developing a strong physician referral network. Physicians still control a high proportion of hospital admissions, although most industry observers see a gradual change coming

as consumers are given incentives to shop and compare hospital services.

- Developing convenience-oriented feeder systems. Free-standing minor emergency centers or hospital-owned HMOs are examples of this element.

As an example of aggressive marketing efforts designed to increase market share, three hospitals in Peoria, Illinois, have been engaged in "a marketing battle that has been far from friendly." The hospitals are offering discounted rates, free physicals, and other marketing inducements. One of the hospitals, St. Francis Medical Center, signed a preferred provider (PPO) agreement with Peoria's largest employer, Caterpillar Tractor Company, which drew antitrust charges from the other two hospitals. Julie Franz concludes that the "three facilities have been openly copying each others' marketing ideas," and that no hospital is able to sustain a market advantage (1984, pp. 94–95).

A few hospitals will, in all probability, achieve some success in attempting to increase their market share through aggressive marketing. However, many others will fail to stem the loss of patient-days. The overall market for inpatient hospital services is declining; the success of a few hospitals will be at the expense of others.

Therefore, as a strategy, efforts to increase market share may pay off for a limited number of well-located, aggressively managed hospitals. For the rest, the results of marketing efforts may, at best, minimize the loss of patients.

6. Physician Bonding. Physician-hospital relationships are one of the key tools available to a health care system in differentiating itself from its competitors. This strategy is premised on the fact that hospitals and physicians face similar challenges in the emerging competitive environment, and physicians continue to play the dominant role in the choice of hospitals and other aspects of the health care delivery system. Many hospitals and physician groups (independent practice associations, hospital medical staffs, group practices, and individual practitioners) are forming joint ventures or otherwise working together to survive. Included in this strategy are a wide variety of financial arrangements, including joint ventures in health plans, medical office buildings, ambulatory surgery centers, extended-hours clinics, and physician office start-ups. The possibilities are nearly infinite.

7. Centers of Excellence. Centers of excellence correspond to Porter's strategy of differentiation from the competition *in a particular market segment.* Many acute care hospitals have been pursuing this strategy for years, and it should pay off. Cleveland (Ohio) Clinic, for example, has developed a specialization in coronary bypass surgery and is performing 4,000 such operations per year; this is one of six centers of excellence at the clinic.

In another example, Alta Bates Hospital (Berkeley, California) identified obstetrics as an area of strength, and has developed a high-risk obstetric/maternity/perinatology program around this strength.

8. Networking. Networking is an increasingly important supporting strategy for hospitals seeking cost leadership or product differentiation. About 90 percent of all U.S. hospitals are either publicly owned or not-for-profit institutions, and this broad group has an additional alternative to consider—joining with other hospitals through a network or multihospital system. As indicated earlier, there are a number of large hospital networks, or alliances, involving not-for-profit hospitals. The two major ones are Voluntary Hospitals of America (VHA), with over 600 hospitals and over 170,000 beds, and American Healthcare Systems (AHS), with 500 hospitals and 98,500 beds.

The advantages of participating in a hospital network usually fall into these categories:

- Economy in purchasing of supplies, equipment, and insurance
- Coordinated establishment of national alternative delivery systems (for example, Partners National Health Plans, established as a joint venture by VHA and Aetna)
- Access to capital as a part of a larger group
- Shared management expertise, including assistance in establishing new ventures (diversification)

- Shared comparative financial data and other useful information
- Joint market research, marketing, and public relations; developing a "brand" name
- Management development and other human resource programs

Recent developments indicate that we will see more joint efforts between not-for-profit and investor-owned organizations. Research Health Services of Kansas City (a not-for-profit organization) signed a joint venture agreement with Hospital Corporation of America (HCA) to construct a psychiatric facility on its campus in Kansas City, Missouri. Intermountain Healthcare, a not-for-profit system based in Salt Lake City, Utah, was involved in the joint development of a hospital in Twin Falls, Idaho, also with HCA. Numerous other examples exist in the area of behavioral medicine, nursing homes, and home health care programs.

9. Being a Low-Cost Provider. Being a low-cost provider is a strategy that every hospital must attempt. However, we question the ability of most hospitals to survive solely on the basis of a low-cost provider strategy. On a nationwide basis, the number of hospital employees per bed has increased significantly since 1965. In that year, there were 1.9 employees (full-time equivalents) per occupied hospital bed. In 1985, there were 5.4 employees per occupied bed, a 184 percent increase in ten years. By contrast, in the United Kingdom, the ratio is 1.7, in France 1.9, and in Japan 2.0 employees per occupied bed (Richter, 1986, p. 7).

These ratios for U.S. hospitals at least partially reflect the increasing intensity of services; hospital patients tend to be sicker under the new, more restrictive environment. This can be seen by tracing the average amount of hospital resources (dollars, staff time) consumed per patient-day; the long-term trend has been upward.

In order for hospitals to be successful in pursuing the low-cost strategy, the medical staff must cooperate by ordering only appropriate tests and by carefully monitoring each patient's progress in order to achieve early discharges. Hospital management must develop better systems for scheduling nurses and other personnel in order to control variable costs. In hospitals, labor costs typically represent 55 to 60 percent of total costs.

10. Downsizing. Downsizing is a necessary supporting strategy for many health care providers, particularly if they are seeking to reduce costs. The key issue in downsizing is finding the optimum level of operation that can be carried out profitably, yet with minimum impact on the quality of care. This will not be a popular strategy, and is probably not appropriate for most small, rural hospitals, but it will often have to be faced given the tremendous excess bed capacity in the nation's acute care hospitals.

It is difficult to generalize on how small a hospital can be and still operate effectively. However, the factors to consider include:

- Size, age, and configuration of existing facilities. Is it possible to close an entire wing, section, or department?
- Potential impacts on the hospital's competitive position.
- Mix of cases currently being handled, and compatibility of these cases in respect to use of facilities and support services.
- Mix of medical and surgical specialities represented on the medical staff, and the impact of downsizing on the staff.
- Size of the administrative structure needed to operate efficiently (medical records, administration, building and grounds, and so on).
- Present debt structure (that is, can the existing debt be adequately serviced if the organization operates on a smaller scale?).
- The permanence of downsizing—whether the space and personnel can be redeployed in a related activity (such as a diversification business), whether the space can be "mothballed" and reasonably expected to be reopened at a later date, or whether the reduction is likely to be permanent.

5

Differentiation on the Basis of Quality of Care

At the dinner program following our monthly trustee meeting, we looked forward to hearing an update from a member of the state hospital data commission. What health care cost information was the state going to collect and publish? Would differences in case mix and the complexity of cases (acuity) be considered? How would HMOs, PPOs, and major employers use the data to "shop" for hospitals?

Our speaker, formerly with a large accounting firm, told us that hospitals need to restructure their cost-accounting systems completely, primarily so that they can figure their marginal costs. "If you don't know how much it costs you to produce an additional patient-day, how are you going to price your services for big buyers (major employers or large PPOs)?" he asked. "If you want to be successful in getting new business, you're going to have to price 'at the margin.'"

Was our speaker correct? Is health care soon to be offered as a commodity with no product differentiation? Is this what industry and the American public want? And is this the way the health care industry, especially hospitals and physicians, is willing to operate? As one physician said, after hearing the accountant speak, "If it comes to this kind of price competition, I think we should lock the doors. I sure don't want to be held responsible for quality of care in this environment."

Gary Strack, president of the Orlando (Florida) Regional Medical Center, says that it is not his organization's objective to be a low-cost provider and to compete on price. Strack says, "There are three ways to compete: price, quality, and service. We'll bet our future on our ability to convince our customers (employers and consumers) that we offer the highest quality and best service. We will not compete on price" (Gary Strack, interview with the authors, Orlando, Fla., July 18, 1986).

A basic thesis of this book is that hospitals and other health care providers need to place increased emphasis on differentiating their products and services. If they fail to, many will be viewed as providers of generic health care products to be sold at the lowest price. For many hospitals, this would spell disaster.

Product differentiation is not a problem unique to the health care industry. Banks, for example, have traditionally faced this same problem, although with deregulation, financial institutions have more latitude to develop and market new products and thus differentiate themselves from their competitors. Banks often attempt to establish a unique identity with impressive buildings, accessible locations, and adequate parking. Some banks are open Saturdays; some provide a convenient network of outlets (branches) throughout their market area. A few banks offer "private banking" services to a select group of high-income, high-net-worth customers (often referred to as the "upscale" banking market—market segmentation in action). The last thing in the world most banks want is to compete on price (lower loan rates, zero service charges); such an approach assures reduced profits, jeopardizes reserves, and threatens capital adequacy.

Theodore Levitt, a professor at Harvard Business School, goes even further. He says there is no such thing as a commodity that cannot be differentiated from its competition. Levitt says, "The usual presumption about so-called undifferentiated commodities is that they are exceedingly price sensitive. A fractionally lower price gets the business. That's seldom true except in the imaginary world of economics textbooks" (1983, p. 73).

But, other than by price, how can a health care provider set itself apart from its competitors? There are many ways, including the following:

- *Location.* By being located in areas that are accessible to large number of physicians and patients, health care providers offer convenience. Most rural hospitals compete on this basis; so do many suburban hospitals.
- *Physical plant and equipment.* The quality and appearance of buildings, and how they are maintained, can be a way to set apart one hospital from another. It is surprising how often consumers mention "cleanliness" or "nice atmosphere" when comparing hospitals. Of course, available equipment and technology can also be the basis for establishing differences among hospitals.
- *Quality.* Quality of care, including service, is the most important factor in differentiating hospitals, physicians, and other providers (for example, urgent care centers); it is the subject of most of the discussion in this chapter.

For many U.S. hospitals located in or near the old central business district, location and the quality of the physical plant are negative factors; these hospitals are no longer convenient to the large numbers of physicians and patients who once supported them. Given the large capital investment already in place, and difficulties in accessing large amounts of new financing (usually in the form of debt), these hospitals are often stuck.

In some cases, these older downtown hospitals have moved or built satellite units (either small acute care hospitals or various outpatient facilities, such as surgery centers or urgent care facilities). Or they have become part of smaller multihospital systems and developed themselves as tertiary care facilities handling the most complex cases or referrals from the less specialized hospitals within their system.

For those hospitals or health care organizations not enjoying a locational advantage, or not blessed with modern and attractive facilities, there are other ways to compete, including specializing (centers of excellence), aggressive HMO and PPO contracting, downsizing, and reducing costs (all strategies briefly described in the introduction to Part Two and discussed in more detail in subsequent chapters).

For those hospitals or provider organizations now enjoying a convenient location or modern facilities, this may form a solid basis for differentiating the organization from its competitors. A locational advantage can be enhanced through building one or more medical office buildings, suburban health parks, a system of minor emergency or urgent care centers, or other ambulatory services. In other words, actions designed to enhance the referral and feeder network are especially effective for the well-located hospital. This is discussed in more detail in Chapter Nine, which deals with the strategy of aggressive marketing.

As this chapter is being written, one of the authors is standing in the "customer services" room at O'Hare Airport in Chicago, waiting to be rebooked on another United Airline's flight to Denver; the previous flight was overbooked by forty-two people. There are over fifty people waiting for their new tickets and their compensatory free tickets or cash rebates; two UAL clerks are processing the tickets. Earlier, there were five at work, but three have left. The small room is smoke-filled, and there is no place to sit. Is there any better example than the airlines of an industry that has ceased catering to its business customers and committed itself to price competition? United lost $400 million last year, with continuing losses forecast for the current year. Quality of service? A differentiated product? Future profits? We do not see these aspects of a competitive business in most airlines.

Most health care systems, and especially the physicians working for them, strive for a better reputation than that of the airline industry; they want to be viewed as different or unique from other health care providers. The remainder of this chapter deals with quality of health care and how quality, or perceptions of quality, can set apart hospitals and physicians.

Perceptions of Quality of Care

We recently had lunch with the head of the medical staff of a large hospital to discuss some of our research findings relative to hospital and physician quality. We noticed, as the discussion progressed, that he was visibly upset by our research findings on quality. "The Joint Commission on Accreditation of Hospitals has very rigorous and specifically defined measures of quality assurance," he said. "I've spent most of my time over the past year trying to get a satisfactory quality assurance system operating in the hospital, and it hasn't been easy. Now you're trying to tell me that the proper measures of quality are drastically different. It doesn't make sense."

We recovered quickly, explaining that our research with consumers, physicians, employers, and trustees deals with *perceptions* of hospital and physician quality; perceptions may or may not be the same as "the real thing." This cleared up matters, but it taught us a valuable lesson. In discussing quality of health care from a marketing or business point of view, the key word is *perception*.

Based upon national research, only about half of all consumers and employer representatives, and two-thirds of all doctors, say they can identify hospitals that stand out based upon quality of care. This leaves the impression that people either do not care about hospital quality, or that it is just too difficult to tell the difference.

However, our focus group research, which probes in greater depth the opinions of fewer respondents, suggests that with only a minimal amount of prompting, most consumers and employer representatives (CEOs, personnel and benefits managers, controllers) are able to identify higher-quality hospitals in their area. Many of the perceptions shared in focus group sessions lacked depth and were based on the most superficial information, but such perceptions nevertheless existed in the minds of most of our participants.

Furthermore, our research and analysis suggest that consumers and business representatives will, in the near future, become increasingly knowledgeable about hospitals and their unique attributes. Awareness of hospital advertising is unusually high, especially among women, and recall of the specific message is amazingly accurate. This is borne out by most health care consumer surveys and has been frequently reported by National Research Corporation in its summaries published in *Modern Healthcare.*

With the increasing role of HMOs and PPOs (discussed in more detail in Chapter Six), consumers will be called upon, to an extent far exceeding anything known today, to select their doctors and hospitals. Under most PPO arrangements, consumer selection of a hospital not on the preferred list provided by his or her health plan will require an extra, out-of-pocket payment (a disincentive to use physicians or hospitals not on the preferred provider list). However, substantial numbers of consumers say they are willing to pay extra for quality; therefore, an increasing portion of the hospital selection decisions made by consumers will require cost versus quality trade-offs. Given the increasing role of HMOs and PPOs, consumers will want to know more about hospital quality as a part of their health plan decision-making process. As an increasing proportion of consumers, and representatives of employers, become more knowledgeable purchasers of hospital services, it is a challenge for hospitals to provide top-quality care and to communicate their unique attributes to consumers and employers and to the various health plans that are marketed to employers.

On this latter point, one personnel manager for a company with 350 employees noted that she kept seeing three hospitals identified in PPO proposals received by her firm. "These three hospitals must be doing something right or I wouldn't keep seeing their names pop up in health plan proposals." This example also illustrates one of the possible ways to communicate hospital quality.

Consumers' Perceptions of Hospital Quality. What are the characteristics of high-quality hospitals? Focus group participants characterized high-quality hospitals as caring, with attentive attitudes on the part of hospital personnel (administrative staff—particularly in admissions—nurses, and physicians). Consumers seem to value small, personal actions directed toward the patient and the patient's family as indicators of quality. Many consumers cited nursing care as a quality characteristic; this is closely related to the caring attitude.

The perception that the best physicians are associated with a specific hospital is also an important quality descriptor. Determination of the "best doctors" is based on personal experience—for example, having an acute episode and recovering, or word-of-mouth reputation from friends and relatives. Many people believe, however, that their physician is the best or one of the best, and expect their doctor to be associated with a hospital that can best take care of their needs.

According to several consumers, specialization in a clinical area is an important attribute of a quality hospital. Consumers want the best, and want to know that if they have a specific problem, the hospital to which they are admitted can deliver the best care. Heart services and maternity care are the two product lines most frequently associated with specific hospitals.

Other indicators of quality were mentioned, but not as frequently. Technology is an important quality descriptor to some consumers, but many believe that the majority of hospitals offer comparable technology. To some, physical facilities—a nice atmosphere or an attractive view—are a consideration. Cleanliness was often cited, especially by women, as a very important aspect of hospital quality.

Men interviewed tended to value outcome as a very important quality characteristic. Men said that, if admitted to the hospital, they wanted to recover as quickly as possible and get out. Although the majority of the men's responses match those of women, this relationship between outcome and the quality of the hospital differs for male participants.

In the focus groups, a second question used a list of fourteen factors that might influence consumers' opinions of the quality of a hospital. Each participant was asked to identify the two most important and the two least important factors. Results are summarized in Table 7.

Table 7. Consumer Rating of 14 Factors as Indicators of Hospital Quality.

| | Number of Mentions | |
| | Most | Least |
Factors	Important	Important
Caring attitude	14	0
Medical staff	13	0
Technology/equipment	10	1
Specialization/scope of services	10	3
Outcome	8	1
Reputation	3	3
Communications	3	0
Nursing	2	0
University/teaching status	1	11
Food	1	16
Facilities/rooms	0	1
Charges	0	3
Size	0	23
Total	65	62

Size of the hospital and the food are the least important determinants of quality, according to individuals in the groups interviewed. In fact, hospital size is apparently unrelated to consumers' perception of quality. According to consumers, hospital food is universally bad, but as an indicator of quality, food is not as important as several other factors. University/teaching status of a hospital does not carry favorable quality connotations to most participants; consumers believe medical education is important, but they prefer not to be the laboratory or guinea pigs.

Interestingly, charges (or cost to consumers) are not viewed as being related to quality. Despite considerable publicity about high health costs, consumers do not appear to be concerned about hospital charges.

A study prepared by the Orange County Health Planning Council identified nineteen indicators of hospital quality (Orange County Health Planning Council, 1985). The indicators, which were not rated in terms of importance, were in the following five general categories:

Hospital Staff and Services

1. Medical staff
2. Nursing staff
3. Scope of services
4. Frequency of procedures performed
5. Laboratory services (clinical and pathological)
6. Radiology services
7. Special certificates (outside review beyond Joint Commission on the Accreditation of Hospitals)
8. Alternative services (diversification or vertical integration)

Hospital Organization

9. Financial condition
10. Governing board
11. Active bioethics committee
12. Professional integration (physician and allied health professionals participating in planning and decision making)

Supplementary Systems/Services

13. Community education
14. Accessibility to social and cultural support groups

Quality Assurance

15. Treatment of patients
16. System of measuring outcomes
17. Medical records completion

Quality at the Operational Level

18. Rate of nosocomial infections (infections acquired while in the hospital)
19. Mortality rates

These indicators represent objective criteria and are comprehensive. It is interesting, however, that they do not correspond to consumer, physician, and employer *perceptions* of hospital quality. Caring attitudes and concern for the patient (high-touch aspects of quality), so important to consumers, are not reflected in these more objective criteria. Nor does the Orange County study discuss technology, equipment, or facilities (aesthetics, cleanliness) as quality indicators; these are also very important quality factors for consumers.

Benefits and Personnel Managers' Perceptions of Quality. In general, employer responses do not differ substantially from those of consumers; employer groups are not obviously more sophisticated in terms of differentiating hospitals on the basis of quality. Employer participants indicated that they value hospital reputation, caring attitude, equipment and facilities, and speciali-zation. Their determination of quality also includes such factors as cost-effectiveness, feedback from employees, and a good emergency room.

Hospital reputation is an important quality criterion for many employers. From their perspective, reputation encompasses many of the more specific factors, such as good physicians and favorable outcomes from hospitalization. A good reputation is earned by quality service and passed about in the company or community through word of mouth. Thus one important quality measurement for employers is employee feedback.

Many employers, like consumers, associate a caring attitude with a good or better outcome and a high-quality hospital. Employers also value equipment and facilities, as well as special-ization, as characteristics of a high-quality hospital. Employer representatives in the focus groups gave heavier weighting to specialization than did consumers. Some of the employers' representatives also noted that they value hospitals that promote preventive medicine.

Several employers indicated that cost-effectiveness is an important quality consideration. However, employer representa-tives could not say how they would measure cost-effectiveness in health care. To our surprise, employer representatives present in the focus groups did not appear to be overly concerned about hospital charges.

Lower-quality hospitals are seen by employers as those that give poor care—lack of attention and the absence of a caring attitude. Public hospitals do not rank high; reasons identified for a low ranking are related to political and funding issues and indigent care problems. One participant stated emphatically that smaller hospitals are satisfactory for routine care, but are inadequate for major surgery or other problems.

Employer representatives in the focus groups were also asked to identify the two most and two least important characteristics that influence hospital quality. In their rankings, caring attitude was the most important factor; medical staff, technology/equipment, and scope of services were equally valued after caring attitude (see Table 8).

Size of the hospital and university/teaching status were the two least important factors influencing employer opinions of quality. Interestingly, employer representatives did not identify cost as an important factor; three said it was among the least important.

Health Care Professionals' Perceptions of Quality. Health care employees (from a hospital and from physician offices located next to the hospital) participating in two focus groups tended to be more emphatic about the importance of a caring attitude and hospital/physician priority on the patients' needs. Health care employee groups, particularly nurses, seem to expect the kind of care that they deliver to patients. The most important aspects of quality, in their view, are care and attention from all levels of hospital personnel, and the atmosphere created by the facilities (for example, pleasant, clean). Most assume that quality hospitals will have state-of-the-art technology for most types of care.

Lower-quality care for this group is associated with inadequate concern for the patients' well-being. Participants specifically mentioned loose management and a lack of responsibility for patients and the mixing of patients with different severity of illnesses in the same room. Such factors make hospital stays unpleasant and leave patients with uncertainty about the quality of care.

When asked to review the list of hospital quality indicators, health care employees indicated that caring attitude was the most important descriptor of hospital quality. Medical staff and

Table 8. Employer Rating of 14 Factors as Indicators of Hospital Quality.

Factors	Number of Mentions	
	Most Important	Least Important
Caring attitude	10	0
Medical staff	6	0
Technology/equipment	6	0
Specialization/scope of services	6	5
Nursing	5	0
Reputation	2	0
Communications	1	0
Facilities/rooms	1	1
Charges	1	3
Outcome	0	1
Food	0	4
University/teaching status	0	7
Size	0	14
Total	38	35

technology/equipment followed caring attitude as important attributes of hospital quality.

Size and university/teaching status were rated as the least important attributes of hospital quality by health care employees.

Overall Perceptions of Quality. Perceptions of consumers and employer representatives, confirmed by health care employees, suggest four major indicators of hospital quality, each one important to significant numbers of people:

1. *Concerned, caring attitude.* Consumers want a high level of personal service and attention. They want the people taking care of them to feel that they, as patients, are important to the hospital employee and doctor. Nursing care is an important ingredient; nurses reflect the overall attitude of the hospital.
2. *Medical staff.* Experience, reputation, expertise, up-to-dateness, specialization, and ability are all part of this category.
3. *Specialization/scope of services.* Consumers want to go where there is a track record of success, and a sufficient volume of

similar cases. Any specialized and renowned service in a hospital appears to have a "halo" effect for other services in the hospital (see Chapter 11). Specialized services attract patients; if their experience is positive, they will likely return to the hospital for other care, or be active in their word-of-mouth promotion of the hospital.

4. *Technology/equipment.* Correctly or not, consumers generally assume that a quality hospital has up-to-date technology and equipment; this is expected of a hospital recommended by their doctor.

Perceptions of Physician Quality

Consumer Focus Group Results. According to consumers, a high-quality physician has a pleasant manner, exhibits a caring attitude, and communicates well with patients and their families. Such characteristics instill in consumers a sense of trust and physician competence and build a good reputation. The majority of consumers indicated that word-of-mouth recommendations from friends and relatives was the customary way of selecting a physician.

Several consumers in each group indicated the importance of preventive medicine and education in the physician's approach to health care. These consumers, primarily women, wanted acute needs addressed but also desired a better understanding of how to avoid illness and enjoy a higher quality of life. Male participants mentioned outcome as a determinant of physician quality more frequently than did women.

The perception of low-quality care is related to a physician's lack of familiarity with the patient, poor communication, and restricted availability.

Consumers were asked to rank the most important and least important factors related to physician quality from a list of fourteen characteristics. According to consumers, thoroughness of the examination and the physician's manner are the two most important attributes. Outcome, communication, preventive medicine, and after-hours service are also valued indicators.

According to consumers, length of wait in the physician's office and handling of insurance forms and billing are the two least important factors influencing their opinion of physician quality. Consumers also indicated that convenience/accessibility, equipment, and charges were not as important as other indicators of physician quality.

Consumer focus group interviews indicate that the physician/patient relationship is the most important determinant of quality. Although many consumers complain about charges, waiting time, and other such factors, those complaints do not appear to be as important, in terms of satisfaction with physicians, as do the other factors mentioned above.

Employer Focus Group Results. The employers we spoke with generally agreed with consumers on attributes of a high-quality physician: physician's manner, caring attitude, and reputation are all important quality indicators. Employers were additionally concerned about the outcome and the physician's sensitivity to the costs of illness and treatment.

In the general discussion of quality attributes, low-quality doctors were identified as those who overtreat patients. Benefits managers were aware of abuses of the system—particularly the abuse of disability insurance, and practices that encourage overuse of the system at the employer's expense.

Only one of the two groups of employers ranked factors influencing physician quality. In that group, thoroughness of the examination and communication were the two most important physician quality descriptors. Not surprisingly, employers identified the handling of insurance claims and billing as an important criterion.

Health Care Employee Focus Group Results. According to health care employees, the physician's manner, caring attitude, and good communication are primary determinants of a high-quality physician. This group identified another unique characteristic of the high-quality physician: the physician's board certification and continued education and training. Characteristics of low-quality physicians identified by the group include a greater interest in a disease, or in the fee, than in the patient's needs. Generally, lack of concern for the patient was a very negative characteristic.

Ranking quality attributes based on the list of factors, health care employees indicated that physician's manner and thoroughness of the examination are the two most important factors influencing their perception of physician quality.

Handling insurance claims and billing and equipment are the least important factors influencing their opinion of physician quality, according to health care employees.

Strategic Implications

Hospitals. Based on focus group discussions and other research, it appears that different marketing approaches can be used to create and communicate different quality attributes. As discussed earlier, important quality attributes include a warm, caring atmosphere, specialty areas, and a strong medical staff. Each characteristic requires a different marketing emphasis.

"Warm and caring" is clearly a dominant attribute of quality, for example. For this reason, it cannot be ignored in any marketing effort directed at consumers and employers. However, media advertising based on "warm and caring" alone has little chance of success. Every hospital can claim atmosphere. The consumer recognizes this and is likely to discount the message. Instead the more concrete attributes associated with quality—such as areas of outstanding competence—should be featured in media-based advertising. These areas should be chosen in part on their ability to benefit the rest of the hospital and medical staff—that is, their halo effect.

The matrix shown in Table 9 represents what we believe to be an appropriate mix of marketing approaches for those hospitals desiring to market major quality attributes. A matrix of this type could be used by many health care organizations as a way to allocate marketing and public relations dollars, or to check on present expenditure patterns. The best approach will depend on local market factors, including an assessment of competing health care organizations and what they are emphasizing.

Table 9. Marketing Approach Matrix.

	Marketing Approach			
Quality Indicator	Advertising	Public Relations	Patient Relations	Word of Mouth
Concerned, caring attitude	*	**	***	***
Medical staff	**	**	***	***
Specialization/scope of services	***	**	*	**
Technology/equipment	***	***	*	**

*** Best approach
** Satisfactory approach
* Least desirable approach

The medical staff's unique attributes can be marketed in a number of ways—assistance to physicians in marketing their practices (patient acquisition), joint physician-hospital advertising, various tours or other public relations activities, and word of mouth by satisfied patients and their families.

The most important quality measure—caring attitudes, concern for patients—can be enhanced through continued employee relations and customer relations programs, employee monitoring, and rewards that encourage this type of behavior by nurses and other employees.

Finally, hospitals could establish joint physician-staff task forces to identify and analyze various approaches to meeting the needs of the relatively large group of consumers who are willing to pay more for top quality. Additionally, such a program could partially offset the negative impacts of ADS discounting and reductions in DRG reimbursement levels.

Physicians. Physicians depend on word-of-mouth advertising for referrals, and their reputation among existing patients is likely to continue to be an important marketing approach. There are additional opportunities for practice building related to quality: concern/caring attitude by physicians and their nurses, thoroughness, and good communication. For primary care physicians, concern for wellness and preventive medicine will be increasingly important.

Marketing medical staff physicians to each other, through educational seminars or social gatherings, will help to promote a tight referral network by encouraging greater awareness and confidence in medical staff peers. The tighter referral network will benefit both physicians and hospital.

For those physicians interested in how they can improve their ability to market quality, hospitals could take the lead in offering seminars for various specialties on practice development, especially as it relates to communicating quality to patients, health plan buyers, and referral sources. Physicians *do* want marketing help from their primary hospital (see Chapter Two).

It is inevitable that certain hospitals, physicians, and health plans will be positioned as quality leaders in the competitive health care marketplace. Others will fall into the good-but-not-superior category.

We believe that quality can be marketed or communicated, and that it is vitally important that most health care providers attempt to gain a competitive advantage by marketing quality of care. Such a commitment must be viewed as a long-term strategic initiative; in a sense, it represents an investment with potential (not assured) returns.

Paul Ellwood, Jr., a physician and one of the leading visionaries in the health care industry, believes that competition in the industry will develop around quality issues. "I am not talking about quality in a narrow sense," he explains, "but across-the-board differences—quality of health outcomes, quality of access and quality of service. The organizations that are able to manage quality best and sell it as a difference probably are the ones which are going to be dominant" ("Ellwood Says 'Supermed' Concept Gaining Ground . . . ," 1986, pp. 9, 11).

6

Pursuit of Alternative
Delivery System Contracts

The subject of the meeting was the development of admissions and patient-days forecasts. The group was the marketing task force formed to assist in developing the hospital's strategic plan. The faces around the table were grim. The hospital was extremely well located, away from downtown but right in a high-income growth corridor. Still, it was losing business.

"To begin with, we know now that 13 percent of the patients in our service area belong to HMOs. With the current contracting practices, we're keeping less than 2 percent of the HMO market in this area. More than 10 percent go straight downtown because of HMO contracting," offered the marketing vice-president. "And PPOs will be the kicker. We're projecting that by 1990, 12 percent of your current patients will be in PPOs that at least in part dictate their hospital choice," said the consultant.

Of the ten health care strategies discussed in Part Two, the alternative delivery system strategy has received the highest health care industry attention over the past three years. A substantial proportion of the health care industry—especially hospitals, investor-owned hospital chains (Humana, Hospital Corporation of America, and others), national not-for-profit alliances (Voluntary Hospitals of America, American Healthcare Systems, and others), physician groups (independent practice associations), and indemnity insurers (Aetna, Prudential, CIGNA, and others)—is concentrating on controlling part of the health care dollar-flow through the establishment of HMOs and PPOs.

As one indication of hospital involvement with alternative delivery systems (ADS), a recent survey of over 700 hospital trustees indicated that 35 percent of the hospitals represented in the survey are organizing or already operating their own HMOs. Over half of the hospitals represented are contracting with one or more HMOs. An even higher percentage of hospitals are planning to start a PPO or already own one.

HMO and PPO growth has been as uneven as it has been explosive. In Minnesota and northern California, HMOs have reached maturity and achieved market shares large enough to change the entire health care delivery market. In other large markets, such as Boston, and midsized markets, such as Norfolk, Virginia, the HMO battle for market share is at a highly competitive level. In other markets, such as Denver, HMOs appear to have lost momentum but PPOs are growing rapidly and competing intensively.

What will happen to the HMO/PPO picture? How big a share of future patients will come to hospitals and physicians via this pathway? Will all markets follow the early, leading-edge markets or will they develop along different lines? How important is it for a hospital or other provider to become involved in ADS? Are ADS a good investment for a health care provider, or is it better to limit ADS involvement to contracting? What are the financial implications of contracting with HMOs and PPOs? How should hospitals and physicians react to potential changes in the HMO/PPO landscape in their markets? These are the issues addressed in this chapter.

The Minnesota Story

As a preface to our discussion of HMOs and PPOs, it may be useful to review briefly the HMO experience in Minnesota, a leading-edge state for the last several years. Minneapolis and St. Paul have been and remain at the forefront of the HMO movement. HMO membership in the Twin Cities was just under 1 million in late 1985, up from 100,000 a decade earlier. About 45 percent of the population are HMO members; this is four times the national average. Richard Reece, M.D., editor of *Minnesota Medicine,* says, "Traditional fee-for-service medicine is dead, or dying. We won't return to it" (Robson, 1986, p. 72; page references in the next few paragraphs are to the same source).

In 1957, there was one organized prepaid plan operating in the Twin Cities—Group Health. Group Health was a staff-model HMO; it hired its own salaried physicians. The medical establishment tabbed Group Health as "mad medicine."

Walter McClure, who worked with Paul Ellwood in what is now InterStudy, said that the strategy was to convince the good doctors that "this so-called 'goofy' and 'dangerous' movement was in their interest. . . . In 1972, doctors in the St. Louis Park Medical Center—a well-respected clinic in operation since 1951—agreed to form MedCenter Health Plan, the first local group-model HMO" (p. 72).

In 1973, a year after MedCenter was formed, federal law was changed to require companies with twenty-five or more employees to include at least one HMO among their health insurance options. Congress also made money available in the form of grants and low-interest loans to stimulate HMO development. As a result, Share Health Plan was formed in mid-1973, and Blue Cross/Blue Shield started HMO Minnesota in September 1974. In 1975, the Hennepin County Medical Society sponsored the creation of Physicians Health Plan for doctors in solo or small-group practices.

Physicians Health Plan (PHP)—with 307,000 members as of year-end 1985, and 3,400 physicians on its panel—is the largest Minnesota HMO. Its physicians receive a standard fee for each of 8,000 medical procedures, but 20 percent of the amount is withheld until the end of the year, when each physician is evaluated on the basis of his or her efficiency.

At the present time, more than 80 percent of the state's physicians are connected with one or more HMOs; this compares with 50 percent nationally. The health care market in Minnesota is a buyer's market: there are roughly 250 doctors per 100,000 residents, as compared to a national average of 225 physicians per 100,000 residents.

The impact of HMO growth on Twin City hospitals has been profound. In 1984, residents of the Twin Cities who were not HMO members spent an average of 1,087 days in the hospital per 1,000 people; this was close to the national average. HMO members, on the other hand, spent just over one-third as much time in hospitals—385 days per 1,000 people (p. 102). Overall occupancy levels in 1984 were 47.5 percent. With lower occupancy and increased pressure on prices, those hospitals still earning a profit (or adding to their fund balance) are earning at very low rates. As a result, half of the region's hospitals will be forced either to merge or to go out of business by the late 1980s, according to the Metropolitan Council.

What Are Alternative Delivery Systems and What Could They Be?

Alternative delivery systems (ADS) is one of those rather odd descriptive phrases that recently became common in the health care industry. In this book, and in normal industry usage, the term refers to HMOs and PPOs. In other words, the term describes an alternative form of health insurance—one in which the consumer's choices of hospitals and physicians are more limited and in which there is likely to be more emphasis on utilization review, prevention of illness, and financial risks for providers. In HMOs, in particular, primary care physicians are usually paid either a salary (closed-panel model), a predetermined amount each month for every patient in the plan assigned to that doctor (called "capitation"), or a fee for service, with a withhold on part of the fee. Therefore, HMO physicians have an incentive to keep healthy patients away from specialists, and out of hospitals.

There are many different types of PPOs. In general, a PPO is an arrangement between a large purchaser of health care services (a major employer, union, or insurance company) and a group of providers (physicians, one or more hospitals, or both). In return for the business, providers usually offer what could be called a volume discount. For example, physicians usually give a 15 to 20 percent discount to a PPO.

Peter Boland, in his *New Healthcare Market,* says that "large [health care] purchasers are beginning to intervene in the market and negotiate contracts with providers, or through intermediaries such as insurance carriers and third-party claims administrators, for medical care at 'preferred' or reduced rates" (1985, p. 2). This is a good working definition of a PPO.

PPOs may also include utilization review procedures designed to cut down on hospitalization and unnecessary treatment, especially surgery or expensive diagnostic services. Both HMOs and PPOs frequently provide what is called "managed care"—*managed* in the sense that a physician, nurse, or plan administrator pays close attention to utilization of health care services.

ADS membership in 1986 included approximately 10 percent of the U.S. population. Changes in HMO and PPO membership from 1975 to 1986 are shown in Table 10.

Several different organizations have forecast ADS market penetration to the year 1990. The most optimistic forecast was prepared by Kenneth Abramowitz of Sanford C. Bernstein & Co., Inc., in 1985. The Bernstein report estimated that HMO penetration would rise from 9 percent of employees in 1985 to 30 percent in 1990. A recent Bernstein research report says that "by 1990, the vast majority of the population (70 percent) will be in some such sort (HMO or PPO) of health care delivery system and fee-for-service medicine as we know it will be dead" (Abramowitz, 1985, p. 11). Bernstein's research is optimistic about HMO growth for several reasons, including Medicare's efforts to encourage its thirty-one million beneficiaries to become HMO members. Medicare HMO contracts are referred to as Competitive Medical Plans (CMPs), and a large proportion of the major players in the HMO market (Kaiser, Aetna, Blue Cross) are offering such plans.

Table 10. ADS Membership in United States, 1975–1986.

| Year | Millions of Members in ADS | | |
	HMOs	PPOs	Total
1975	5.7	—	5.7
1980	9.1	—	9.1
1981	10.3	—	10.3
1982	10.8	—	10.8
1983	12.5	—	12.5
1984	16.7	1.3	18.0
1985	18.9	5.8	24.7
1986	21.0	9.0	30.0

Bernstein predicts that 25 to 30 percent of Medicare beneficiaries will be enrolled in HMOs by 1990.

Todd Richter of Morgan Stanley says, "We expect total [HMO] enrollment to exceed 50 million—22 percent of the population— by the close of 1990. This extraordinary growth rate includes a more than four-fold increase in the number of Medicare recipients participating in HMO plans. By year-end 1990, we believe nearly 10 percent of the Medicare-eligible population— about three million individuals—will be HMO members" (Richter, 1986, p. 20).

The Congressional Budget Office (1986) has estimated that HMO enrollment will be forty-seven million by 1990 (about 20 percent of the U.S. population), while Frost & Sullivan, Inc., a consulting firm, predicts forty million (17 percent) (Tatge, 1985). Neither of these groups has published estimates of PPO penetration by 1990.

Growth in HMO membership is expected to be primarily in the independent practice association (IPA) models. Closed-panel models, such as Kaiser, are expected to grow, but at a slower rate. Physicians are jumping on the bandwagon for the IPA-model HMOs; they view the closed-model HMOs as a serious source of competition.

Leonard Schaeffer, former president of Group Health in Minneapolis and currently president of Blue Cross/Blue Shield of California, has a different view of the future of HMOs. "From where I sit, the HMO industry has been oversold, and employers are beginning to react. But the bloom is off the rose just about everyplace. . . . The HMO industry will grow, I believe, but its savings to employers will be less than they anticipated and the complexity of making it work is really awesome" ("HMOs and Hospitals: An Update," 1986, p. 12).

The question of ADS penetration levels is further complicated by the types of cost-containment provisions included, especially in PPOs. For example, if a PPO has strong disincentives for employees using physicians or hospitals not on the preferred list, it may be less acceptable to employers and their employees. An 80/60 PPO plan is an example of one with a strong "steering mechanism"; such a plan would provide an 80 percent copayment by the employer for use of a preferred provider, but only a 60 percent copayment for other providers. A 100/90 plan (that is, a plan that pays 100 percent when preferred providers are used and 90 percent when employees use other providers) has fewer "teeth" in it and is less likely to lead to substantial cost-containment benefits (Elizabeth Igleheart, Partners National Health Plans, interview with the authors, Dallas, Tex., July 14, 1986).

Largely because major players in the insurance and health care industries are committing large amounts of capital to ADS, we believe that the Congressional Budget Office and Frost & Sullivan projections could be on the low side. At the same time, our own observations of the growth of ADS and our recent focus group research among employers, benefits consultants and brokers, and consumers indicate that large increases in ADS market penetration will not happen without huge marketing efforts and significant financial incentives to both businesses and employees. Therefore, we believe the Bernstein projection of 70 percent of the U.S. work force (including dependents) in ADS by 1990 is too high.

A more realistic estimate is that HMOs and PPOs combined will have 30 to 35 percent market penetration among the population as a whole (or close to triple the present levels) by 1990, and perhaps as much as 55 to 60 percent of the market by 1995. This represents a very significant change in the marketplace, and one with tremendous financial implications for physicians, hospitals, and other health care providers.

In addition to—and in response to—the growth in ADS, traditional indemnity insurers are shifting rapidly to "managed care," which gives them a more active role in utilization review, concurrent review, and other measures to reduce physician and hospital use. Indemnity plans have traditionally been "passive," but change is coming fast. The impact? Less use of hospitals (fewer admissions and shorter stays) and less demand for medical specialists (surgeons and others).

Our research indicates that about half of all physicians participate in HMOs, and an equal percentage participate in one or more PPOs. However, HMOs and PPOs represent only a small fraction of the patient load of most doctors' practices. Consequently, physicians' willingness to grant relatively large discounts—15 to 20 percent being common—to ADS companies has not yet had a significant financial impact on most doctors.

The results of our research among employers indicate that over half of the larger firms in the United States offer one or more HMOs. HMO penetration decreases with size of firm; for example, we estimate that fewer than 5 percent of all businesses with ten to thirty employees offer HMOs.

The challenge facing HMOs is twofold: first get a foot in the door via a contract with the employer, and then sell employees on the HMO option. Data from one of our current HMO clients illustrates how the typical HMO attracts business. This HMO has 25,000 subscribers (about 10,000 employees and 15,000 dependents). Among the over 200 firms it has under contract, the HMO has an 8 percent penetration level among employees. This represents a big improvement; two years ago the HMO had only 4 percent penetration among eligible employees.

PPO penetration among businesses is much lower—less than 10 percent for U.S. firms with thirty or more employees. Even for larger firms (500 employees or more), fewer than 20 percent offered PPOs to their employees in 1986.

A new approach to the establishment of PPOs is taking place in California's Silicon Valley. If successful, it could speed up the adoption of PPOs. "A group of seven Silicon Valley employers that includes Apple Computer Company, Lockheed Corporation and Xidex Corporation announced they had formed the 'Preferred

Connection' and had negotiated discounts with every major hospital and physician group in the Valley. The three companies alone represent 40,000 workers. The employers are aided by the American Electronics Association (AEA) and A. S. Hansen, Inc., a Chicago-based health care management consulting firm. AEA has 900 member companies in the Silicon Valley, a 60-mile strip that stretches from San Francisco to San Jose, and 2,800 nationwide" (Moore, 1986, p. 1). Given the large number of trade and industry associations in the United States, the implications of the AEA thrust are profound for the future of health plan coverage.

Some large firms are making HMO membership mandatory. Lockheed took such a step with 6,287 new employees; after a one-year trial, 95 percent stayed in HMOs even when they could switch to indemnity coverage (Rundle, 1986b, p. 29). If this type of move becomes popular, HMO membership growth could be given a substantial boost.

By 1990, the picture is expected to be much different; nearly all U.S. firms with 500 or more employees are likely to offer either an HMO or a PPO, or some combination thereof. ADS penetration among physicians should exceed 80 percent.

Investing in HMOs and PPOs

Many health care providers have considered in the past, or are currently considering, whether or not to invest in ADS companies. Investment can take many forms, from an acute care hospital and its medical staff putting up the needed capital to start an HMO, to a group of physicians and a hospital forming a joint venture to contract with PPOs.

Our research and experience indicate that the front-end investment needed to start an HMO is in the $3 million to $5 million range. In markets characterized by severe price competition (for example, Chicago), it can be even higher. Most of the capital is needed for establishing the organization, marketing (including a direct sales force), and covering operating losses until break-even is attained. There are no pat answers on the number of members required to break even; the lowest numbers we have heard are from 12,000 to 15,000. Break-even depends on premium rates, utilization by members, types of contracts negotiated with physicians and hospitals, the level of marketing effort, and, of course, the number of members.

The previously mentioned Bernstein Research report is pessimistic about the earnings outlook for all elements of the health care industry (hospitals, doctors, supply companies) other than the large proprietary HMO companies. It believes that these companies (U.S. Health Care Systems, Maxicare, HealthAmerica, United Healthcare, and Safeguard Health Enterprises) represent an excellent investment opportunity. However, this optimism is largely based on the potential increase in HMO companies with a national presence. Locally owned HMOs with small markets are not expected to do well in future market conditions, in part because they have little ability to compete for large national contracts and generally have less leverage with physicians.

Many hospitals and health care systems that are part of the two largest networks—Voluntary Hospitals of America (VHA) and American Healthcare Systems (AHS)—have invested in alternative delivery system ventures sponsored by the two groups. VHA, for example, raised $40 million for its half of the joint venture with Aetna to establish Partners National Health Plans. The typical VHA hospital electing to participate invested $200,000 to $330,000.

When an IPA or physician joint venture is formed, primarily to contract with one or more HMOs or PPOs, physicians are often asked to invest in the venture. The amounts are usually low; the $500 to $2,000 range is common. Once contracts are signed, however, physicians can be at risk financially in terms of some form of capitation (payment of a fixed amount per month per ADS patient) or the withholding of part of their fee-for-service reimbursement. The objective of most organizers of HMOs and PPOs is to increase the risk for physicians and to increase the incentive for physicians to practice cost-effective medicine.

Investing in an HMO is, in our opinion, very risky. There are many things that can go wrong—price competition, difficulty in signing cost-effective contracts with physician groups and hospitals, inadequate utilization review, the need to spend large sums on advertising and direct marketing efforts, and shifts in utilization in the event of adverse selection (less healthy employees signing up for the plan).

The upside potential, from a financial viewpoint, is that HMOs sell at excellent multiples of future earnings. It is not uncommon for one of the large national HMOs, insurance carriers, or proprietary hospital chains (American Medical International, for example) to acquire a successful HMO at prices ranging from $300 to $600 per member. A relatively small HMO, with 25,000 members, would sell for $7.5 million to $15 million. These amounts would normally represent substantially more than has been invested in the HMO. But will these kinds of premium prices continue into the future? We doubt it. Most HMO industry participants expect an industry shakeout, with the stronger national firms able to pick up the pieces at substantially less than historical prices.

Whether or not an HMO or PPO represents an acceptable financial investment may be of less concern to investors than participation in the health insurance part of the health care marketplace. The intention of HMOs and PPOs to direct their members to designated physicians and hospitals scares most hospital administrators and governing boards. Therefore, the strategy of vertical integration into ADS (discussed in more detail in Chapter Eight) has to be seriously considered; ADS decisions made can have significant impacts on the long-term viability of many hospitals and medical practices.

ADS Implications for Hospitals

Hospital managers and trustees should be concerned with several marketing and financial implications of HMOs and PPOs. For example, given the projected rapid growth in ADS market penetration, what will be the impact of ADS on inpatient-days? What are the likely financial impacts on hospitals offering sizable discounts to HMOs and PPOs? What are the best strategies for hospitals to use in meeting the ADS challenge without "giving away the store"?

Current Example. A hypothetical U.S. hospital with 125,000 patient-days in 1986 might experience the payer mix shown in Table 11. These estimates reflect various hospital usage factors for groups covered by different types of health plans and those having no insurance. In this example, utilization by persons covered by HMOs and PPOs (13 percent of the market) would result in only 6 percent of patient-days. At this stage of their development, HMOs and PPOs tend to attract younger members, those who are less likely to require extensive hospitalization.

The Situation in 1990. The hypothetical hospital is likely to find that its patient-days have been reduced to 100,000 by 1990. The payer mix in the hospital's market area will have moved to a much greater emphasis on ADS, with steep discounts and extensive utilization review procedures.

What will this hospital's payer mix look like in 1990? Table 12 projects one scenario. Under Table 12's estimates, ADS patient-days will have increased from 7,500 (6 percent of compensated patient-days) in 1986 to 40,000 in 1990. This dramatic increase (433 percent) in patient-days subject to ADS discounts will have tremendous financial repercussions for most hospitals. The combination of Medicare, ADS, and uncompensated care would represent 74 percent of total patient-days in 1990; the similar ratio for our hypothetical hospital in 1986 is 55 percent.

Dealing with Discounts. We have heard several industry experts say that hospitals and physicians are adept at getting around discounts by making up the financial shortfall through increased intensity of tests and ancillary services. Max Fine, one of the contributors to *The New Healthcare Market,* says that "a hospital can recover any discount it offers by keeping patients an extra day, thereby running up plan costs" (1985, p. 207). While this may have been true in the past, we expect that concurrent review procedures, capitation, and overall monitoring of hospitals and physicians participating in health plans will close the door on this unethical behavior.

Table 11. Hospital Payer Mix, 1986.

Health Plan Coverage	Market Area Health Plan Coverage	Percent of Patient-Days	Patient-Days
Medicare (not covered by HMO)	25%	45%	56,250
Indemnity insurance	55	45	56,250
ADS (HMOs and PPOs)	13	6	7,500
Uncompensated care (no insurance)	7	4	5,000
Total	100%	100%	125,000

Table 12. Hospital Payer Mix, 1990.

Health Plan Coverage	Market Area Health Plan Coverage	Percent of Patient-Days	Patient-Days
Medicare (not covered by HMO)	15%	30%	30,000
Indemnity insurance	33	26	26,000
ADS (HMOs and PPOs)	55	40	40,000
Uncompensated care (no insurance)	7	4	4,000
Total	100%	100%	100,000

As we mentioned previously, Bernstein Research characterizes hospital prices as "unstable." The Bernstein report says that, given the excess capacity in the health care system, employers and health plans will increasingly "whipsaw" hospitals and physicians on their prices—not a pleasant prospect, but one that could very well come true in the next three to five years.

Future Implications of ADS. In the future we expect to see more, not less, differentiation in HMO and PPO penetration and pricing from market to market. Consider the following:

• We predict substantial price differentials among three types of markets: urban competitive markets, urban stable markets, and rural markets. The highest hospital prices will be in the rural areas, where providers have little incentive to grant discounts but will go along with PPO contracts at token discounts in order to make it convenient for local employees of national companies. Prices will be lowest in selected growth markets where national chains compete head to head and there is an oversupply of physicians. In these markets, there will be a two-staged effect on pricing: providers will grant large discounts, and the ADS themselves will accept lower margins as they seek to capture market share. As an analogy to this particular competitive issue, we offer the recent airline industry experience.

• We predict a large number of markets in which HMOs will never be successful. In many markets, PPOs may arrive first and preempt enough market share to discourage the establishment of HMOs.

• We predict, in many markets, a period of low prices to the consumer, followed by gradual price increases. After a period of intensive marketing by competing "franchises," the winners among HMOs and PPOs will be identified. ADS operations at or near break-even will be sold at less than current price levels to the survivors. Relationships among consumers, payers, and providers will be established, and there will be costs and inconveniences attached to changing them. However, the payers and providers will be doing poorly relative to their peers in other markets. With relationships established, hospital prices will gradually increase.

ADS Implications for Physicians

The two family practice physicians sat across from one another, flanked by mostly older specialists on each side. Each was male and roughly thirty years old. The setting was a physician focus group in a midsized midwestern market. One said, "I'll never join any of the three plans, even if it means I have to go out of business. They can't tell me how to practice." The other said, "Well, I've joined all three, and if three more come along I'll join them too! They *are* my business."

As HMOs and PPOs cover increasing numbers of patients, the price pressure on physicians, and on the overall economic condition of their practices, could present serious problems to some doctors. This may be especially true for primary care physicians, many of whom are already struggling to establish and maintain a practice.

There is no consistency in physician responses to the various ADS initiatives now confronting them. However, our research across numerous markets shows that physicians tend to react in accordance with the four personality profiles we described in Chapter Two, and on that basis we can predict how each profile will respond to ADS options.

- *Early innovators.* Look to these physicians to lead in formulating an ADS strategy in local markets, but do not make the mistake of assuming that they are representative of the general medical staff.
- *Joiners.* Members of this group will join anything that might forestall the coming decline; thus we expect them to participate in ADS.
- *Traditionalists.* These physicians intend to hold out to the end and "just practice good medicine." Many traditionalists are excellent physicians, and leaders of their medical staffs. However, their counsel on ADS issues, like that of the early innovators, can be misrepresentative of other medical staff members.
- *Pure practitioners.* Many of these physicians are looking for a refuge from the business issues of their profession in a group-model HMO, a hospital-based practice, or a position in a large-group practice. They will go along with an IPA-model ADS, but this is not the answer to their needs.

As indicated by these four examples, physicians of the same age and specialty may fall into different categories. However, there is a strong tendency for the early innovators to be younger and the traditionalists to be older.

In a few cases, doctors are actively resisting HMOs and organizing themselves to combat prepaid health plans. At a meeting of 250 Los Angeles physicians, Morris Katz, a family practice doctor, drew applause by saying, "We must hang together or assuredly we will hang separately" (Hull, 1986, p. 25). Katz was referring to the power of corporate medicine as represented by HMOs. In Honolulu, 100 physicians are forming a group to support traditional fee-for-service medicine. "One local group with a particularly strong voice is the Committee to Save Private Patient Care, based in West Palm Beach, Fla." (p. 25).

Despite these limited examples of organized resistance to ADS, we believe that most physicians will respond to the ADS marketplace in one of four ways:

- Sign contracts with all available HMOs and PPOs in order to maintain patient load. Based on our interviews with physicians, the attitude of most is "Why not take some additional business? It won't cost me much. HMOs and PPOs represent a very small percentage of my patient load, and I'm not going to worry about them."
- Work with their primary hospital in mutually developing an ADS strategy. One common way to do this is to form a joint venture between a select group of doctors (or an independent practice association) and the hospital. In other words, hospitals and doctors will be joining together to compete for ADS business.
- Although it is inconvenient and time-consuming, seek active status on the medical staff of several hospitals. We believe there is the beginning of a trend in this direction; physicians will feel pressured into following their patients.
- Do nothing; continue to serve Medicare and fee-for-service patients.

The ADS trend, particularly HMOs, often places the primary care doctor in a pivotal "gatekeeper" position. He or she is likely to control referrals to specialists and, increasingly, to be involved in hospitalization decisions. And, since the compensation of primary care doctors is likely to be on a capitated basis (for example, $20 per month per patient), or at risk as a part of a joint venture or IPA, primary care physicians will want to limit use of costly resources, especially the use of specialists and inpatient-days in a hospital. Many primary care doctors are already having a difficult time economically; they are likely to be diligent in protecting their income stream.

Strategic Implications

Most hospitals and physicians, especially younger doctors seeking to establish or build a practice, have little choice but to pursue business (patient acquisition) agressively through ADS contracting. Those hospitals that do not participate face dramatic decreases in patient-days; doctors who do not participate face the loss of patients. Hospital financial managers, CEOs, and governing boards will need to develop strategies to minimize the potential adverse impacts of price discounts on an increasingly large share of their hospital's business. Although there are no easy answers, here are a few suggestions.

- *First, size up your market and your own position in the market.* How fragmented will the market be? How many ADS entries can survive? How many national, as opposed to purely local, employers are present? Is your market share and/or reputation for quality such that an ADS competitor would be at a disadvantage not to include you? Do you have room to discount and still make a profit (or positive contribution to the funds balance, in the case of a not-for-profit health care provider)? Are you already a low-cost provider (see Chapter Thirteen)? Will new ADS contracts improve or create problems in your relationships with your medical staff?

Certain hospitals, because of their competitive position, will be able to dictate their ADS positioning. We recommend that they:

- *Offer only shallow discounts.* Compete wherever possible on the basis of quality, geographic coverage, or market share, not price. Lessons learned from other industries (airlines, apparel, and steel manufacturing) suggest that price competition can be disastrous.
- *Do not grant any HMO or PPO an exclusive agreement.* Be

willing to accept contracts with all the ADS players. (Why cut yourself off from part of the market if you do not have to?)

- *Purchase minority ownership positions in one or more HMOs or PPOs.* You may have something to offer a new ADS because of your market position and prestige. You also have something to gain. Minority ownership ties payers more closely to you, and may make it less likely that they will work out agreements elsewhere because of small price differentials offered by other health care systems.

- *Avoid majority ownership/managerial roles in most ADS entries.* There may be exceptions, but in most cases the opportunities to lose financially by offending admitting physicians exceed the opportunities to gain from ADS profits. In fact, it may be a long while before ADS firms make a profit, if ever.

In negotiating ADS contracts, certain hospitals may be able to capitalize on their status as low-cost providers. While this may be a good position to be in and to retain, it does not assure survival. Hospital profit margins tend to be slim—less than 10 percent of revenues—and substantial price cutting will quickly absorb available margins. Therefore, even low-cost providers should offer resistance to pressure to cut prices.

Given the projected fivefold increase in the proportion of patient-days covered by HMOs and PPOs, and the anticipated price discounts, low-cost hospitals should certainly move away from a cost-based pricing mentality. Cost-based pricing does a disservice to lower-cost hospital providers.

Obviously, not all hospitals are in a position to dictate the terms of their ADS agreements. However, we hope our basic message is clear. Even if a health care system finds it necessary to compete on the basis of price, it should start working for the day when this will no longer be necessary. If a health care system or hospital has no choice but to give large discounts in exchange for admissions, it may be time to consider downsizing, sale, or closure.

Similarly, most physicians will not be in a position to dictate terms. At this point, many physicians can afford to grant 15 to 20 percent discounts to ADS payers because their usual and customary fees are not based on cost and the proportion of total income from ADS payers is still small. Our advice to physicians is to seek negotiating leverage other than price, or attempt to become a low-cost provider.

In summary, patient acquisition through ADS is an appropriate strategy for many hospitals and physicians. Yet the practice of granting large discounts in order to obtain this type of business is fraught with dangers. Careful negotiation is essential. Those hospitals aggressively pursuing ADS contracts must be prepared either to cut costs or to make up for the discounts by raising prices elsewhere. Joseph Califano refers to this latter practice as the "health care shell game"—but show us an industry that is profitable that doesn't price its products or services differently for varying segments of the market.

7

Diversification: Exploiting New Business Opportunities

At a semiannual trustees' retreat, our guest speaker, Michael Annison of Westrend (formerly with John Naisbitt, of Megatrend fame), challenged trustees, hospital managers, and medical staff leaders to speculate about the future of the "bed business." Annison asked, "As you look ahead five years, what percent of your business will come from outpatient services or from diversification?" The responses varied from 5 percent to 50 percent. Annison then asked, "What percent of the health system's profits in 1990 will come from new ventures, perhaps business you can't visualize today?" Once again, responses varied—from "No profits; we'll be lucky to break even," to "More than half of our earnings will come from new business."

The key issues facing a health system considering diversification as a survival strategy are these:

- What are the reasons to proceed with new business opportunities?

- What kinds of diversification ventures are most appropriate?
- How should a diversification strategy be implemented to increase its chances of success?
- What can realistically be expected from diversification efforts?

Background

We have been analyzing diversification strategies in different industries for the past twenty years. In the mid to late 1960s, at a time when it looked as if arms control would reduce the need for a massive defense industry, we were involved in a research project that examined the diversification experiences of fourteen large aerospace companies, including Boeing, Lockheed, and AVCO. More recently, we have worked with both the telecommunications and banking industries as they have gone through periods of tremendous change. The factors impacting these industries are familiar to those in the health care industry:

- Excess capacity
- Increased competition
- Deregulation
- Rapid technical change
- Difficulty in differentiating products
- More aggressive marketing

But when an industry undergoes dramatic change—as have telecommunications, banking, and health care—opportunities for new business ventures are created.

The presence of threats to core business (in the case of hospitals, inpatient-days), and the presence of numerous opportunities, leads almost inevitably to consideration of diversifying a health care system's revenue mix and finding new sources of profitability.

Russell Coile, a highly respected health care industry futurist, thinks that health care systems can, and must, more aggressively diversify out of the inpatient business. He says, "As competition intensifies and traditional revenues shrink, health care organizations will expand their definition of health products and services. Health testing and self-diagnostic equipment are product lines that could expand any health care company's portfolio.

"Diversified health care companies will seek revenues from unrelated businesses as well. Information systems, staff leasing, and real estate development are but a few examples of nonhealth activities that may provide a broader revenue base for tomorrow's health care organizations. By 1990 the combination of related and unrelated new business will reduce the average hospital's dependency on inpatient care from 95+ percent to 85 percent. For larger multihealth corporations, non-inpatient revenues could account for 25 to 40 percent or more of all revenues by 1990" (1986, p. 27). Coile and many other industry observers feel that this shift can be accompanied by profits. We have reservations about this conclusion; it will be much easier to generate revenues from diversification than an adequate return on investment. One of the purposes of this chapter is to suggest how local health care systems can control losses from diversification, and eventually manage new ventures in ways that contribute to the health care system's bottom line.

What Is Diversification?

When hospital administrators decide to pursue diversification seriously, they ask themselves what the most appropriate definition of diversification is, and whether the best approach is through new product development or acquisition.

Definition of Diversification. There are many ways to define *diversification*. At Swedish Health Systems, we evaluated a number of alternatives and came up with this: *"Diversification is a strategy that attempts to spread financial risk by taking advantage of new market opportunities."* The concept of risk spreading is important; it distinguishes diversification from vertical integration (discussed in Chapter Eight). Vertical integration in the health care industry usually refers to an attempt to control all aspects of health care delivery, from health insurance through the continuum of care.

New Products Versus Acquisition. Some organizations have a bias against acquisition. "If it's so good, why do the present owners want to sell?" they ask. "Why buy someone else's problems?" On the latter point, we have worked with a rapidly expanding, very successful bank holding company. Most bank holding companies expand by acquiring banks, but this firm will not consider acquisition. The president's reasons relate to management style, corporate culture, and the potential for inheriting a portfolio of bad loans.

The question of new product development versus acquisition should not be a major problem; despite the banker's reservations about acquisition, most health care organizations need to consider both.

Diversification Versus Incremental Changes in Product Lines. What are the major differences between diversification and making incremental changes in existing product lines? Two examples will serve to illustrate. In one hospital we work with, the distinction was an important one: individuals responsible for product line management wanted the freedom and encouragement to pursue products that could enhance their specific product lines without falling under the more rigorous structure used in analyzing and assessing new business ventures. As an example, the women's health product line formed a joint venture with the two OB/GYN physicians to establish an infertility program. Is this diversification or extension of a product line? We tend to view it as product line development.

In another example, a hospital was approached to establish, on a joint-venture basis with another major health care organization, a low back institute for persons with failed back syndrome. There was a heated turf battle on this one, especially among the neurosurgeons, orthopedic surgeons, and affiliated rehabilitation hospital. A task force was appointed to see what could be done. Is this an example of diversification or is it simply expansion of existing product lines? Since the institute would open a new market, we would categorize it as diversification.

Geographic Expansion. Given increased competition among health care providers in a given market area, hospitals frequently attempt to extend the geographic coverage of their market area as a response against intrusions by others. Such an expansion can often involve a system of urgent care centers, financial arrangements with primary care physicians, development of a health park, or establishment of other ambulatory services.

In one sense, geographic expansion can be considered to be diversification: it provides services or product lines to submarkets not previously having convenient access to these services. Hospital staff who are responsible for major product lines, and the extension of these product lines into new market areas, often do not look at the situation in this light, however.

Reasons for Diversification

In our research and analysis, we find it useful to identify the various reasons an organization might want to diversify. One good way to do this is to assess past diversification efforts in terms of the reasons they were initiated. When we did this recently at Swedish Health Systems we identified seven major reasons the system had diversified into the new businesses. These were:

1. *Community Service.* Address health care needs of the population that would go unmet without hospital action.
2. *Competitive Positioning.* Maintain or improve the health system and medical center's competitive position.
3. *Innovation.* Operate at the cutting edge of new products, technology, and services in order to identify emerging new business opportunities.
4. *Profit Augmentation.* Replace expected revenue and profit reductions in traditional areas (for example, inpatient services).
5. *Risk Management.* Minimize overall organizational risk by spreading risks among a variety of ventures and markets.
6. *Operating Economies.* Achieve operating economies (reduce costs) and improve utilization of existing resources (facilities, staff, and so on).

7. *Medical Staff Relations.* Improve relationships with medical staff members, or augment their practices.

It is also interesting to compare the initial reasons for establishing a new venture with the reasons for a business's existence today. In our studies we have found that frequently either the initial reasons for starting a new venture were not well defined or, with the passage of time, there have been significant changes in these reasons.

For example, one hospital established a system of four urgent care centers. This was accomplished several years ago with the intent of better serving the community by making outpatient services more convenient to the public. These centers were innovative at the time they were established; very few other hospitals were using this approach in serving patients.

As we look at these centers today, they are far from innovative. In reality, their purpose now is to act as a feeder network for the medical center. They also serve a competitive purpose, in that their presence discourages other health care organizations from establishing urgent care centers in the market area of the hospital.

What are the lessons learned by looking back at past diversification attempts? The first is that there should be one or more solid reasons for embarking on a new venture. If there is no intention that the new venture make a profit, this should be clearly understood by all concerned—not only at the time the initial decision is made, but in the future, when budget review comes around. On the other hand, new enterprises established with the objective of making a financial contribution should not later be justified on the basis of goodwill or community service.

Implementing a Diversification Effort

Scale. A well-designed strategic plan normally has estimates of the "scale"—or size in relationship to revenues or profits of the entire organization—of new ventures considered by the health care system. This plan might also include general targets for the scale of potential future ventures.

To illustrate this point, we have a continuing relationship with one of the large television networks. This organization has approximately $3 billion in annual revenues. A $30 million per year new venture was proposed: the investment would represent about 1 percent of our client's annual revenues; the projected $5 million annual profit would represent slightly more than 1 percent of corporate profits.

This would appear to be an attractive new business venture for a major broadcasting company. Yet we recommended that our client not get into this business for two major reasons: the new venture was not big enough to justify the capital investment and top-management time required, and without adequate funding or management, its probabilities of success were low.

At the same time, a local health care system should not put all of its eggs in one basket. Given the odds against success in most new ventures—the batting average is usually in the 10 to 20 percent range—this would be foolhardy. In fact, Peters and Waterman, in *In Search of Excellence* (1982), point out that the most innovative companies, those with the greatest number of success stories in terms of new product development, have one theme in common: they all attempt to develop large numbers of new products. To successfully develop a significant number of new products requires the initiation of a very large number of new product development efforts; it is a numbers game.

Initiating New Ventures Versus Reacting to Proposals. In health care, we hear business described in terms of "a deal a day." For midsized to large hospitals in metropolitan areas, this is probably an accurate description; hospitals are bombarded by a variety of proposals, all of which may involve committing funds, establishing new businesses, and entering into new types of arrangements with physicians, other health care organizations, and even for-profit institutions.

Given that deal-a-day bombardment, how much of a proactive stance should a health care organization take regarding diversification? Every health care system desiring diversification needs systematically to identify and rank, in order of priority, the kinds of businesses and product lines it wants to develop. When this is done the list will usually exceed 100 potential candidates. But there are only a few potential activities that hold promise for making significant financial contributions. Rehabilitation hospitals and nursing homes stand out as diversification activities that have the potential to make a big difference. Those opportunities appearing to be most attractive should be the subject of systematic analysis, careful management and trustee decision making, and the development of realistic business plans.

However, our experience indicates that most proposals coming across a CEO's desk are not part of the hospital's strategic plan; instead, the ideas originate with external sources. These proposals require a response by the hospital, and on a timely and businesslike basis.

Screening Criteria. It helps to have criteria for screening proposed new ventures. Every organization will have different criteria. The seven screening criteria listed below are used by one health care system:

- Consistency with strategic plan
- Adequate return on investment (payback in three to five years)
- Evidence of market demand (market research)
- Quality (consistent with present health care system's standards)
- Control (ownership of an adequate amount of equity to exercise control)
- Use of management resources; avoidance of spending too much time on ventures with limited potential (scale)
- Risks (moderate to low)

R. Neal Gilbert, in "Hospital Revenue Diversification" (1986), spells out the criteria used by a hospital he consulted with:

Financial

- Break-even in three years
- Investment per new venture not to exceed $2 million
- Payback in five years

- Return on investment in the fifth year to exceed 150 percent of hospital's long-term interest rate

Nonfinancial

- Support of basic philosophies and goals
- Direct or indirect relationship to health care
- Enhancement or protection of market share and image
- Availability of nonhospital management
- Compatibility with medical staff relationships

In Gilbert's example, the financial criteria are specific and rigorous (breaking even within three years and paying back the investment within five years). This hospital also insists that nonhospital management expertise be available to manage the new business and that the investment not threaten or jeopardize medical staff relationships.

Screening criteria, normally applied early in the evaluation process, represent a quick way to decide whether or not to invest resources in testing the feasibility of a new venture and then going ahead with preparation of a business plan. They represent general guidelines and are not intended to be rigidly applied.

Market Research and Segmentation. Objective market and economic feasibility analysis is an area in which the health care industry lags well behind other industries. We are shocked at the number of important decisions made in hospitals without the benefit of rigorous marketing and economic analysis (see our more detailed discussion in Appendix B). Our observations indicate that economic feasibility studies for proposed new ventures or major capital improvements are most often deficient in terms of their estimates of demand. Market segmentation is often poorly done, yet given the changes in payment mechanisms taking place (for example, HMOs and PPOs) it is especially important to consider the payment capabilities of the market segment being analyzed.

The list below shows examples of marketing segmentation related to several potential new ventures that we evaluated:

Proposed New Venture	*Market Segment*
• Mobile breast diagnostic center	• Women forty and over with primary care physician
• Ambulance company (acquisition)	• Number of emergency and transport cases
• Medical office building	• Physicians in area, and those who are likely to move to the area
• Outpatient surgery center	• Proportion of surgeries now performed that could be shifted, plus new business potential
• Low back program	• Portion of regional population with failed back syndrome
• Magnetic resonance imager (MRI)	• Percentage of cases requiring MRI imaging (physician referrals key)
• Regional diagnostic center	• Several submarkets, each with a different market area
• Health maintenance organization (HMO)	• Firms of over twenty-five employees in the area served

For example, the proposed mobile breast diagnostic center noted above was targeted at women forty and over who had a primary care physician. The reason for this segmentation was that the van holding the mammography equipment was to be parked adjacent to physicians' offices. Incidentally, we did not recommend that the hospital proceed with this new venture; physicians did not support it because they felt the quality and service provided would be inferior to the hospital's breast diagnostic center.

The feasibility of a magnetic resonator (MRI) depends on the percentage of cases in an area that require the type of imaging at which MRI has an advantage over CAT scans. In order to estimate the market for this $1 million to $2 million piece of equipment, we performed an analysis of CAT scan utilization data and conducted focus group interviews with physicians in specialties likely to make referrals to an MRI (oncologists, neurosurgeons, and others).

For a proposed new HMO, the target market includes firms with twenty-five or more employees—and, as a submarket, those employees in these firms that are expected to sign up with an HMO once it has a contract with the business (mainly younger workers not having established relationships with physicians).

We recently talked with the chairman of the board of a specialized hospital in the Midwest. He told us that the hospital had disbanded its corporate staff, the group responsible for ten different new ventures that the hospital system had attempted to establish over the past four years. He said that the fundamental problem was that the staff jumped into too many businesses without adequate assessment of the need and potential payoff of these ventures. In other words, there was inadequate market research and economic feasibility analysis.

Review Procedure. Any hospital or local health care system considering a significant number of different diversification alternatives should have an organized approach for handling such proposals. Here is the approach we recommended for one health care system:

1. A seven-member capital priorities committee should be created by the system president. Members should include representatives of the medical center—finance, planning, marketing, and medical staff. The committee should meet twice a month at a regularly scheduled time.
2. Although the system president may, from time to time, desire to meet with the committee, we recommend that the chief financial officer chair the committee.
3. The committee chair may appoint task forces to pursue certain proposals.
4. It is the responsibility of the chair to maintain an up-to-date data base of potential capital investment opportunities for the system. The purpose of this data base is to be able to assess any new proposal in the context of overall health care system needs and opportunities.

5. The committee should have a budget for use in requesting market, feasibility, planning, or engineering assistance that is beyond the scope of system staffing capability and availability. We recommend $100,000 for the first twelve months.

Relationship to Strategic Plan. We mentioned earlier that diversification efforts should relate to the health care system's strategic plan. Diversification should do more; it should *enhance* other competitive strategies in specific product lines or other businesses (see Chapter Sixteen).

Managing New Ventures

One key to successfully establishing new ventures is attracting and motivating key people: the entrepreneurs. This is an especially difficult problem for hospitals; the types of individuals likely to be successful in running new ventures probably will not fit into the hospital's culture.

Appropriate Management Style. It is important that the management system for new ventures be different from that used in the hospitals. About five years ago, one of the authors was asked to serve on the board of directors of an HMO started by two hospitals and an independent practice association; each group owned a one-third interest. The board meetings were conducted like hospital board meetings: very formally, with detailed minutes. In addition, there were finance, marketing, quality assurance, and executive committees. At the time, the HMO had 1,100 subscribers and annual revenues of less than $1 million. This is an example of transferring hospital management techniques to a market-oriented small company needing a much simpler management style. Fortunately, things have changed and the HMO is now run more like a small business. The present CEO and his marketing director would probably not get along within the typical hospital environment, but they are doing an excellent job in the highly competitive health plan marketplace.

Adequate Capitalization. Neal Gilbert, in the article referred to earlier (1986), suggested that the hospital should set aside 150 percent of any new venture funding requested, to make sure that adequate dollars are available. It may not be necessary to be this rigid, but we agree with Gilbert that inadequate capital is the biggest single problem with new health care ventures.

Over the years, our consulting firm has been associated with the establishment of a number of commercial banks. Financial projections prepared for a newly established commercial bank usually indicate losses for the first one or two years of operation, with break-even in the third year. Most banks move solidly into the black by the end of their third or fourth year of operations, but there are many exceptions. It is frequently necessary to request additional capital from shareholders in order to maintain capital requirements at the levels required by regulatory authorities, and to ensure the viability of the shareholders' initial investment. We have never seen a group of bank stockholders enjoy having to ante up more capital, but they are locked into doing so once they make their initial investment.

The same is true of trustees; they do not appreciate requests for additional capital to keep a venture going. In the future, trustees are likely to take a much tougher stance on additional funding requests. Therefore, it behooves health care systems active in establishing new ventures to assure adequate capitalization in the first place, thus minimizing the possibility of having to go back for supplementary funding.

Commitment Without Loss of Objectivity. There needs to be top-management and trustee commitment to newly established ventures. Yet at some point, trustees and managers need the objectivity to recognize that there are problems and accept the need to phase out marginal new ventures. In health care systems with a number of different boards, members of specific boards tend to become advocates of the venture or ventures under their scrutiny. They lose their objectivity. This can be positive in the sense that the management of the new venture can be assured of whole-hearted support from the board having oversight responsibilities for their venture. However, it poses problems for the overall health system and its CEO in cases where objective analysis might indicate radical change or termination.

Realistic Expectations from Diversification

To the best of our knowledge, there have been no comprehensive studies of the success or failure of health care industry diversification efforts. The conventional wisdom is that there have been many more failures than success stories. But the question is "What are the criteria for success? If you are talking about ventures that could be called a huge financial success, there probably aren't many. However, if success is measured in terms of community service, patient referrals, public relations, or tying in the medical staff, there may be quite a few successful diversification efforts" (Morlan Lewis, managing director, VHA Enterprises Consulting Services Division, interview with the authors, Dallas, Tex., July 14, 1986).

Comparison of Economic Factors. A brief comparison of the economics of inpatient versus outpatient services shows why it is often more difficult for new outpatient diversification efforts to be profitable. The economic factors shown below are important to the financial success of almost any new business.

Economic Factor	*Inpatient Services*	*Outpatient Services*
Capital requirements	High	Low
Competition	Increasing	Tough
Payment mechanisms	Established	Improving
Location/convenience	Important	Critical
Prices	Becoming important	Important
Referral network	Established (but changing)	Developing

For example, capital requirements are high for inpatient activities but usually fairly low for most types of outpatient business. Related to this is the ease of entry; it is much easier to enter a new business that has low capital requirements than one in which capital needs are high. In addition most outpatient services are likely to be faced with very tough competition. This is not to suggest that inpatient business is not competitive; however, in most markets it is not usually as competitive as the outpatient business.

The pricing structure of inpatient business is weakening because of DRGs and the discounting typically associated with HMOs and PPOs. However, the pricing structure of the inpatient side of the business has not yet begun to crumble, at least not in most markets. If hospitals exert good economic judgment, they should be able to maintain adequate pricing for their inpatient business. Pricing for outpatient services is more subject to competition, and there will be a continuing need to respond to providers who choose to compete on a price basis.

Accepting Risk and Failures. We have already discussed the need to accept risk and the inevitable failures that go with any diversification program. One has only to look at the experience of venture capitalists and why they succeed. Venture capitalists recognize that most of the businesses they invest in are going to either fail or be marginally successful at best. However, if one or two out of ten of their investments are highly successful, venture capitalists can experience financial success on their overall investment portfolio.

Although trustees do not like to dig into the hospital's financial resources to come up with additional capital for businesses that have failed to achieve their pro forma projections, they are likely to welcome the opportunity to invest additional funds in ventures showing unusual promise. For example, one health care system was asked to invest an additional million dollars in its HMO, in order to compete more effectively within its market area. The value of the HMO would be enhanced through marketing efforts designed to increase its subscriber base.

Strategic Implications

Proper Scale. We previously discussed the importance of scale. Proposed new ventures should not be so large that they put the entire health care system at risk should they fail, nor should they be so small that they lack the potential to make a significant impact on the future of the system. In one hospital we work with, there is a continuing outflow of cash into a wellness program that does not appear to have significant profit potential. Furthermore, this program, even though it represents a fraction of 1 percent of total revenues, absorbs a disproportionate amount of top-management time. Such programs are candidates for closure.

Management Resources. Although there is considerable management talent in the health care industry, there are very few people with the experience to manage the variety of new ventures represented in an active diversification program. Therefore, it is extremely important to protect management against the time and energy drains that occur with the proliferation of marginally successful small businesses.

Go with Strengths. In evaluating the diversification experience of the "excellent" companies, Peters and Waterman (1982) found that such firms identify their strengths and go with them. In other words, top companies do not spend large amounts of time and effort trying to beef up their marginal product lines. It would be better, according to the findings of Peters and Waterman, systematically to identify the areas of greatest strengths of the hospital or health care system and then build a diversification program around these strengths. For example, a hospital that has a strong women's health program could establish one or more outpatient diagnostic, clinical, and educational centers for women.

Tie to Strategic Plan. It is important to be aware of competitors' actions and to have a strategic plan flexible enough to respond to competitors' moves, but to respond to every competitive action on an ad hoc basis is not a strategy that will assure survival. Trustees often listen to discussions about how their hospital needs to respond to various competitors' actions. Recently, a major hospital located less than two miles away from its main competitor spent $100,000 to purchase the medical practice of a primary care physician. This led to a proposal to the board of the impacted hospital that it should set aside $500,000 for purchasing primary care medical practices. Yet the hospital's strategic plan does not include guidelines on purchasing physician practices.

Quickly Terminating Losers. Accepting failure in a diversification program is difficult but increasingly common for hospitals and major health care systems. If a new venture has been operating for two or three years with little evidence of being able successfully to meet its objectives, serious consideration should be given to termination. The best market research is to actually test a new product or service in the marketplace; health care managers and trustees need to pay close attention to the data generated from this sort of "real world" research.

In assessing the hospital industry's batting average in diversification, Morlan Lewis says, "For every success story there are three or four failures. The main reasons for failure are a lack of understanding of the market, poor financial analysis, and lack of understanding of management requirements." Lewis also points out that most health care organizations have no bail-out strategy in case the new venture is failing (interview with the authors, Dallas, Tex., July 14, 1986).

Earlier in this chapter we described a hospital's attempt to establish a system of four urgent care centers. As a result of in-depth analysis and an inability to come up with a business plan that could convert these centers into profitable operations, one of the centers was closed, one has been temporarily closed but will reopen in a new location, and another is moving to a more convenient location; only one is operating at break-even. These are tough decisions, particularly for the CEO who originally made the decision to establish the centers.

Is diversification a strategy that most health care systems should pursue? The evidence to date is not promising; many new ventures are struggling. Some should be terminated. Profits have been very slow to materialize. Yet there are many opportunities available to aggressive health care systems and hospitals. Given careful screening and selection, objective marketing and economic analysis, and well-managed implementation, diversification efforts represent a promising alternative and may contribute to the long-term viability of many health care organizations.

8

Vertical Integration

Vertical integration differs from diversification. As defined in the previous chapter, diversification is a strategy designed to spread risk. Vertical integration, as practiced in the health care industry, is usually a strategy designed to control a significant portion of a local or regional market by integrating health plans (ADS), primary care physicians, urgent care centers, acute care hospitals (and their medical staffs), and other types of care, such as home health care or long-term care.

As a health care strategy, vertical integration often relates back to earlier diversification efforts. Many local health care systems and hospitals have invested in closely related ventures that were perceived as targets of opportunity or as businesses that would feed patients into the hospital (a series of urgent care centers, for example). HMOs, nursing homes, and rehabilitation hospitals have been popular diversification moves; viewed in today's environment, they often form important building blocks for a vertically integrated health care system.

Jeff Goldsmith, author of *Can Hospitals Survive?* (1981), says that *vertical* integration in the health care system "involves linking together different levels of care and assembling the human resources needed to render that care" (p. 136). He defines *forward* integration as reaching toward the patient through physicians and their offices, emergency rooms, ambulatory care systems, and HMOs. *Backward* integration in industry usually involves securing sources of supply; in health care, Goldsmith relates this to the need to secure an adequate supply of physicians, nurses, technicians, and other allied health personnel (p. 144).

Gerald McManis stresses the need for health care providers to become part of what he calls "integrated health care clusters" ("CHA President: The For-Profit Threat Is a Myth," 1986). McManis says that this is one of the critical strategies for survival for many organizations. McManis defines an integrated health care cluster as a strategic business unit made up of a number of health care providers, usually in metropolitan areas where the population exceeds 200,000. According to McManis, a cluster could include a tertiary care hospital, several community hospitals, a long-term care facility, urgent care centers, and a psychiatric facility. The group would also offer one or more health plans.

Michie Hunt argues that HMOs and hospitals will soon "take the next step: integration into regionally based systems that can create efficiencies unavailable to independent HMOs and hospitals." She goes on to say, "HMO and hospital managers should seek to form regionally based, multi-unit systems whose scale advantages can both learn and profit from an HMO. As price competition escalates, the cost savings that such a system provides will make the difference between extinction and survival" (1985, pp. 20–24). We do not agree with Hunt's conclusions about scale economies; however, her prognosis on the rush toward vertical integration is representative of much of the current thinking in the health care industry.

From a local health system or hospital perspective, there are two aspects of vertical integration: integration forward into the patient acquisition chain to achieve greater control of health plans and primary care physicians, or integration backward toward control of the continuum of care (acute care hospitals, long-term care, home health care, and so on). In our view, opportunities for successful forward integration are limited to a few players who begin with substantial market power. Opportunities for successful backward integration, however, are available to many health care systems in both large and small markets.

Forward integration emphasizing control of the buyers (employers and employees) is a deadly serious game in the health care markets in which this type of competitive approach is being played out. There most certainly will be winners and losers; not every physician group or hospital will be able to retain market share in the face of strong efforts by major health care industry players backed by huge amounts of capital. The most important element of the strategy, and one in its early stages of development in most metropolitan areas, is to control significant numbers of consumers through the health plans they participate in and thus direct patients to selected physician groups, ambulatory facilities, and acute care hospitals.

In markets where this type of competition is developing, many providers feel they have little choice but to follow a similar course in order to protect market share. This strategy is being carried out in a variety of ways, including the integration—through contractual arrangements or joint ventures—of hospitals and physician groups with HMOs and PPOs, hospitals working with such large national systems as VHA and AHS in the development of their health plans, and hospitals seeking provider contracts with the most successful ADS competitors.

The Experience of Other Industries

Vertical integration, as a general business strategy, has been analyzed by Robert Buzzell (1983), a Harvard Business School professor. Buzzell based his analysis on a study of 1,649 manufacturing/processing units and on a review of the business literature on vertical integration. In describing his findings, Buzzell defines vertical integration as "the combination, under single ownership, of two or more stages of production or distribution (or both) that are usually separate" (p. 93). He identifies five pluses and four minuses associated with vertical integration:

The Pluses	The Minuses
1. Reduced transaction costs (buying and selling costs)	1. High capital requirements
2. Supply assurance (raw materials)	2. Potential for unbalanced throughput
3. Improved coordination	3. Reduced flexibility and increased risk
4. Increased technological capabilities	4. Loss of specialization
5. Higher entry barriers for competitors	

One of the major conclusions of Buzzell's research is that high levels of vertical integration are often accompanied by high levels of investment; therefore, return on investment may be reduced. He says, "The lesson seems clear: if a company's management can carry out a strategy of increasing [vertical] integration without greater investment intensity, this strategy usually leads to higher profitability. But the data also show that the winning combination of high value added as a percentage of sales and low investment intensity is uncommon" (p. 96).

Strategies of Investor-Owned Systems

All four of the large proprietary chains are pursuing vertical integration, although each describes it in somewhat different language:

- Humana is combining its Humana Care Plus health plan, extended-hours clinics (called Humana MedFirst), and eighty-seven acute care hospitals into an aggressive, forward-integrated health care system.
- Hospital Corporation of America (HCA), the largest investor-owned chain, is strengthening its regional health care systems, with the focus on acute care hospitals and somewhat less emphasis on either forward or backward integration. However, HCA's latest annual report also mentions forward integration:

"In each region, HCA hospitals are being linked with a broad range of health plans and financing options, strong physician relationships, and alternative delivery service to create a system providing multiple levels of quality health care services in a range of cost-effective and convenient settings" (Hospital Corporation of America, 1986, p. 8).

- American Medical International (AMI) is developing regional health care delivery networks to work in conjunction with insured medical benefit plans. The networks encourage forward and backward integration. The objective is to dominate selected attractive markets.

- National Medical Enterprises (NME) is emphasizing a backward, continuum of care approach; it is developing a number of medical campuses that will include long-term care facilities, specialty hospitals (psychiatric and rehabilitation), home health care, pharmacies, and an acute care hospital.

The eight largest investor-owned hospital corporations had this pattern of vertical integration in 1983 (McNerney, 1986, p. 40):

426 acute care hospitals
272 long-term care units
234 hospital management contracts
163 medical office buildings
103 pharmacies
102 psychiatric hospitals
89 ambulatory care centers
34 alcohol or substance abuse centers
38 home health agencies
62 dialysis centers
32 clinics
3 radiology units
2 medical laboratories
1 freestanding diagnostic center

Each of the large proprietary chains has identified certain market areas as targets for its vertical integration strategies. AMI, for example, has targeted Miami, Houston, southern California,

Denver, Omaha, and New Orleans. Humana is marketing its family of Humana Care Plus health plans in fifty markets.

Strategies of Not-for-Profit Systems

The not-for-profit sector is responding in similar ways by providing outpatient facilities (urgent care and diagnostic centers, specialty hospitals, and arrangements with primary care physicians) and by establishing medical campuses or health parks. With such systems in place, many not-for-profit organizations are also attempting to control ADS (forward integration) in order to direct patients to their facilities.

Among the multihospital systems, Voluntary Hospitals of America—the largest alliance, with over 600 not-for-profit hospitals—has over thirty regional health care systems. Partners National Health Plans, a VHA-Aetna joint venture, will be marketed in each of the VHA regions. Partners represents a national effort at forward integration that is potentially more ambitious than that of any of the investor-owned chains. The VHA regional systems are also developing a large number of additional services to facilitate backward integration into long-term care by its member hospitals.

The HealthWest Foundation, a five-year-old not-for-profit system headquartered in southern California, is aggressively pursuing what it calls a "vertically integrated healthcare system emphasizing 'managed care' continuums" (HealthWest Foundation, 1985, p. 4). This $300 million (in revenues) system says that it recognizes "that the network must seek creative ways to seize marketshare from others just to stay even" (p. 32).

The key to HealthWest's strategy is UniHealth, a group of HMOs and PPOs packaged under the brand name of CareAmerica. HealthWest has earmarked $40 million to spend on CareAmerica over the next thirty months (p. 10). CareAmerica is capitating both its physicians and hospitals and is installing a variety of cost-containment controls. CareAmerica will be offered in each of HealthWest's targeted markets (Washington, Oregon, California, Arizona, Texas, New York, New Jersey, Ohio, and Pennsylvania).

CareAmerica also includes a health plan for seniors, called ElderMed.

The wording used by HealthWest to describe its objectives is ambitious, and somewhat vague, yet it conveys its vertical integration strategy: "It [HealthWest's mission] calls for our pooled resources to be redirected to a new generation of fully integrated continuums of managed care wherein tertiary hospitals, physicians, ambulatory outreach programs, home care, rehabilitation, mental health, substance abuse, transportation and health promotion are all clustered under a single umbrella. The UniHealth arm of HealthWest strategically packages this interactive network of providers into risk assumption arrangements that may include indemnity products, insured premium PPO's or capitated HMO's. UniHealth then markets these seamless managed care continuums to self-insured employers, third party payers, HMO's and other major purchasers of healthcare" (p. 52).

In an example of the continuum of care approach to vertical integration, Providence Hospital of Mobile, Alabama, is building a "medical mall" that includes acute care and rehabilitation hospitals, long-term care facility, restaurant, hotel, medically oriented retail shops, and a fitness area. The medical mall is designed to offer one-stop shopping for comprehensive health care services (Super, 1986). In a sense, medical malls or integrated regional clusters represent vertical integration, but on a metropolitan or regional basis.

Longer-Term Approaches to Forward Integration

Several industry observers are predicting that the major insurance companies, with their huge equity bases, will soon become a major force pushing vertical integration. Except for major insurers, the health care industry is fragmented—6,800 hospitals, over 400 HMOs, and nearly 550,000 physicians. Even the four major investor-owned chains are relatively small—$13.5 billion in revenues in a $420 billion industry. The big insurance companies have the financial base to acquire hospitals if it fits their vertical integration plans.

Richard Averill and Michael Kalison, in a provocative article entitled "Present and Future: Predictions for the Healthcare Industry," predict widespread use of capitation of both physicians and hospitals by the mid-1990s. "By accepting payment for their services on a capitation basis, hospitals will in essence become insurers" (1986, p. 52). Averill and Kalison go on to predict that hospitals, in order to survive, will become health care organizations (HCOs). They define an HCO as the conglomeration of a hospital, nursing home, hospice, primary care center, and home health care service under one corporate structure. Physicians delivering services to an HCO will become employees; thus the HCO will be similar to a closed-panel HMO in that it will be responsible for all the health care needs of its enrollees.

Commercial health insurers and Blue Cross fit into this picture as health care corporations (HCCs). HCCs will, according to Averill and Kalison, become a chain of HCOs; they will acquire hospitals and HMOs. "Existing hospitals will either have to evolve to become an HCO or be purchased by an HCC. By 1995 any major metropolitan area will have several independent HCOs and several HCOs that are part of a national HCC. Many employers will use several HCOs, giving their employees a choice among competing HCOs" (p. 53).

Eric Schlesinger of the Boston Consulting Group comes to a different conclusion. Looking at the health care industry from an insurance company or health plan perspective, he says it does not make sense for insurance companies to acquire hospitals. "It makes more sense to purchase marginal [hospital] capacity, which is readily available on the open market, than to own specific capacity" (1985, p. 5).

We agree with Schlesinger, and see several problems with the Averill and Kalison scenario. First, Averill and Kalison assume that a single acute care hospital can effectively serve a large metropolitan area. Our experience is that a competitive delivery system must have hospitals conveniently located to most major population concentrations within a large metropolitan area of one million or more people. Given this requirement for an adequate network of physicians and hospitals, it is difficult to accept the proposition that most metropolitan areas could support several

HCOs and HCCs. Nor do we believe that employers would give employees a choice of HCOs. Based on the present interest in PPOs, we expect that large employers will work with a single provider network; those employees who choose to go outside the preferred network will be penalized financially by being only partially reimbursed for health care services used.

Strategic Implications

When it comes to vertical integration, there is a wide range of situations facing health care systems, hospitals, and physicians. Several large metropolitan areas have already been designated as targets of one or more investor-owned chains or large not-for-profit systems; in these situations local hospitals and their medical staff are faced with the need to respond to new competitors or face a loss of market share. Louisville, Houston, Denver, Phoenix, and Dallas are examples of these types of areas. In many other metropolitan areas, it is still possible for a local system to gain an advantage over potential competitors by initiating some type of vertical integration strategy. For many smaller areas with a population of less than 100,000, the need to consider any type of vertical integration may still be in the future.

Metropolitan Areas That Are Under Attack. For those providers in metropolitan areas that have already been targeted for forward integration, it may be too late to develop a successful vertical integration counterattack. It is costly to initiate a new health plan ($3 million to $5 million is the usual start-up capital required for an HMO through break-even; and it normally requires several years to attract a significant number of members).

One alternative available to those hospitals that are members of one of the national alliances (for example, VHA or AHS) is to participate aggressively in the health plan products being developed and marketed by these organizations. Participation in these plans requires substantially less capital than going it alone, and the risk of failure is reduced. The biggest problems faced by local health care systems desiring to participate in national plans are organizing the medical staff as a provider group and obtaining adequate geographic coverage for their provider network within the metropolitan area. Adequate coverage often involves contractual arrangements with hospitals and IPAs that are affiliated with other national systems. Even in metropolitan areas targeted by investor-owned chains, physicians often do not recognize the seriousness of the situation and are thus not eager to participate in new health plan joint ventures.

Another strategy open to hospitals and physician groups in larger metropolitan areas is to stay out of the health insurance business and concentrate on becoming preferred providers for the numerous plans battling it out for market share. This is an especially attractive alternative for those health systems (including hospitals and their medical staffs) that are low-cost providers, those who can compete on price and still make a profit. This is a defensive strategy, but in many instances involves less risk. (There is, for example, no need to provide capital for starting one or more health plans.)

Another approach is to join with other hospitals and physician groups and attempt to control all or major portions of the health care delivery system. By acting in unity, providers can try to avoid the fragmentation and bidding against each other that typically play into the hands of alternative delivery systems. This cooperation can be a delicate situation, given potential antitrust considerations. However, there are hospitals that are networking with other hospitals in order to present a stronger position in their negotiations with ADS.

A group of physicians in San Antonio, Texas, have taken a still different approach to dealing with a large national system intent on its vertical integration strategy. According to a *Wall Street Journal* story, "Many local physicians view Humana's expansion in San Antonio, and particularly its clinics and HMO, as a threat. When a local oncologist, Stephen Cohen, called a meeting last spring to air concern about the increasing corporate control of medicine, some 300 physicians showed up. Dr. Cohen urged doctors at the meeting to refer patients to locally owned hospitals instead of facilities owned by large corporations like Humana. Several who attended the meeting subsequently resigned from Humana's HMO and began using non-Humana hospitals"

(Hull, 1986, p. 25). This seems to be a relatively isolated uprising; we do not believe it is an indication of typical physician reaction to ADS and forward integration.

Less Competitive Metropolitan Areas. There are a large number of metropolitan areas with populations in the 100,000 to 500,000 range that have not yet been targeted by large health care industry players, particularly the investor-owned chains. In these areas, there may yet be opportunities for local systems to control their own destiny using some type of vertical integration strategy.

One strategy that might be pursued under these circumstances is to attempt to gain a strong enough market position to be able to discourage new market entrants. For example, it is unlikely that one of the major investor-owned systems would target a small to midsized metropolitan area, and spend millions of dollars in developing its health plans and delivery systems, if a strong and unified local group had already seized a substantial share of the market.

If a metropolitan area is not currently the target of national health care systems, there may be time for one or more local systems, hospitals, or physician groups to gain competitive advantage by initiating an aggressive vertical integration strategy. This could involve joining one of the large national alliances, networking with other providers in the area to establish one or more health plans, or making sure that the system has a strong areawide delivery system (ambulatory services, primary care physicians, extended hours, and so on).

Smaller Areas. In metropolitan areas with 100,000 or fewer people, and in rural areas, there is usually less urgency in the need to control the market through payer-oriented vertical integration. In many of these areas there are one, or at the most two, hospitals; there the emphasis for survival should be on other strategies designed to retain market share (keeping costs down, aggressive marketing, diversification, and backward integration by providing a continuum of care).

This does not mean that hospitals in smaller areas should not be available to contract with ADS; they should. But the need to try to control the market through aggressive ADS and payer-oriented vertical integration strategies is much less.

Health care systems and physicians in smaller areas have other serious problems, such as keeping patients from being drawn to nearby metropolitan areas, dealing with a higher proportion of Medicare patients and indigents, and accessing capital for modernization.

Backward integration appears to be a useful strategy in nearly every type of market situation. Although there are dangers—tying up too much capital in developing a continuum of care, and the loss of flexibility (both described earlier in this chapter, in the review of industrial experience with vertical integration)—there appear to be substantial backward integration opportunities for many local health care systems.

9

Aggressive Marketing of Services

Near the close of a recent trustee meeting, a knowledgeable member of the board and a partner in a Big 8 public accounting firm said, "Last year we voted to spend nearly $1 million for marketing this hospital in the coming twelve months. Basically, it was done on faith. But next year, when they come to us with a budget request, I want to see some answers to these questions: What are we accomplishing with our marketing dollars? Are we gaining any competitive advantage? How much is enough?"

The trustee's questions are not unique to one health care system. One *Hospitals* magazine cover story in mid-1986 describes a slowdown in marketing while hospitals take a look at the value received from their marketing efforts. Has hospital marketing reached the age of accountability? the story asks. Lauren Barnett, director of American Hospital Association's Society for Hospital Marketing and Public Relations, believes that it has. "The ability to measure and evaluate results is critical to any marketing effort. Merely saying, 'We know it worked' isn't going to convince CEOs and boards of trustees anymore." She adds, "Marketing executives are going to have to justify the expenditure of human and financial resources in very quantifiable and easy-to-understand terms" (Powills, 1986, p. 51).

To make matters even more difficult, the health care market is more complex than most, primarily because of the role of the physician. At this time, doctors are the most important customer group for nearly all hospitals. (See Chapter Two for a discussion of physicians as a market segment.) Physicians admit patients to hospitals and refer patients to other doctors; the whole complex issue of referral patterns enters into the health care marketing puzzle. However, third-party payers (mainly HMOs and PPOs) are becoming a much bigger part of the health care marketing system.

One of the strategies for survival described in the introduction to Part Two is to increase market share, at the expense of competitors, by more sophisticated marketing, by spending more dollars on advertising and public relations, and by doing a better job of "patient acquisition." We have observed this approach being attempted in other industries, and with mixed results. To gain a bigger share of a static or declining market like health care represents a very difficult challenge. The key economic issue is this: what are health care providers willing to pay for an additional percentage point of market share? Is the marketing investment justified by the potential return?

We believe that the trustee's three marketing questions can be satisfactorily answered in most health care organizations. Well-conceived and well-planned health care marketing efforts can make a substantial difference. Furthermore, the various health care market segments may not yet have been saturated with advertising and promotional pitches. Yes, the complexities of the health care industry "market" can be understood, and it is possible to design marketing programs to reach each segment. This is being accomplished by some hospitals and other providers.

How much is enough? How many dollars should be spent? There can be no one answer applicable to all hospitals or other health care providers. The answer is best found by isolating the probable impact of proposed marketing efforts, assigning a value to the additional business likely to be generated (contribution to overhead and profit would be the normal measure), and comparing these benefits against proposed marketing costs. This can be accomplished on a hospital- or systemwide basis, or on a product line basis; the appropriate level of detail depends on the size of the organization and the amount of marketing dollars available. Of course, the accuracy of the data (on the benefits side) may not satisfy our trustee/accountant friend, but this lack of precision should not deter an effort to meaningfully evaluate the costs versus the benefits of marketing, both for the past year and for the future.

Another approach to measuring the impact of a marketing program is to compare actual inpatient admissions, patient-days, outpatient activity, and other appropriate measures of volume against projections of what is likely to have happened without marketing. In a declining market such as inpatient-days in most parts of the United States, aggressive marketing may be successful if it reduces the rate of decline in patient-days. It is incorrect to judge the effectiveness of marketing by comparing patient-days this year against those a year ago. One useful technique for making these types of comparisons is called the Box-Jenkins forecasting model, named for George Box and Gwilym Jenkins, Princeton University mathematicians who developed the technique. This statistically based forecasting methodology is described in more detail in Appendix B.

This chapter is not intended to be a "how to" discussion of health care marketing; for that we refer you to two recent books devoted to this subject (Hillestad and Berkowitz, 1984; Cooper, 1985). Instead, we are assessing marketing as one of the strategies for survival and asking how it can be used to gain a competitive advantage. We are also focusing on the economics of health care marketing. Is it a good investment? Will it provide adequate returns? What are the risks of failure?

Understanding Market Segmentation

We have found that the first and most basic step in any market research and planning project is to develop a matrix showing each market segment and subsegment in correspondence with the various product lines and specialized services offered. As we prepare this chapter, we are performing this very task for a group of four hospitals—a children's hospital, an acute care institution, and two rehabilitation hospitals, each with different specialties—that want to form a joint venture to market and deliver their services. It will be a "rehabilitation center of excellence" (one of our tasks, not yet completed, is to come up with a suitable name). The CEO of one of the four hospitals, which specializes in severe spinal cord injuries, said, "We are most concerned about insurance companies; they represent our primary market and they're located all over the United States. We don't try to market to doctors; it hasn't paid off." Another CEO said, "Our market is that relatively small group of referring physicians in this metropolitan area. Without their referrals, we've had it." All four institutions have different reasons for wanting to participate in the rehabilitation consortium and for how they perceive their specific markets.

In another example of the matrix approach to market segmentation by major hospital product line, Table 13 identifies six major markets (and eleven submarkets) for six hospital product lines. The number of crosses (+) in each slot indicates the extent of market potential. For example, the neurosciences product line has very little applicability to consumers, from a market point of view; thus that slot has no crosses. Primary care physicians on the medical staff, on the other hand, rate very high as a target market segment for neurosciences; that slot has three crosses.

One large hospital in the southeastern United States has a physician-oriented marketing program that segments physicians into three groups—new additions to the medical staff, the established group of big admitters, and the "recovery" group. The latter physicians are those who, at some point in the past, used the hospital but had a bad experience or were antagonized. The marketing department has specific programs designed for doctors in each of these categories. In addition, each year the hospital interviews 160 to 170 physicians in the community, asking about hospital admission patterns, practice volumes, and attitudes toward hospitals and other providers.

Theodore Levitt, in his book *The Marketing Imagination*, says, "If you're not thinking segments, you're not thinking. To think segments means you have to think about what drives

Table 13. Evaluation of Opportunities to Increase Market Share of Selected Product Lines.

Market Segments	Women's Health (OB/GYN)	Neurosciences	Orthopedics	Emergency	Vascular	General Surgery
1. Consumers:						
a. Women of Medicare age	+++		+++	+	+++	+
Other women	+++		+	++		+
b. Hospital patients, present	+++		++	++	+	+
Patients within past 3 years	+++		++	++	+	+
c. Users of primary care physicians on medical staff	+++	+	+++	++	+	+
d. Noncustomers (no physician, or physician not on medical staff)	+		+			
2. Physicians:						
a. Medical staff (primary care)	+++	+++	+++	+++	+++	+++
b. Medical staff (specialists)	++	+++	++	+	++	++
c. Other service area; physicians not on medical staff	++	+++	++	+	++	++
3. Business/Industry:						
a. Participant in hospital-owned HMO	++	+	++	++	+	++
b. Some connection with hospital (trustee, wife of CEO in auxiliary)	++	++	++	++	++	++
c. Other businesses in service area	+					
d. Other businesses in metropolitan area				+		
4. Employees of hospital or physicians in medical office building	+++	+	+++	++	+	++
5. Other providers (for example, specialty hospitals in regional partnership)	++	+++	++		++	++
6. Third-party payers, including HMOs and PPOs	++	+	++	+++	+	+

+ + + Excellent opportunity to impact market
  + + Good opportunity
    + Fair opportunity

customers, customer groups, and the choices that are or might be available to them. To think segments means to think beyond what's obviously out there to see" (1983, pp. 128–129). Levitt goes on to say that what sets people and organizations apart from the ordinary is the ability to see beyond the normal descriptors of market segments (demographics, user groups, and the like) and to identify the simple appeals that turn people on to a product or service.

Our experience convinces us that marketing in the health care industry is well behind other competitive industries, particularly in its ability to understand and implement market segmentation. There are many "pathways" to the hospital—primary care physicians, specialists (including surgeons), emergency rooms, other outpatient services, health plan "steering" to preferred providers, consumer preferences, and the normal return business from satisfied patients. Each of these needs to be understood in depth, and marketing programs need to be developed to maximize the potential to attract patients. For most health care systems and hospitals, the marketing surface has just been scratched. This is understandable; most health care providers had no formalized marketing function four years ago.

Allocating Marketing Resources Using Product Life Cycle

Steve Hillestad and Eric Berkowitz, in *Health Care Marketing Plans: From Strategy to Action* (1984), have provided a useful conceptual framework for allocating marketing resources to specific product lines or health care ventures. Their approach is based on the product life cycle, a concept that has been used by business analysts for the past twenty-five years. We first became familiar with the value of this concept in the early 1960s, when studying the special problems of financing small business.

The theory of a product life cycle suggests that the four distinct phases any product or service passes through are start-up, growth, maturity, and decline (see Figure 2). Hillestad and Berkowitz have categorized several marketing strategies based on the stage of a product or service in the product life cycle (pp. 79–93):

Figure 2. Product Life Cycle.

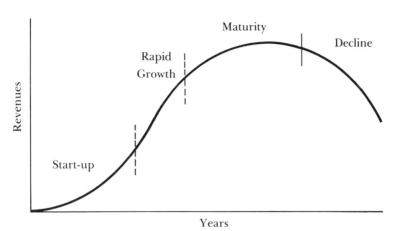

- *Go for it.* This strategy is best implemented in the start-up or introductory stage, when overall market demand is beginning to develop and when a new health care product or service has just been introduced. In many market areas, the introduction of magnetic resonance imaging (MRI) in the 1984–1985 period was prompted by the "go for it" strategy.
- *Differentiation.* This strategy is most appropriate for the introductory and growth stages, when it is desirable to differentiate product lines from those of competitors. Normally, price would not be a key differentiating factor in this stage of growth. On the other hand, advertising is usually effective in differentiation.
- *Necessity.* When an organization enters a market late (usually when the market is maturing) out of a necessity to match competitors, there is still an opportunity for significant market penetration and profitability. When using the necessity strategy, it is usually desirable to match the prices of competitors.
- *Maintenance.* This strategy is best suited for a mature market and product; the strategy is to "keep what you've got." In this stage, extra dollars spent on marketing and advertising are

unlikely to result in increased demand but are necessary to
maintain existing market share.
- *Harvest.* This is the phase-out stage, when business volume
  and profitability are declining. Little effort in public relations
  and advertising is warranted.

This brief overview is intended to stimulate interest in the
potential value of assessing current and planned marketing efforts
using the product and market life cycle conceptual model.

Pricing

Most of the health care industry marketing professionals we
have talked with are not involved in pricing decisions. One
marketing vice-president told us, "Our emergency room dropped
its prices, and it was three months before I heard about it. When I
asked them why they did it, they said that it would attract more
business. It seems to me that that is marketing judgment, and we
should have been consulted." This example, which is not unusual,
says something about the state of marketing in the health care
industry in the mid-1980s. In other competitive industries, the
marketing staff normally has a great deal of influence on pricing
strategies.

It is difficult to identify an area of health care management
in which more immediate short-term benefits could accrue to the
organization than in pricing. Based on our experience, most
hospitals are missing opportunities to charge more for certain
types of services, although the investor-owned chains have been
more aggressive in their pricing of ancillary services (see Chapter
Thirteen). The continuing criticism of the press and such industry
observers as Joseph Califano (1986) has made some hospital
managers and trustees gun-shy about raising prices.

Pricing may not be a critical issue today, but it certainly
will be in the near future, as HMO and PPO penetration increases
and the federal government becomes increasingly restrictive about
Medicare DRG payment levels. For most hospitals, the day is not
far off when three-quarters of their patients will be receiving care
on some form of discounted basis. Combine this with indigent

(uncompensated) care, and a serious problem is looming in the future.

Some industry observers believe that despite increased competition, health care industry prices are arbitrarily propped up. They expect a dramatic fall in prices as the whole industry price structure begins to crumble. There is little doubt that some areas of the country will soon experience severe price competition, particularly when there are investor-owned hospitals active in the market. The HMO industry has already experienced this type of price competition in certain markets (for example, Chicago), and the results can be ruinous.

Russell Coile urges local health care systems and hospitals to develop contingency plans for price wars: "Price competition can be expected. Major purchasers are already fomenting bidding wars between hospitals for preferred provider status. For-profit chains are repositioning themselves to be low-cost producers and low-price competitors. Discounting and price-specific advertising in all media, including television, should be expected. Hospitals should prepare contingency plans in anticipation that competitors may initiate price wars. Hospital boards should begin to address the issues of discounting and advertising on price now, instead of having to react under pressure for a competitor's initiative" (1986, p. 28).

Most hospitals operate with less than an 8 percent profit margin (profits divided by revenues). It will not take much in the way of price discounting to force substantial personnel and expense cutbacks or wipe out profit margins. As trustees of not-for-profit hospitals, we worry more about the threat of price competition than any other factor. It can happen, and happen fast.

There are two basic approaches to survival in a health care market subjected to severe price competition. The first is to do everything possible to differentiate products and services from those of competitors, with special emphasis on quality. The second is to seek opportunities to increase profit margins on selected products or services, or to start new services that will allow greater margins (for example, a special wing of the hospital for patients who are willing to pay more for quality). Trying to compete on price will create severe problems for all but the lowest-cost providers; it is not an attractive alternative for most hospitals or health care providers.

Market Research

The critical starting point (and mid- and ending-point) for marketing is market research and analysis. Based on the health care market research reports we have seen, market research in the industry is not yet well developed. One medical center we work with conducted its first consumer survey (600 telephone interviews in its market area) in mid-1985.

Peters and Waterman, in *In Search of Excellence* (1982), state that one of the characteristics of an excellent company is closeness to its customers. That can mean formal market research, or increased informal communications, or simply asking doctors on a one-on-one basis what the hospital can do to get more of their business. Talking to patients—and really listening to their comments and suggestions—is an excellent way to stay close to the customers. And how about health insurance companies, HMOs and PPOs; do health care providers really know what they want? How about employers?

With one exception, the market research techniques typically used in health care are similar to those used in most other industries. Telephone interviews, self-administered questionnaires, and consumer and employer focus groups are all being successfully used in the health care industry. But health care research has a secret weapon: the focus group interview with physicians. We have found that doctors like to participate in these sessions—even though their typical late arrivals and early departures suggest otherwise. They love to have someone listen to their opinions. Furthermore, the cost of physician focus groups can be minimized by having the hospital administrative staff make the arrangements and recruit the doctors to participate.

Peter Steiner, the CEO for Immediate Care Centers of Louisville, Kentucky, says that market research is the most important aspect of marketing, especially in outpatient services. When a group of physicians purchased Immediate Care Centers in 1985, they had marketing research carried out by a professional firm. "Understanding what the community market requires and how people make health care decisions will help to target the market," Steiner says. "The market research has been very beneficial in management decisions. It helps us determine the prices and how long the center should be open each day" (Copeland, 1986, p. 9).

Another lesson that can be learned from other industries is that to be most valuable, market research needs to be carried out continuously over a long period of time; it is not a one-shot proposition. The health care marketplace is rapidly changing, and the more sophisticated organizations are constantly monitoring these changes.

In an effort to monitor consumer attitudes continuously in its marketplace, the Orlando Regional Medical Center has seven to ten part-time people conducting telephone interviews each evening. The center has created a company called Community Health Surveys, and one individual in its marketing department heads up this company and its monitoring efforts. The total cost for this activity is about $70,000 per year, or about $1.70 per completed survey (well below the $8 to $25 per interview charged by most survey research firms). The director of marketing says, "We like to keep our fingers on the pulse of this community. A hospital is like a lightning rod in that it attracts controversy" (John Elver, interview with the authors, Orlando, Fla., July 18, 1986).

Market research should play a key role in helping a health care organization evaluate the effectiveness of its advertising and marketing efforts. What difference has the past year's advertising program made in the minds of consumers and employers? Were "awareness" objectives met? How good a job did our competitors do? Has our image as a quality provider been enhanced? Has our overall competitive position changed?

Finally, there is the important task of analyzing and reporting market research data. This is the key to success—pulling out all the insights possible from the data collected in the research process. Analysis can often be enhanced through the use of such sophisticated statistical techniques as cluster analysis and multiple regression analysis (discussed in Appendix B). More often, a trained analyst simply needs to pore over the data, asking, "What are the strategic implications of this research data base for our organization?"

It seems to us that most of the emphasis in health care market research is on data collection, mainly through surveys. This is understandable for an industry in which the application of marketing and market research is relatively new. But the emphasis in the future will be on interpretation and analysis. "The difference between data and information is that while data are crudely aggregated collections of raw facts, information represents the selective organization and *imaginative interpretation* of those facts. This requires knowing, in some sort of direct and systematic way, the work with which one presumes to deal. It requires getting inside the lives and work of the people one is trying to understand" (Levitt, 1983, p. 138; italics added).

Other Elements of Health Care Marketing Strategies

Other marketing elements—applicable to both health care systems and physicians—include advertising, direct marketing, public relations, physician practice support, expanded geographic coverage, and enlarging the referral network.

Expansion of the geographic boundaries of a health care organization's market area may, in some cases, be feasible. This can be accomplished in a number of ways, including establishing urgent care centers or health parks, encouraging physicians to start satellite offices in outlying locations, and spending more on advertising and public relations in geographic areas targeted for expansion. These strategies are commonly used by hospitals or groups of doctors located in or near the central business districts of metropolitan areas. Like banks or retail stores, health care organizations in these kinds of undesirable locations feel the pressure to follow their customers to the suburbs.

Enlargement of the referral network is being attempted by a large number of hospitals and physician groups. For example, a group of cardiac surgeons in Denver make regular trips to Rapid City, South Dakota (400 miles to the north), to cultivate relationships with cardiologists and internists in the Black Hills area.

Some larger tertiary care hospitals participating in one of the more than thirty regional partnerships established within the VHA system are hoping for, among other benefits, referral business from smaller, less specialized hospitals. A group of urologists in several Rocky Mountain states recently decided to avoid competing with each other for kidney stone business and instead formed a joint venture to operate a lithotriptor machine located in Denver. The economic feasibility of the project depended on a large base of referrals from several surrounding states.

Commercial banks catering to the consumer market often obtain the names and addresses of new residents from "newcomers" organizations and then call on the newcomers to solicit their checking or savings accounts. A Louisville, Kentucky, health care provider, Norton Hospital, follows a similar practice. It has a nurse visit the home of new residents to encourage their use of the hospital and its outpatient services. The Louisville health care market, with four Humana hospitals competing with several not-for-profit institutions, is one of the most competitive in the United States. This type of direct marketing is expensive, however. Does it pay off?

Strategic Implications

There is little doubt that hospitals and other health care organizations are committing themselves to marketing, and on an escalating scale. A 1986 survey of 740 trustees conducted by the American Hospital Association showed that over 90 percent of the trustees expected their hospital's marketing budget to increase in the years ahead (the opinions of trustees are discussed in greater detail in Chapter Eighteen).

Will this increased emphasis on marketing allow health care organizations to gain a competitive advantage? In some cases, yes. But there will also be those who lose ground despite spending more effort and dollars on marketing. After all, health care is not a growth market, at least in most regions of the country. Our conclusion is that aggressive marketing is a high-risk strategy, especially if pursued in a vacuum (without consideration of other, complementary strategies, such as development of centers of excellence). Large-scale marketing expenditures can, in fact, weaken some health care systems and physician groups by taking away from the bottom line and reducing financial reserves.

However, aggressive marketing that is focused on specific market segments, is highly imaginative, and is used to complement other competitive strategies can further and may in fact be critical to a hospital's success. Hospitals need to enhance their ability to attract and retain customers in the highly competitive health care marketplace. Marketing expenditures, like investments in the other strategies described in this book, require a return. To measure such returns, marketing efforts need to be continually evaluated to determine whether or not marketing goals have been attained.

To the question of how much is enough? we do not know the answer. Russell Coile suggests that hospitals should spend 2 to 5 percent of their revenues on marketing, compared with 1 percent today (1986, p. 28). This is unrealistic; it would wipe out the bottom line for many hospitals. The proper level of effort has to be determined through analysis of many of the market and competitive factors discussed earlier, as well as the financial capability of the local health care system to support additional marketing. This is an important strategic decision.

The questions raised earlier in this chapter by the hospital trustee are good ones. They need to be answered, and not just once a year.

What is being accomplished with the marketing dollars being spent? This question can be answered if specific programmatic goals are established at the outset of a marketing program. In other cases, simple documentation of increased admissions or outpatient visits for a marketed service will show achievement.

Are we gaining competitive advantage? Answering this question requires careful documentation across several variables that can be used to assess competitive status, including name recognition and market share. It is difficult, if not impossible, to isolate the impact of a marketing strategy on the institution's overall competitive position if, at the same time, other strategies have been implemented.

How much is enough? Most informed opinions suggest that marketing expenditures should range from 1 to 2 percent of revenues. There is no magic number, however, nor is the same amount appropriate for every institution. The amount allocated should be commensurate with the type of return anticipated. This question is related to the previous questions about identifiable accomplishments and likely competitive advantages to be gained by a marketing program.

10

Forming Alliances
with Physicians

Leland Kaiser, a consultant, lecturer, and professor at the University of Colorado, says, "Physicians must learn to 'think organization' and view their destinies as interlinked with the destiny of the hospital" (Eisele, Fifer, and Wilson, 1985, p. 331). Conversely, hospitals will find it necessary to establish stronger bonds with their medical staff if they are to survive. Given the historical tension (in some cases, downright animosity) between the two, will it happen? Will the competitive threats faced by both doctors and hospitals force the two groups to join together, to recognize that their economic well-being is linked? For those groups that are not able to arrive at new types of partnership arrangements, the future is bleak; those hospitals and medical staffs that can effectively combine their efforts will gain a clear-cut advantage over those who do not work together.

This chapter describes a wide variety of physician-hospital partnership arrangements and assesses the present and future prospects and impacts of such arrangements. What will work and what is unlikely to work? From a hospital management and trustee point of view, where do physician-hospital partnerships fit into the overall strategic plan? What are appropriate levels of resources, both financial and managerial, to invest in these types of partnership arrangements? For physicians, is the time and effort associated with these partnerships likely to pay off financially?

The Size of the Medical Staff

Our research indicates that about 40 percent of all physicians have staff privileges at two or more hospitals. In our judgment, the proportion of doctors spreading their patient referrals to multiple hospitals will increase in the years ahead. The primary reason for the shift is the expected rapid growth of HMOs and PPOs, and the efforts of these types of health plans to direct subscribers to more cost-effective physicians and hospitals. Physicians not on the staff of preferred hospitals will be motivated to seek admission to ADS-designated hospitals or face the prospect of losing substantial numbers of patients. As Leland Kaiser pointed out in an Estes Park Institute conference on medical staff issues of the 1980s, "One new HMO in a community can disrupt physician and hospital referral patterns that have existed for years" (1986). The other side of the coin is, of course, that medical staff membership carries certain requirements (attendance at section meetings, and so on) that can be a burden, and a nonreimbursed one at that.

Some industry observers believe the movement will eventually be in the other direction; that is, physicians will tend to limit the number of hospitals they work in and develop stronger ties with a single, primary institution. The reasoning behind this viewpoint is that physicians and hospitals are going to have to work more closely together in order to compete effectively. We do not disagree with this rationale, but we believe that a large number of physicians, especially surgeons and other specialists, are likely to continue to fragment their hospital relationships in order to make themselves available to a larger number of patients.

There is a key strategic issue at stake: should hospitals attempt to be more selective in their screening and credentialing procedures, or should they open their doors to all who apply? There are strong arguments on either side.

Reasons for Restricting Medical Staff Privileges. The reasons for being more rigorous in the selection of physicians for medical staff privileges bear on quality of care, the potential for malpractice suits, the creation of increased competition for present medical staff members, and the need to build tighter physician-hospital relationships. A hospital attempting to enhance its reputation for quality care may suffer from a policy of opening its doors to all comers; its image will suffer in the eyes of physicians who are well aware of the groups in the community who are delivering the highest quality of care. And with a larger number of physicians practicing at a hospital, the chance of a quality breakdown, and subsequent malpractice suits, increases. The present medical staff will not appreciate the host of new competitors being welcomed by the hospital; thus the chances of building a stronger sense of partnership between a hospital and its medical staff will have diminished.

Arguments for a More Open Policy. On the other side, a hospital adopting a policy of exclusivity (not necessarily taking the more extreme position of closing its medical staff) runs the risk of substantial short-term reduction in patient-days, as well as lawsuits brought by physicians denied staff privileges. On the last point, the expected surge in newly graduated doctors will put added pressure on hospitals to allow access to the newcomers; those physicians denied admission to the medical staff are likely to claim antitrust violations (restraint of trade).

Hospital managers and trustees, in consultation with medical staff leaders, will need to assess the situation in their market area carefully and come up with appropriate policies concerning medical staff membership. Trustees are likely to give more weight to the shorter-term business aspects—keeping beds full and maintaining a strong bottom line. Medical staff leaders are likely to favor a more restrictive approach, often justified on the basis of quality of care.

Physician-Hospital Joint Ventures

Physician-hospital joint ventures are popular for a number of reasons, including a desire on the part of many hospitals to strengthen their ties with their medical staff, another source of equity capital, and the possibility of jointly beneficial economic returns (in other words, expectations of profits).

Types of Joint Ventures. Joint ventures can take a variety of forms. Robert Rosenfield (1986), an attorney specializing in the health care industry, breaks joint ventures into two general "models"—*micro* (a small number of doctors and discrete projects) and *macro* (hundreds of doctors and multiple projects). An example of a micro joint venture would be the establishment of an outpatient surgery center by 15 to 25 surgically oriented doctors and one hospital. An example of a macro venture would be 150 physicians joining with a hospital to form a managed care group for the purpose of contracting with a number of different HMOs and PPOs.

For the micro joint venture models, Rosenfield describes three common approaches: contract (between a hospital or health care system and a physician group), corporation, or partnership. In the latter form, the hospital is usually the general partner and the doctors are limited partners.

The macro joint venture model can resemble a venture capital corporation, with a hospital system and a large group of physicians (sometimes the entire medical staff) investing substantial financial resources to create a pool of money for new ventures. In a second macro model, large groups of doctors and their hospitals are forming ventures to compete for HMO and PPO contracts. Under the VHA and Aetna $80 million venture into ADS, many VHA hospitals have taken the initiative in setting up physician-hospital joint ventures to form a provider base.

Problems That Typically Occur in Joint Ventures. Our focus group research with physicians and a review of the experience of many physician-hospital joint ventures suggest that there are several problems that typically occur:

- Many physicians either lack the funds or are not interested in investing significant dollars in health care–oriented ventures. With physicians' earnings continuing to decline, the availability of funds for investment in joint ventures may decrease.
- Many physicians remain unconvinced that a group of doctors, and their hospital, can establish and operate an economically viable new business. Health care systems need one or more success stories in order to build credibility with their medical staff.
- The potential to antagonize a portion of the medical staff exists; in fact, antagonism is *likely* to occur unless there are well-established criteria for screening physicians to identify those who will be invited to participate in specific joint ventures. Our experience indicates that most physicians would be upset if their hospital started a joint venture and they were not asked to participate.
- Lawsuits from disgruntled investors (physicians) are likely when the joint venture experiences managerial and financial problems. Again, recent experience strongly suggests that problems do occur, and on a frequent basis.
- Recent changes in the tax laws reduce the attractiveness of physician participation in joint ventures. These include loss of investment tax credits and lower depreciation allowances.

Successful joint ventures require a willingness to participate (based on identified or perceived benefits of such ventures to all parties) and an appropriate match of physicians with the objectives of the venture. In our work, we have observed a few successful and many unsuccessful joint ventures. The probability of success is clearly determined by many factors, including documentation of the need (or demand), adequate capitalization, good management, and an appropriate organizational and business structure.

Economic Feasibility. Analysis of the venture's feasibility is critical to its success. The fundamental question is "Do the potential returns sufficiently match the hospital's and the physicians' objectives and expectations?" Different types of ventures will have substantially different benefits to participants, in terms of the immediacy and magnitude of return on investment. In the feasibility analysis, potential benefits of the venture can be described and quantified; identification of benefits is critical for both physicians and hospitals in their decision whether or not to participate, and may also help in the selection of the appropriate investment vehicle. Such an analysis should critically examine issues of demand for the type of venture proposed. The impact of the complex regulatory environment should also be examined in the feasibility analysis. Such considerations vary by state but include rate setting, certificates of need, licensing, JCAH standards, malpractice suits, and others.

Investment Vehicles. Selection of the appropriate investment structure requires an examination of various financial and tax considerations. Some ventures will be highly tax-oriented and others will not. In tax-oriented arrangements, key considerations will be mechanisms that effectively pass along tax benefits and cash and property distributions to physicians who can best use these benefits. In other types of investments, business factors such as liability, management, control, and transferability of interest will be primary selection criteria. The principal advantage of incorporation is limited liability. However, the tax disadvantages (double taxation) of a corporation often limit its use for ventures involving real estate, equipment, or leasing. In general partnerships, partners share profits and losses equally and have equal rights in the partnership's management. A special type of organization, the limited partnership, is widely used for raising capital; the general partner(s) is responsible for the management of the partnership's business affairs, while the limited partners do not participate in the venture's management and are financially liable only to the extent of their investment (although the limited partners *do* share in the tax benefits and profits).

Physician Attitudes Toward Joint Ventures

As expected, physician attitudes toward joint ventures vary enormously. However, even some physicians who disagree with the concept of joint ventures participate in joint ventures as a way to keep pace with the changing environment, as the high level of physician involvement in ADS suggests. Opportunities for participation in the other types of joint ventures are not as widespread but continue to increase rapidly.

As with any other investment, participation in a joint venture depends on matching the risk of the venture with individuals' or organizations' comfort levels with risk. Our physician focus group research indicates that doctors evaluate joint ventures with the same criteria used in evaluating other investment opportunities. The risks and rewards of the venture must be equal to or better than other potential investments.

Physicians typically rely on their own personal financial advisers (CPAs, brokers, attorneys) in evaluating joint venture proposals. This forces health care systems to be more rigorous in their market, economic, and financial analysis of prospective ventures. If the joint venture is to be successful, it has to be well conceived, and structured in a way that will benefit all parties. One of our trustee friends who is in the oil and gas business put it this way: "We put together dozens of deals a year. Our investors have to trust us, and we have to make sure they come out winners." The same is true of health care system and physician joint ventures.

The MeSH Approach

The MeSH concept was developed by the physician Paul Ellwood in response to the increasingly fragmented approaches being made by health plans to hospitals and their physicians. Ellwood's concept is based on the belief that hospitals and physicians need a strong central organization in order to compete effectively and to pursue the economic interest of both hospitals and physicians. The MeSH organization would be responsible for management, planning, marketing, financial systems, and utilization control in areas relating to new health plans and payment systems (DRGs).

Practice Building and Joint Marketing

Although younger physicians are especially interested in marketing, marketing activities transect all levels of experience, and almost all specialties, with primary care physicians somewhat more aggressively pursuing practice building. Most hospitals realize that a busy medical staff will lead to an increase in the flow of patients, so they too are becoming increasingly involved in the marketing of physicians' practices.

Hospital assistance to physicians in practice building can take a variety of forms and requires differing amounts of funding depending on the arrangement. Practice-building arrangements may vary from the hospital providing computer and support services to physicians' offices to offering discounts on office space in medical office buildings owned by the hospital to purchasing physicians' practices and, in return, receiving physicians' inpatient admissions. This latter approach appears to be increasingly popular, especially with some of the investor-owned chains.

Primary care physicians just establishing their practices are often interested in such arrangements; most have accumulated large debts during medical school and have borrowed even more to start their practice. Many are looking to their hospital for assistance. For physicians, assistance in the form of services, office space, or practice purchasing can be very helpful. The hospital's investment is usually small—at least for services and office space— and may, in the long run, be highly rewarding for the hospital as well.

Such financial arrangements may enhance a hospital's ability to fill beds, but they can also lead to tensions within the medical staff. Many physicians view such arrangements as inequitable, benefiting only a few physicians. In fact, some physicians believe that such arrangements are unethical. If a hospital elects one of these options, it must form policy guidelines and criteria to make sure there is a lack of discrimination against certain physicians or physician groups.

Joint marketing between physicians and hospitals, however, is usually less controversial and can be of potential benefit to a larger number of physicians. Many physicians are looking to their hospital for its expertise in marketing. Physicians in virtually all specialties and with different levels of experience are anxious to market their practices more effectively. Health care systems and hospitals can help physicians develop marketing programs and work with them in implementing such marketing efforts. Joint marketing programs can include a full range of activities, from community service programs to the development of brochures to sponsorship of radio or television programs that feature members of the medical staff.

Physician-Hospital Financial Arrangements

The local health care system's strategic planning retreat had been going well; there was little disagreement about the corporate mission statement or the need to expand market area boundaries and move more aggressively into product line management. When the physician relations task force made its report, the word *subsidy* was used to describe the system's support of several primary care doctors. The roof blew off; very few of the trustees had any idea that some physicians were being subsidized. This had never appeared as a line item on the budget!

The discussion settled down as several trustees articulated their ideas on how the hospital and other parts of the health system should seek to work with physicians on a businesslike basis (avoiding the word *subsidy* like the plague!). Loans were satisfactory; so were partnerships to establish a practice. Absorbing the first year's rent on office space would be permissible as long as there was at least a three-year lease.

But one year later the problem has not gone away in this hospital; in fact, it has intensified. It is becoming increasingly difficult, in hospitals across the country, to deal with the myriad of proposals from physicians without an overall policy guiding physician-hospital financial arrangements.

One useful step in the development of a policy on financial arrangements is to have the hospital staff prepare a series of brief case studies of what various hospitals, including their own, have actually done with their medical staff. These case studies can then be analyzed with the intent of identifying common themes that might form the basis of a policy statement.

Here are three slightly abridged "real world" examples (names disguised) of one hospital's proposed financial arrangements with doctors:

Case #1. Dr. Ronald Jones, a family practice doctor with an office in the medical office building adjacent to the hospital, is selling his practice and moving to a warmer climate. His price is $100,000, and he approaches his hospital to buy it; he has an offer at his asking price from a nearby competing hospital. In order for the hospital to pay Dr. Jones $100,000 for his practice, it would have to find another physician to take over the practice; without the new doctor, the value of the practice would shrink to zero.

Case #2. Three OB/GYN physicians, all large admitters to the hospital, are interested in opening a second office in a building located four miles from their present office. They want to lease 1,200 square feet and have approached the hospital to pay for half the finishing costs ($35,700 ÷ 2). The new office will allow the three physicians to serve more patients; hence there will be more admissions to the hospital. The doctors point out that the hospital often purchases expensive equipment for use of the other specialists; they say that helping them expand their practice is no different.

Case #3. Dr. Joan Gibbs is an internist operating a general practice in a small office building ten miles east of her hospital. She is a graduate of the intern program at a large downtown hospital that was recently acquired by one of the large investor-owned chains. Dr. Gibbs has an $18,000 loan from the downtown hospital, with monthly payments of $404 spread over five years. She presently admits 60 percent of her patients to her primary hospital and 40 percent to the downtown facility owned by the chain. Her primary hospital has been approached by Dr. Gibbs with a request to loan her enough money so that she can pay off her loan from the downtown hospital. Her reason for the request: she does not like the implied obligation to admit patients to the downtown hospital, which is twenty miles from her office; she would rather switch all of her referrals to her primary hospital.

The three examples have these common themes:

- All the physicians are (or have been, in the case of Dr. Jones) loyal to their primary hospital and prefer to admit their patients to this hospital.

- In terms of marginal revenues (value of patient-days generated by the referrals from the three practices, less direct costs), all three ventures will, in all likelihood, pay off for the hospital.
- All three examples carry potential financial risks. In particular, the question of the purchase of Dr. Jones's practice carries the greatest financial risk; the potential loss of patients should a competing hospital acquire the practice would be serious.

The hospital is moving ahead with all three proposals; they all fit within the broad policy guidelines approved by the board of trustees.

Strategic Implications

Relationship Management. Ted Levitt, the Harvard Business School professor who created the term *marketing myopia,* has a chapter in his book devoted to relationship management. Although Levitt's suggestions are not oriented toward the health care industry, they are relevant to physician-hospital relationships. Levitt says that "... a company's most precious asset is its relationship with its customers" (1983, p. 120). This statement could apply equally well to a hospital and its greatest asset, its medical staff. Despite the increasingly important role of ADS, and the fact that consumers are also playing a bigger role in physician and hospital selection, physicians are currently the most important customers for hospitals.

Physician-hospital bonding will happen only over a long period of time. "Clearly relationship management requires not just the care of little things day in and day out but also the cumulative constructive management of all things large and small throughout the organization. The idea is to build bonds that last, no matter who comes and goes" (p. 120).

Joint Ventures Make Economic Sense. From an economic point of view, joint ventures between hospitals and physicians are a natural. The strengths and weaknesses of the two parties often blend exceptionally well. Hospitals usually have large capital resources, organizational ability, and long-term, well-established reputations in the community. Physicians have access to patients, entrepreneurial ability, and an innovative spirit. The two parties may more frequently find that it is in their mutual economic advantage not to conflict but to join forces to compete in an attempt to increase market share.

Physician-hospital joint ventures will lend themselves not only to a physician bonding strategy, but to other competitive strategies, such as diversification, vertical integration, and centers of excellence. The mutually beneficial joint venture will be a way to achieve goals in each of these areas. Strategies requiring capital and management time will need to be carefully integrated in order to maximize the use and benefits of the limited resources of physicians and health care systems.

Health care systems and hospitals in highly competitive market areas, those targeted for vertical integration by major investor-owned chains, will need to budget for medical staff financial arrangements and joint ventures. The stakes are likely to be high; several hundred thousand dollars per year for a midsized hospital (250 to 400 beds) is not unusual. These types of investments need to be specifically identified so that potential risks and returns can be related to the amount earmarked for specific programs. The use of funds is related to the overall capital budgeting and priority-setting process for the health care system, described in Chapter Sixteen.

For physicians, the payoffs from physician bonding arrangements—joint ventures, financial arrangements, and the like—can be high. Physicians in different stages of their practice will respond more favorably to different types of arrangements. Physicians just starting into practice will clearly be interested in financial arrangements, office subsidies, and shared services to ease their entry into the marketplace. Joint ventures related to the development of a center of excellence may be of great interest and value to specialized physicians with well-developed practices. From the hospital's perspective, the range of interests of physicians will facilitate a diversified approach to the physician bonding strategy.

Strategically, closer bonding between a hospital and its medical staff can represent a successful approach. Our experience indicates that more effort should be devoted to identifying opportunities systematically and then ranking them in terms of economic feasibility and overall desirability in terms of meeting strategic objectives. This ties into an important matter discussed in Chapter Sixteen—the necessity of having physicians be a part of the strategic planning process.

11

Developing Centers
of Excellence

The table was cluttered with printouts as managers, marketing staff, and consultants looked at the latest national consumer and employer awareness data. One person said, "Humana has almost doubled both its awareness and quality ratings! It doesn't make sense." The consultant responded, "It's easy to see. It's the artificial heart transplants. They're affecting public awareness and the quality image of the whole chain."

Humana's heart transplant efforts represent one example of a center of excellence strategy. Centers of excellence can be closely related to differentiating on the basis of quality of care, the strategy discussed in Chapter Five. The difference is that with centers of excellence, investments in quality are heavily focused in carefully chosen areas. Centers of excellence are also closely related to an increasingly popular tactical health care concept—product lines. As a tactical matter, a hospital may choose to market, analyze, or manage itself using product lines. As a strategic decision, a hospital may choose to focus resources on a small number of product lines to achieve excellence.

Many health care systems have centers of excellence, and they are attracting patients because of such centers. Examples include excellence in emergency medicine and the service network (ambulances, paramedics, helicopters), OB/GYN, geriatrics, pediatrics, surgery, orthopedics, and oncology.

One key advantage to using the center of excellence strategy is the potential positive impact on other services: a good center of excellence has a halo effect. A health care system may focus resources on a center of excellence that will attract a high volume of patients (for example, women's health or orthopedics). If the patients' experience is good, the hospital has achieved an advantage in terms of word-of-mouth advertising and the future use of the system's inpatient and outpatient services.

The centers of excellence strategy is receiving reinforcement from the increased use of "product line" marketing and management by hospitals. Rather than viewing the hospital as a series of departments (nursing, housekeeping, supply, finance), there is a strong movement toward defining a health care system or hospital in terms of what it provides—that is, in terms of its product lines.

In assessing the value of the center of excellence (or product line) strategy, health care systems need to consider the following questions:

- Do we have existing strengths that could be built up into one or more centers of excellence?
- What would it take in the way of managerial and financial resources to achieve excellence in our market area?
- From a customer (consumers, employers, and health plans) point of view, would it really matter if quality were improved for particular product lines?
- How would a center of excellence fit into our overall plans for product line development and management?
- What kinds of impact could be expected if we were successful in differentiating one or more centers of excellence? What would be the payoff?

What Are Centers of Excellence?

Product line and *center of excellence,* both popular terms in other industries, have been enthusiastically embraced by the health care industry. Unfortunately, there are no commonly accepted definitions of these terms within the context of health care delivery.

A product line discussion typically refers to a tactical approach, that is, how to implement an institution's strategies. However, the term, product line, is used in different organizations to mean an analytical approach, a marketing approach, a management approach, or all of the above:

- *An analytical approach.* In this approach, the hospital would define a product line for analytical purposes, such as better understanding costs or tracking admissions and outcomes by physician for specified groupings of DRGs. Organizations using this type of approach do not have to go through the trauma of reorganization.
- *A marketing approach.* Repackaging existing hospital services—perhaps uniting newborn deliveries, gynecological services, and breast cancer screening, and marketing them as a women's health center—employs the marketing approach.
- *A management approach.* The hospital using this approach would assign a single individual the responsibility for coordinating marketing, pricing, facilities planning, cost controls, staffing, and physician relations for a specific product line (for example, orthopedics). This approach is similar to industry's use of the profit center concept.

Under the right circumstances, each of these concepts represents a potentially worthwhile management initiative. We believe that analyzing health care markets and systems in terms of product lines almost always makes good business sense. Similarly, marketing a hospital's capabilities in terms of one or more product lines is likely to be effective in nine out of ten urban or metropolitan markets. The third approach, product line management, requires substantial managerial and financial commitments and has more serious implications for most hospitals.

A center of excellence discussion may refer to:

- *Strategic focus on a particularly important product line.* For example, the center of excellence could be a highly specialized product line with state-of-the-art equipment and facilities. Efforts to increase the large numbers of admissions and qualified physicians may result in an enhanced reputation, higher quality, and improved profitability. The improved profitability may result in part from greater economies of scale. With increased volume, or scale of operations, resources may be used more efficiently and costs per unit of production reduced.
- *Focus on a combination of related product lines,* such as neurosciences and orthopedics. This might include investments that could benefit both product lines, such as improved rehabilitation capabilities.
- *Focus on a small innovative area with marketing potential.* Examples of centers of excellence with a marketing value might include pioneering efforts with a small number of patients in such areas as artificial hearts or liver surgery. Although small in admissions and often "loss leaders" in terms of profitability, these programs may be highly beneficial in terms of enhancing the hospital's image (as in the previous Humana example).

A center of excellence specializes in the care of patients in a clinical area but additionally focuses hospital management and financial resources, sometimes disproportionately, on that particular area in order to achieve increased volumes of patients, higher quality of care, enhanced visibility, or all three. That focusing of resources is intended to enhance the service or product line so that it is distinguished within the community for its quality, high standard of excellence, or innovative nature. As we discussed in Chapter Five, the perception of quality of care is critical to the future success of most health care systems and hospitals. Centers of excellence can provide some institutions the opportunity to deliver especially high quality care, and to get credit for it. For example, the heart transplant activities of the 1960s at Baylor Medical Center in Dallas went beyond establishing the center's reputation and patient volume for cardiology; they enhanced the prestige of the entire institution. Similarly, Humana's artificial heart transplants in the 1980s have extended name recognition and an image of quality beyond the Human Heart Institute to the entire Humana system.

Identifying Strengths and Level of Effort Required for a Center of Excellence

Product line analysis has been with us almost as long as Cadillacs, Buicks, and Chevrolets. In its basic form, product line analysis begins by grouping closely related individual products and targeting them toward particular market segments. The factors affecting the business—projected demand, unit revenues and costs, production capacity, and other key variables—are analyzed separately for each product and product line. In the automobile industry, product line analysis was followed by product line management, including development and maintenance of product line distribution systems (dealerships), development of marketing programs and cost controls (including parts standardization), and delegation of profit-and-loss responsibility to product line managers.

In the health care industry, the product line focus has shifted now that hospitals are competing with one another in earnest. Health care product line analysis is beginning to look increasingly like that carried out in other industries. DRGs, for example, are often grouped into product lines; the marketing and delivery of services and the future demand for each product line are taken into consideration.

A typical outline for a product line analysis is shown in Exhibit 1. Using this type of format, an analysis of the product line or potential center of excellence could lead to the identification of strengths and weaknesses, and to the appropriate level of effort needed to distinguish the service from its competitors within the market area (local, regional, national). The health care system

Exhibit 1. Elements of a Product Line Analysis.

I.   Product Line Definition
      • Key products
      • How product line is defined and why
II.   Current Business Assessment
      • External trends
        — Demand trends: market segments utilizing product line, service
          area demographics, total utilization projections, factors
          affecting utilization (outpatient surgery, insurance/payer
          pressures)
        — Competitors: present and projected services, marketing efforts,
          clinical strengths, insurer relationships
        — Technology: expected advances, equipment requirements
        — Summary of opportunities and threats
      • Internal trends
        — Hospital/system capabilities: equipment, trained staff, treat-
          ment capacity
        — Physicians: physicians and their capabilities, referral base
        — Marketing: current effort, currrent market share within service
          area
        — Patients: origins
        — Finances: present and projected charges, costs, payer mix,
          discounting to payers, net operating revenues
        — Summary of strengths and weaknesses
III. Strategic Options (for example, recruiting new medical staff, adding
      a new product, intensifying product line marketing, reducing costs,
      enhancing quality of care, communicating quality)
      • Benefits of options (strategic implications, benefits to service area
        residents)
      • Feasibility of options (costs, revenues, consistency with current
        capabilities)
      • Other factors (political considerations within medical staff, effects
        on relations with other hospitals, regulatory requirements)
IV.   Recommendations

---

must then ask whether the level of effort required is feasible: Are the managerial and financial resources necessary to excellence available within the health care system? Can the allocation of resources to the planned center of excellence be justified in terms of its upside potential?

Before moving ahead with a center of excellence, management must ask itself: What will be the effect on the rest of the system—including the effect on morale—of investing heavily in one or more designated centers of excellence?

St. Joseph's Hospital in Denver is one of many hospitals nationwide that responded to the new competitive environment with a well-marketed women's health product line. Partially as a result of its Women's Pavilion packaging and marketing initiative, St. Joseph's is now one of two Denver area hospitals with the best reputation for providing quality women's health services. Later women's health marketing efforts by several other hospitals have not been successful in closing this perception gap. Both St. Joseph's Hospital and its medical staff have benefited.

The concept of product line packaging is straightforward and appealing: a health care system first identifies a market segment that it really wants to serve; then it identifies not one but several services that can be delivered to that market segment at different points in time. The focus is on building relationships with each market segment, not on marketing a simple service. This makes marketing more efficient and often more effective.

Installing and Promoting Centers of Excellence: Lessons Learned

In order to be effective, centers of excellence should be matched to the appropriate customer group. In some cases, the customer will be a segment of the consumer market; in other product lines, physicians may be the primary market. In other situations, payers or employers may represent the target market. The strongest and most appealing products are used to lead marketing efforts, with the weaker or less appealing services pulled along. Success in building a strong image for any product line will often result in a halo effect on the hospital's image and that of many of its other services.

In pursuing a center of excellence approach, each health care system must decide which market segments and product lines should be selected. It comes as no surprise that women's health is one of the most popular areas. In the early 1980s, it met the key prerequisites for an attractive product line:

1. Profit potential is high. The high-volume services—normal newborn deliveries and gynecological surgery—usually have a favorable payer mix and high net revenues per patient-day.

2. There is a strong demand. With the late arrival of the postwar baby boom's baby boom, it is not uncommon for women's health–related admissions to represent 25 percent of all admissions in a market area. For some hospitals, a 10 percent improvement in their market share of women's health admissions could mean the difference between red and black ink.

3. The appropriate market segments are clearly identifiable and are thought to be receptive to a product line approach. Consumer research shows that women are more health-conscious and place more importance on their choice of health care providers than their male counterparts (see Chapter Three). The women's movement appears to have further increased concerns over health and to have produced some shifts in women's relationships with their physicians based on philosophical and personal compatibility.

4. There is a strong possibility that a favorable experience at the hospital will lead to a favorable perception of all the hospital's services. Consumer research shows that the woman is usually the dominant family decision maker on choices of all health care providers. Establishment of a good relationship with the key female decision maker in a household can lead to a relationship with the whole family. In addition, normal deliveries provide hospitals with an excellent opportunity to highlight their warm, caring environment. Research shows a warm and caring attitude among staff to be the most important characteristic in the minds of consumers in determining the overall quality of a hospital (see Chapter Five).

5. The women's health product line can be publicized with a splash. In many markets, no clear leader in women's health has yet emerged.

6. The product line can be marketed as an example of unusual competence.

With respect to points 5 and 6, "me too" promotions, which imitate another hospital's promotion in the same market, and efforts to promote services that are not well established cannot be expected to succeed.

Alliance Health System in Norfolk, Virginia, provides one example of how a center of excellence strategy is working within a diversified local health system. Alliance includes two acute care hospitals, several specialty facilities including a world famous in vitro fertilization institute, and several alternative delivery systems. Alliance's flagship acute care hospital, Norfolk General, initiated a marketing and management program for twelve product lines in early 1985. At least three of the twelve product lines have sufficient reputation, capabilities, patient volume, and management emphasis for them to be considered centers of excellence.

Four examples illustrate the manner in which the centers of excellence integrate strategically into the larger local system:

1. The centers of excellence are used to convey the desired overall image of Norfolk General Hospital. The hospital's marketing campaign is coordinated to simultaneously emphasize a desired image and a product line. For example, women's health services are used to convey a warm and caring image, cardiac surgery is used to convey up-to-date facilities and high-tech competence.
2. Norfolk General's image is used to convey the overall quality represented by the system, including its suburban hospital and its alternative delivery systems.
3. Other system components are used to reinforce the centers of excellence. The in vitro fertilization institute and on-campus children's specialty facilities reinforce the women's health center.
4. Centers of excellence are used internally to spearhead the overall move toward product line management. Product lines are grouped together for managerial purposes. The centers of excellence provide focal points for these groups.

At University Hospital in Cleveland, Ohio, product lines have been initiated as a means of improving managerial accountability. This system was influenced by a board chairman who was a former General Motors manager. Direct line reporting through product line managers is used. Everyone working in an area, including department directors and physicians, reports to one of six product line managers. This system is heavily oriented toward innovation and patient and market responsiveness. The product line managers maintain their offices near the wards with which they are the most closely associated.

There are numerous examples of incremental improvements associated with designating and focusing resources on centers of excellence. We are aware of no total failures. While some organizations may choose to implement broad-based product line marketing and management, others may choose to simply designate and work with one or two centers of excellence. For organizations without systematically identified product lines but with a potential competitive advantage in a focused area, it may be best to move now with centers of excellence and later with well thought out product lines.

Strategic Implications

Centers of excellence can be a particularly valuable strategy for teaching and tertiary care hospitals. The level of resources required to develop or promote a center of excellence will generally be lower for tertiary care hospitals than for others; centers of excellence enhance the specialized and technological image that should already exist for these types of hospitals.

Community hospitals can also successfully implement a center of excellence strategy, if they have the basic building blocks needed to establish one or more centers. The investment in such centers has to be analyzed carefully to make sure it is commensurate with the potential gains. In a highly competitive market, a center of excellence may confer a more concrete and distinctive character to a community hospital, thereby helping it stand up to pressures to reduce prices.

The center of excellence strategy is not likely to be as successful for rural hospitals. Regional medical centers will be competing for specialty patients through their own centers of excellence, and it is unlikely that many rural hospitals have the size, resources, or potential volume of business to compete at this level.

The center of excellence strategy is closely related to at least two other competitive strategies—quality of care and aggressive marketing. Use of the three strategies in concert should maximize financial and managerial resources: a high-quality product will attract attention to a hospital's image as a quality institution; and with an aggressive marketing strategy, a disproportionate amount of marketing resources may be committed to a specific center of excellence, particularly if that center has the potential for high volume and high margins.

Centers of excellence may also complement the physician bonding strategy described in the previous chapter. New equipment or facilities will often be a part of the development of a center of excellence, and new physicians may be recruited to further specialize or broaden the center's capabilities. Focusing on quality of services encourages more positive physician-hospital relationships.

12

Networking
Among Organizations

This chapter discusses multihospital systems and alliances and their potential for helping a local health care system and its medical staff prosper and survive. Two out of five not-for-profit hospitals are members of multihospital systems or alliances.

The American Hospital Association (AHA) refers to multihospital systems as those organizations that own or manage hospitals. In 1985, AHA identified 249 such systems (American Hospital Assocation, 1985). Of these, 30 were investor-owned. The multihospital system group represented 35.5 percent of all U.S. hospitals and 37.2 percent of hospital beds (p. 6).

For the purposes of our analysis, we have included alliances as part of multihospital systems. The two largest alliances— Voluntary Hospitals of America (VHA) and American Healthcare Systems (AHS)—together account for well over 1,000 hospitals and 250,000 hospital beds (more than one-quarter of all beds in the United States). VHA and AHS are described in more detail later in this chapter.

Among the Catholic multihospital systems, Mercy Health Services is the largest, with 43 hospitals and 15,000 beds (Anderson,

1986b). Among other church-related systems, the four Adventist Health Systems combined are by far the largest, with 69 hospitals representing 10,000 beds (American Hospital Association, 1985, p. 20).

Other large not-for-profit systems include the New York City Health and Hospital Corporation (12 hospitals with 9,400 beds), Kaiser Foundation Hospitals (27 hospitals with 5,700 beds), Intermountain Health Care, Inc. (described later in this chapter), and Lutheran Hospitals and Homes Society of America (43 hospitals and 2,600 beds).

This chapter focuses on the two largest multihospital alliances in some detail, summarizes key aspects of three smaller systems, and assesses the advantages and disadvantages of being part of a multihospital system or alliance from the perspective of a local hospital or health care system and its medical staff.

Voluntary Hospitals of America

VHA, formed in 1977, is the largest alliance of not-for-profit health care organizations, representing over 600 facilities with over 170,000 beds in forty-seven states. VHA claims that it is larger, in terms of hospital beds, than the four largest investor-owned chains (AMI, HCA, Humana, and NME) combined. VHA hospitals represent over one-sixth of the acute care beds in the United States, and the gross revenues of its member hospitals surpass $26 billion per year.

VHA hospitals are distributed as follows into three categories:

Shareholders	85
Affiliates of shareholders	150
Hospitals in regional systems	400

VHA shareholder hospitals pay an initial fee of $200,000 and an annual assessment of around $50,000. Most are relatively large—500 beds or more—and are located in major metropolitan areas, distributed so that they do not compete with one another. To qualify as a shareholder, a hospital or local health care system has to have a reputation for delivering high-quality care. A substantial proportion of VHA's core group, the shareholders, are teaching hospitals; they include Massachusetts General Hospital, Johns Hopkins Hospital, and Baylor University Medical Center.

VHA's basic objectives are to "provide the resources, systems and unity necessary to strengthen our shareholders', affiliates' and regional partners' competitive advantage and to enhance the voluntary sector of the health care industry." To accomplish these goals, VHA has stated nine business fundamentals:

1. Strong corporate/institutional management
2. Productivity/quality control programs
3. Human resources programs
4. Financial systems
5. National purchasing agreements
6. Corporate capital financing
7. Insurance programs
8. Internal and external image programs
9. Access to strategically important information

VHA is also heavily involved in ADS, having formed a joint venture with the Aetna Insurance Company to market a series of PPO and HMO products through Partners National Health Plans.

VHA has subsidiary companies that provide a wide variety of consulting services (VHA Enterprises) and access to capital (American Health Capital). Other elements of the VHA system include Behavioral Medical Care (a joint venture with a large firm in the alcoholism and drug abuse treatment business), a physician placement service, and a partnership with ServiceMaster Industries to provide housekeeping and related services. VHA also provides market research information to the various elements in the system through its Market Monitor.

In reflecting on the rapid growth of VHA, and the growing commitment of shareholders to the VHA system, Don Arnwine, chairman of the board, said that two events had had momentous impact. The first was the decision in December 1984 by the board of the 798-bed Wesley Medical Center, Wichita, Kansas, (a founding member of VHA) to sell to HCA. Wesley's departure represented a stunning blow to VHA and its shareholders (Bark-holz, 1985). Several weeks later, HCA announced plans to merge with American Hospital Supply, driving home the point that independent hospitals will have an increasingly tough time competing.

American Healthcare Systems

AHS, formed in August 1984 as a result of the merger of Associated Health Systems and United Healthcare Systems, is the second-largest system in the United States, with a membership in excess of 500 hospitals. The AHS network of systems and hospitals breaks down as follows:

Shareholder systems	35
Shareholder owned, leased, or managed hospitals	500
Other hospitals accessing AHS programs	950

Owned, leased, and managed hospitals of the 35 shareholder systems represent 98,500 beds and annual revenues of $14 billion. The 35 systems in 43 states employ 277,000 persons.

AHS criteria for becoming a shareholder are the following:

- Reputation for high quality
- Two or more hospitals owned, leased, or managed
- $100 million or more in annual revenues
- Separate corporate office
- Not-for-profit status
- Strong management and financial position

AHS has issued shares valued at $125,000 twice in the past two years, with additional stock offerings planned.

The basic objective of AHS is to "improve the competitive and economic condition of our shareholders." AHS goes on to say that "to [meet this objective], we treat the business of health care like business. We run lean, we manage tough and we retain control of community health at the local level" (American Healthcare Systems, 1986, p. 1). To achieve its purpose, AHS operates a variety of programs, including group purchasing of supplies, formation of alternative delivery systems, development of capital sources, and federal policy impact through its American Healthcare Institute located in Washington, D.C., AHS also offers a marketing system, called the Futures Program, to track health care industry trends.

Moving into the field of ADS, AHS has formed a joint venture with Transamerica Occidental Life of Los Angeles and Provident Life and Accident of Chattanooga, Tennessee, two of the ten largest investor-owned insurance companies in the United States. The joint venture, called American Healthcare Plus, is initially forming PPOs; it will eventually establish a national network of HMOs. The joint venture partners each invested $10 million in the venture (for a total of $30 million).

In a recent article, Samuel Tibbitts, AHS chairman, outlined six factors critical to the success of multihospital corporations (small regional systems or clusters):

1. *Size.* At the regional level, Tibbitts suggests that a multihospital corporation should operate six to ten hospitals with total annual revenues of at least $250 million.
2. *ADS.* Each multihospital corporation should develop an HMO or PPO with at least 100,000 members.
3. *Corporate practice.* By negotiating contracts with professional medical corporations, or putting physicians on the payroll, Tibbitts says that multihospital corporations should gain control of the type and quality of care offered.
4. *Information systems.* Using telecommunications and satellite communications, multihospital corporations should be linked with their members and with a larger system such as AHS.
5. *Central finance.* Multihospital corporations should centralize financial control and access to capital.
6. *Core values.* According to Tibbitts, core values will bind the large, decentralized company with its hospital components.

AHS appears to be assisting its shareholders to achieve these success factors.

Small Regional Networks

SunHealth, Inc. Established in 1969, SunHealth is a network of thirty-five acute care hospitals in the southeast and mid-Atlantic regions of the country. SunHealth's objectives are to provide programs and services for member hospitals and to provide a vehicle or network for working together. According to SunHealth's annual report, "On any given day, more than 375 health care facilities are using one or more SunHealth services" (1986, p. 1). SunHealth recently sold equity shares to its hospital members, making it a for-profit multihospital system owned by not-for-profit hospitals. (It is similar to VHA in this respect.)

Services provided by SunHealth include contract management of hospitals, consulting services in diversification and corporate reorganization, physician recruiting, ADS development, productivity enhancement, group purchasing, facilities consulting, and pooling of hospital bond issues to obtain better terms for financing.

Intermountain Health Care, Inc. Intermountain Health Care (IHC), established in 1975, is the parent company of five entities:

- *IHC Health Plans.* Established to provide HMO and PPO coverage to persons in Utah, southern Idaho, and western Wyoming, this organization has 800 physicians in its network. Its HMO, IHC Care, was established in mid-1985 and had 11,000 members within six months. Health Choice, the PPO, was started a year earlier and had 38,000 members as of year-end 1985.
- *IHC Hospitals.* This subsidiary owns twenty-four acute care hospitals and a number of related facilities, including seven urgent care centers, women's health services, psychiatric and behavioral health services, and medical equipment and supplies.
- *IHC Professional Services.* This group includes several freestanding outpatient surgery centers and an occupational health division.

- *IHC Affiliated Services.* Group purchasing is the largest element of this subsidiary.
- *IHC Foundation.* This foundation serves as a resource for the foundations of individual hospitals.

IHC says that its mission is "excellence in the provision of health care services to communities in the western United States" (Intermountain Health Care, 1986, p. 51). IHC's major strategic initiatives include joining forces with physicians through a newly formed Medical Executive Council, increasingly emphasizing HMOs and PPOs, merging the delivery and financing of health care, and developing women's health services.

Consolidated Catholic Health Care. In June 1985, nineteen Catholic multihospital systems formed Consolidated Catholic Health Care (CCHC) for the purpose of strengthening Catholic health care ministries. There are 301 health care facilities in the system, and they represent 52,500 beds; 180 of the facilities are acute care hospitals.

Initial planning indicates that CCHC will be developing a variety of services, including alternative delivery systems, group purchasing, marketing, and management and diversification activities (Doody, 1986). Each participating system provided $250,000 in start-up capital. According to Sister Kathleen Popko, chairperson of the alliance, the new group has the potential to be stronger than other alliances because its members share "such a strong faith commitment to the ministry of Catholic healthcare" (Anderson, 1985).

Strategic Implications

Our contacts with multihospital systems and alliances and their members (either smaller systems or local hospitals) indicate an overall satisfaction; benefits have so far outweighed the costs (initial stock purchase, annual assessments, CEO time to participate on committees and in governance functions). Most participants are generally optimistic about the future of multihospital systems and alliances and their ability to bring meaningful assistance to shareholders and other members.

In assessing the large alliances, with special emphasis on the two megasystems, VHA and AHS, there appear to be four major problems, however.

• *Developing a brand name or identification that is of value to shareholders and others in the system.* As of the mid-1980s, there was virtually no name recognition among consumers, employers, or even physicians for either VHA or AHS. Both alliances plan to develop brand names, but the cost will be substantial (in the tens of millions). Humana's success in establishing a brand name— largely due to the publicity surrounding its artificial heart transplants—appears to have whetted the appetite of VHA and AHS for similar brand-name recognition.

• *Developing and maintaining a consensus on strategic initiatives, and obtaining the necessary commitment to implement new programs.* Members of large alliances tend to look after their own interests first, relegating those of the system to secondary importance. This is especially evident as both large alliances attempt to establish national HMO and PPO provider networks; some member hospitals are struggling with certain of the exclusivity provisions—for example, restrictions on contracting with other national health plans, such as Humana Care Plus.

• *Gaining support from the staff in member hospitals or health care systems.* For example, shareholder CEOs in VHA attend semiannual board meetings and are generally tuned in to VHA programs. But hospital and health care system staff members a step below the CEO generally lack in-depth knowledge of VHA and AHS. Medical staff members have generally seen no impact from their hospital's participation in a multihospital system; in many cases, they are totally unaware that such networking exists.

• *Accessing capital.* Adequate capital is a critical problem for smaller hospitals, and most large multihospital systems are attempting to assist, with some success. For example, VHA's American Health Capital provides financial expertise on a consulting basis to VHA institutions, and it has negotiated a preferred letter of credit management with Mellon Bank in Pittsburgh. American Health Capital has also assisted several VHA regional systems in forming capital pools, which are especially beneficial to smaller hospitals. Yet to have a major impact on their shareholders' ability to survive, multihospital systems will need to develop more innovative, large-scale efforts to make capital available.

An additional, less troublesome problem with alliances is that they move too slowly to suit some members. HealthWest Foundation, a member of AHS, is moving ahead with its own insurance products. "Our concern about being a member of an alliance is that every marketplace is moving at a different pace," explains Paul Teslow, HealthWest's president. "Given the high velocity and competitiveness of Southern California, we can't build our short-term insurance strategy around AHS" (Shahoda, 1986, p. 57).

On the positive side, there is little doubt that shareholders and other participants have received substantial benefits from the large-scale purchasing programs of the multihospital systems. These programs have had an impact in terms of volume purchasing, with the savings accruing to members. AHS claims that it saves its hospitals $13 million annually in pharmaceutical purchases alone.

Much of the current emphasis in multihospital systems is on their efforts to establish national networks of HMOs and PPOs. As indicated earlier, progress has been slow, and the final outcome is by no means certain given the tremendous competition in the health plan marketplace. Sanford Bernstein, the Wall Street investment firm that has published predictions of a massive shift toward HMOs and PPOs by 1990, predicts that Partners National Health Plans, the VHA-Aetna joint venture, will have seven million members by 1990, or 9.2 percent of the ADS market. But will this be sufficient to satisfy VHA's constituent hospitals, which have high, and perhaps unrealistic, expectations of what they will receive in the way of patients from Partners?

Will VHA make it? Will AHS fall apart? We think that both organizations have shown their ability to adapt to change, and on a timely basis; we expect both to survive as major players in the health care marketplace. Furthermore, we believe that participation in such organizations has the potential to provide a competitive advantage to those health care systems and hospitals (and their medical staffs) that elect to participate. From the local health care system or hospital viewpoint, being in a multihospital system or alliance is a relatively low-cost, low-risk strategy, with benefits usually outweighing costs.

13

Being a Low-Cost Provider

As discussed earlier, we are opposed, except under very unusual circumstances, to a health care institution initiating strategies based on price competition. Yet many industry observers predict that the health care industry, and hospitals specifically, will soon be competing on a price basis "at the margin" (that is, with prices equaling marginal costs). If this does happen, we are convinced it will spell disaster for many organizations.

Health care systems and hospitals need to know how they would stand up under price competition. Seeking to be a low-*cost* provider—which is not the same as being a low-*price* competitor—may be a useful objective for many organizations.

Daniel Nimer, an authority on health care pricing, hit the nail on the head. "Yes, costs are important to test the price—but not yours. Your competitive cost position doesn't mean you have to be the low *price* supplier, it just gives you more options than your competition. If, in fact, you do have lower costs, meeting the competition's price will give you more profit at that level. The decision can then be made as to whether to keep these incremental revenues, invest them in incremental marketing programs, or do both" (1986, p. 23).

The problem is in determining the low-cost providers in each market area. One hospital we work with is considered by many health insurance companies and PPOs to be a low-cost hospital within the context of its market. But how do we really know? And will the institution retain this advantage over the long run? It would be disastrous for a hospital to consider its low-cost provider status as the cornerstone for its strategic planning, only to find later that its costs were not really as low as previously thought. If a hospital's occupancy rate were to drop from, say, its present 65 percent to 45 percent, it might suddenly find itself much more expensive; fixed costs—such as management salaries, interest expenses, utilities, and insurance—would be spread over fewer patients, and therefore unit costs (or prices charged) would have to increase in order to maintain profit margins.

Is the fact that a hospital is able to make money on DRGs, or that its costs on specific DRGs are lower than those of its competitors, an indication that it is a low-cost provider? Not necessarily. DRG payments have proven to be generous, at least for many hospitals. This may be lulling certain hospitals to sleep.

A big part of the problem in knowing whether or not a hospital is a low-cost provider relates to the accounting system being used. Most hospitals' accounting systems were designed for cost reimbursement and are intended to allocate overhead in ways that maximize collections from Medicare and third-party payers. Under prospective pricing, accounting systems must carefully separate fixed and variable costs by product line. In order to make intelligent pricing decisions, health care system executives need to know incremental costs, and how much will be contributed to overhead and profit at a specific price. Given appropriate cost data, we might discover that a hospital is a low-cost provider in some of its product lines, but not in others (Morlan Lewis, managing director, VHA Enterprises Consulting Services Division, interview with the authors, Dallas, Tex., July 14, 1986).

A Review of Concerns About Health Care Costs

Until recently, the focus of research on health care costs has been on questions relating to why health care costs were escalating so rapidly, and cost comparisons between investor-owned and not-for-profit hospitals. The emphasis has not been on individual hospitals and how they might be able to survive as low-cost providers under conditions of price cutting.

Martin Feldstein, in his 1981 book *Hospital Costs and Health Insurance*, says that increases in hospital costs have occurred for fundamentally different reasons than inflation in other sectors of the economy. "The unusually rapid increase in the cost of a day of hospital care reflects a change in the character of hospital services rather than a higher price for an unchanged product" (p.19). Feldstein says that only 25 percent of hospital cost increases over the 1950-1975 period were due to increases in input prices (wage rates) in excess of the general increases in consumer prices, and that 75 percent of the increase in average cost per patient-day was due to greater inputs, especially more full-time-equivalent employees and more technology (p. 28). He goes on to say, "The essence of the explanation is that the explosion of hospital costs reflects a rapid growth in the quality and style of hospital care, not an increasing cost of providing the same product" (p. 133). Feldstein's last point is relevant to current concerns about the low-cost provider strategy: are we comparing apples with oranges in terms of the "products" being delivered?

Various studies comparing the economic performance of investor-owned versus not-for-profit hospitals also shed light on the overall issue of hospital cost-effectiveness. The most thorough analysis was carried out jointly by Lewin and Associates, the Johns Hopkins Center for Hospital Finance and Management, and the Department of Health Policy and Management, Johns Hopkins University; the results were summarized in a *New England Journal of Medicine* article (Watt and others, 1986). The study involved eighty matched pairs of hospitals in eight states during the 1978-1980 time period; it represented an early attempt to adjust for case mix (similar health care products).

The study found that the investor-owned chains charged higher prices—22 percent more per admission—than did not-for-profit hospitals in the same community. "Nearly all the difference in inpatient charges was attributable to differing charges for ancillary services" (p. 91). The study went on to say that investor-owned hospitals employed significantly fewer full-time-equivalent staff members per adjusted average daily census, but they paid higher average salaries and benefits than did their not-for-profit counterparts. The net result was personnel costs that were comparable.

Other factors were also evaluated—income and property taxes paid, size and age of physical plant, and debt service—but variability was relatively minor. Nearly 90 percent of the differences in inpatient charges could be explained in charges for ancillary services. The study noted that "these results strongly suggest the existence of a strategy by the investor-owned chain hospitals of setting competitive prices for the more visible 'room and board' services while setting higher prices for ancillary services, which are less easy to compare from hospital to hospital" (p. 95).

A study for the Hospital Alliance of Tennessee, carried out by Booz-Allen & Hamilton Inc. (1984), compared prices among seventy-three not-for-profit hospitals and sixty-five proprietary hospitals (data are for 1981 and 1983, prior to prospective payment). The study, which made comparisons on a case-mix basis, found that not-for-profit hospitals generally had lower costs and charges per admission. Another finding was that proprietary hospitals had higher administrative costs, higher capital costs (debt service), high ancillary charges, and more favorable profit margins (p. 4).

The Committee on Implications of For-Profit Enterprise in Health Care identified six studies of price differences between for-profit chains and not-for-profit hospitals. "The studies consistently found that prices of for-profit chain hospitals were substantially higher than prices of not-for-profit hospitals—chain or independent" (McNerney, 1986, p. 80).

The point in reviewing these older studies is not to debate the merits of investor-owned versus not-for-profit hospitals. In fact, for an era dominated by cost reimbursement, the results are not surprising. The main reason for revisiting these studies is to show the kinds of price and cost comparisons typically made as late as 1984, and to point out that most of the differences in pricing among hospitals appear to have been deliberate attempts to maximize earnings; the differences do not appear to be based on widely varying cost structures. In fact, we could argue that the data from both the Lewin/Johns Hopkins and Booz-Allen studies show that costs for the investor-owned chains and matched not-for-profit hospitals are comparable. The data raise the question: are there significant cost differences among similar types of hospitals? From there we must ask, is a strategy based on low costs likely to be successful?

Factors Currently Impacting Hospital Costs

Like other businesses, hospitals experience cost-related factors that are controllable and some that are beyond the control of the organization (for example, mix of customers, bad debts, reductions in the volume of patients in the overall marketplace). It appears that several of the uncontrollable factors may be more important in determining a hospital's cost status than those that can be controlled.

Indigent (Uncompensated) Care. For hospitals having to serve a significant number of indigents, and without special gifts or donations (or in the case of government-owned hospitals, substantial appropriations), costs must be shifted to paying patients and their insurance companies.

University/Teaching Affiliation. The director of nursing at a 500-bed Ohio hospital told us, "We're a high-cost hospital, mainly because of our teaching status. We have a large number of interns, and they order lots of tests." In other words, prices charged patients (or third-party payers) may be high because of the training and research roles of many hospitals.

Teaching and research hospitals face an especially difficult problem in dealing with HMOs and PPOs. The problem is so serious that some industry observers fear for the future of teaching and research. In Minneapolis-St. Paul, for example, Physicians Health Plan (PHP)—the largest HMO in the Twin Cities, with over 300,000 members—has decided whenever possible not to use University of Minnesota hospitals for its members. "In a competitive market, we can't afford their rates," PHP CEO Richard Burke

says simply. "They are not market-oriented, they are not respon-
sive, and they are high cost." He blames costs not just on teaching
and research but on inefficiency. "The problem is going to get
worse before it gets better," he says. "I don't know who ought to
have to pay the difference [in cost]. We are certainly not going to
volunteer" (Robson, 1986, p. 70).

   Medical Technology. The relationship between medical
technology and hospital care has had a powerful effect on hospital
costs, demand for services, and overall national health care
expenditures. The use of new technological services often creates
additional revenue flows and generates both direct and indirect
expenditures. Such expenditures include the direct acquisition of
capital equipment in terms of the initial outlay, interest, and
depreciation expenses; additional operating costs, including new
employees, training, supplies, and other incidental expenses;
additional expenses incurred because the new service leads to the
provision of complementary services (for example, heart bypass
surgery following cardiac catheterization); and new demand for
other services (for example, increased incidence of Caesarian
sections following routine use of fetal monitors).

   The development of medical technologies (and the incentives for hospitals and physicians to use the latest technologies) has
resulted in the improved treatment of various diseases and
improved outcomes. However, incentives for improved outcome
and use of technologies have led to dramatically expanded use of
ancillary services and increases in hospital service intensity and
costs of hospital stays. Various studies estimate that 10 to 25
percent of hospital cost increases over the past decade are the result
of new medical technology (Vignola, 1984).

   Payer Mix. There are large variations in the Medicare case
load of hospitals, depending on the medical specialties offered and
the demographics of the hospitals' market area. Those hospitals
with a higher than average Medicare patient load have been at a
disadvantage because of Medicare's resistance to full reimbursement, especially for capital-related costs. Under the DRG system,
financial pressures have increased for some hospitals, while other

institutions have benefited. In the future, however, it appears that as the federal government continually squeezes funds available for Medicare, it will be increasingly difficult for most hospitals to benefit from their Medicare business.

Up until now, the discounts typically provided to HMOs and PPOs have posed no financial problems for most physicians and hospitals. The percentage of patients covered by ADS is typically small, and the extra services provided by some hospitals more than make up for the discounts (see Chapter Six). However, as the proportion of patient-days covered by ADS increases, and as ADS companies tighten up on the ordering of ancillary services, some hospitals will be hurt financially; they will be required to spread their costs over other patients, thus increasing their overall cost structure.

Case Mix. Certain types of cases require more expensive equipment and facilities—coronary bypass surgery, for example. The case mix of a hospital is obviously a key factor influencing its cost structure. Large tertiary care hospitals, with a higher proportion of complex cases referred to it by outlying physicians, will almost always have a higher cost structure.

Severity of Illness. In our view, severity of illness differs from case mix. A hip replacement for an eighty-year-old woman, for example, may require more hospital resources than a similar operation for a sixty-year-old man.

Medical researchers are now paying more attention to the severity factor and how it affects length of stay and consumption of resources (ancillary services, special care). For example, Paul Gertman and Steven Lowenstein (1984) argue that severity of illness measures, although imprecise, need to be incorporated into the DRG system. Indexes of severity of illness have been developed, and several are described later in this chapter; it is our belief that some measure of severity will be phased into the DRG system, thus making comparisons among hospitals and physician groups more equitable.

Medical Staff Practice Patterns. As increasingly sophisticated data bases are being developed, it is becoming more and
more obvious that there are major differences in practice patterns
among doctors, or groups of physicians, around the United States.
The way physicians practice medicine—including hospitalization
decisions, utilization review, and the ordering of various tests—has
a major impact on a hospital's status as a high- or low-cost
provider. We hope that these physician practice patterns will
change, come more into line, thus reducing their impact on
hospital costs. Certainly a hospital coveting a low-cost provider
status needs the full cooperation of its medical staff.

Controllable Cost Factors. In this category, we are including
salaries of management and supervisory personnel, debt service,
utilities, insurance, and a host of other costs incurred simply to
keep the doors open. Direct labor and expenses include all nursing
and other personnel directly associated with patient care, as well as
supplies, food, cleaning services, and ancillaries that are typically
a function of patient volume and intensity.

In such highly competitive health care markets as Minneapolis and Los Angeles, hospitals have successfully shifted a
substantial proportion of their direct labor costs from a fixed to a
variable basis. In Minneapolis, for example, only 23 percent of all
hospital nurses are employed on a full-time basis. The remaining
77 percent are on flexible schedules that depend on patient
demands (Nelson, 1986b, p. 22). In effect, hospitals have put nurses
"at risk"; their earnings depend on the success of the hospital in
attracting patients.

Better Defining the Health Care Product

In addition to the Medicare DRG system developed by
researchers at Yale University, several other systems have been
formulated to measure health care resources consumed in the
treatment of various diseases. Resource consumption is an
extremely important aspect of hospital reimbursement under
prospective payment and other fixed-price systems (such as ADS).
These efforts are all designed to better define the "product" so that

comparisons among different institutions can be improved. University and research hospitals have been the most active in these efforts and have the most to gain.

Health Data Institute. The Health Data Institute (HDI), organized in 1981 and located in Newton, Massachusetts, has been a leader in collecting and analyzing health care cost data. Chrysler was one of HDI's early clients, and HDI's studies led to substantial changes in worker hospitalization and treatment patterns in that firm. The HDI data base, national in scope, is largely developed from insurance claims. HDI has a heavy emphasis on physician input supported by economic and statistical analysis. After Medicare's DRG system, HDI's data base and analytical services appear to be the most widely used in the health care industry, especially by insurance companies and large employers.

Disease Staging System. Ernst and Whinney, a Big 8 accounting firm with one of the largest health care consulting practices in the country, has joined with Systemetrics to computerize a disease staging system. The staged diseases identify patient groupings that require common treatment procedures and services. Disease staging is linked to codes of the International Classification of Diseases, Ninth Revision (ICD-9), to come up with severity of illness measures.

MEDISGRPS. Alan Brewster and his associates at the Medical Illness Severity Grouping System (MEDISGRPS) have developed and applied a system that is based on an initial classification at admission to a hospital, followed by measurement of changes in severity of illness during the hospital stay. This system differs from others in that it is not disease-specific; however, results can be significantly correlated with charges and length of stay.

Codman Research Group. Another approach to the collection of useful data for controlling health care costs has been developed by John Wennberg and his associates at the Codman Research Group, Inc. (CRG), in Hanover, New Hampshire. CRG conducts small-area analysis of the patterns of statewide and local utilization of health care services. CRG reports compare hospital service area rates for admissions, patient-days, length of stay, and reimbursement or costs for all medical causes of admission and surgical procedures, using the DRG classification system; DRGs are adjusted for age and sex to make more accurate comparisons among small areas. Phillip Caper, a physician with CRG, says, "The data allow us to understand physicians' professional decision making much better than has ever been possible. We've heard for years that the quality of medical care would suffer if cost containment were imposed, and it's always been difficult to dispute that." But, Caper goes on to say, the small-area (micro-level) comparisons have been fed back to physicians to help them change their practice patterns. "Small area analysis provides a way to get objective data concerning physicians' practice styles and their relationship to costs on the table. Then dialogue can occur on the basis of those data, as opposed to there being just two sides asserting their opinion" (Wennberg and Caper, 1985, p. 90).

Severity of Illness Index. Susan Horn and a team of researchers, physicians, and nurses at Johns Hopkins University developed a Severity of Illness Index that is a refinement, based on patient severity, of DRGs. Its purpose is to refine prospective payment so that resources allocated reflect the severity of the patient's illness. The system, now being offered to health care systems, was developed with two key evaluation criteria in mind: medical meaningfulness of the categories, and the homogeneity of resource consumption within each of the case-mix groups. The team developed its index on the basis of a severity scoring of patients across seven dimensions. Using data from fifteen hospitals, Horn and her colleagues showed that DRGs explained 28 percent of the variability in resource use per case, while severity of illness-adjusted DRGs explained 61 percent of the variability in resource use (Horn, Horn, and Sharkey, 1984).

Other Systems. Other systems have been developed by Jefferson Medical College (Joseph Gonnella), Blue Cross of Western Pennsylvania (Wanda Young), and George Washington

University ("APACHE," developed by William Knaus and Douglas Wagner).

All of these efforts have as their objective a better definition of the health care "product." This definition is basic to the development of an equitable system for payment and is especially important to hospitals that deal with more complex cases. In the future, as price competition heats up, the success of these types of classification systems will determine whether or not certain types of hospitals have a fair chance of competing.

Health Care Data Collection and Reporting

There has been increased emphasis by state and local government, employers, health care coalitions, health plans, benefits consultants and brokers, and hospitals to collect and analyze the kinds of data that will allow buyers to know they are receiving the best possible value for their health care dollars.

Health insurance companies, often in association with efforts to form PPOs or to convert traditional indemnity plans to a managed care (or cost-containment) basis, have been the most aggressive in analyzing claims data to better identify cost (or charge) patterns. For example, across the United States Blue Cross and Blue Shield are pooling claims information for 78 million subscribers; this constitutes the nation's largest health care data base. The objectives of the expanded data base, which is capable of recording 170 data elements per claim, are to identify inappropriate utilization, better measure the effectiveness of several health care cost-containment strategies (including preadmission certification and second opinions on surgery), and compare experience among employers in the same locality or with a work force having similar characteristics (Moore, 1985).

Several states have implemented state data commissions. Although the legislative intent and statutory authority may differ among states, the data commission mandates generally require providers to give utilization and charge data to the commission for publication. The intent behind publishing such data is to encourage more prudent purchasing of health care. But it is still too early to determine whether or not such systems make a difference in the cost of health care.

One major problem with the present widely used data collection and reporting systems is that they do not appear to give adequate weight to severity of illness. As noted earlier in this chapter—and it is consistent with the experience of those physicians and hospitals that offer tertiary care to Medicare patients—some patients are sicker than others and less able to respond quickly to treatment. Hospitals handling large numbers of these more difficult cases are being penalized by prospective payment (DRGs, ADS) and will be impacted even more in the event of price competition.

Competing on the Basis of Price

When it is necessary to compete on a price basis, there are several actions a hospital or health care system can take to minimize the adverse effects:

1. Aggressively seek opportunities to increase prices in less price-sensitive market segments or services. This is what the investor-owned chains have done for years; they have maintained competitive prices for room charges but raised prices for less visible ancillary services. In Chapter Five we talked about the existence of a quality-conscious market segment that will pay extra, out of pocket, for private rooms and other special services.

2. Transfer fixed costs to a variable-cost basis. This is what Minneapolis hospitals have done in shifting 77 percent of their nurses to flexible, part-time schedules.

3. Work with the medical staff to tighten up even more on the use of inpatient-days, tests, and ancillary services.

4. Carefully control overhead, including management and supervisory staff, utilities, interest and debt service, and other fixed-cost items.

5. Eliminate unprofitable ventures or services (see our discussion of diversification strategies in Chapter Seven). The days of cross-subsidies within a health care system are over.

Strategic Implications

It appears to us that most hospitals have the potential to further reduce their costs. However, most will not, or in some cases cannot, make significant cost reductions without continuing data in the form of declining census, and reduced bottom line indicating that further reductions are needed. For example, the medical staffs of most hospitals are likely to strongly resist reductions in staffing levels, especially in nursing and equipment budgets; they will equate such cuts with lowering the quality of care. Since physicians are the main "customers" for most hospitals, it may not be worth jeopardizing the relationship with physicians in order to reduce costs. It may take several shocks to the local health care delivery system before the stage is set for additional reductions. This is what happened in Minneapolis-St. Paul: reductions in utilization so impacted the entire hospital industry that it became acceptable for individual hospitals to make rather drastic cost reductions.

We contend that most comparisons of hospital charges are superficial. As illness classification systems are refined, however—especially with better quantification of severity of illness—and as hospital medical record and cost-accounting systems are merged and improved, it will be possible to develop better comparisons of hospital charges. We believe that these increases in sophistication will narrow what are now perceived as major differences in costs. Some hospitals that have considered themselves to be well positioned as low-cost providers may find their perceived advantages evaporating.

We also believe that the dissemination of hospital charge data, adjusted for case mix and (in the future) for severity of illness, will tend, over a period of time, to reduce regional differences in physician practice patterns. As a consequence, hospital costs will come into line; there will be fewer and fewer extreme differences. It will be increasingly difficult to gain competitive advantage by virtue of low costs.

At the same time, quality of care differences will become increasingly important as a way of differentiating among hospitals and physicians. The advantages some hospitals will seek by reducing staffing and by other cost-cutting measures will be offset by greater consumer and employer recognition of the impacts of these cost reductions on quality and service.

For some hospitals, there may be a two- to three-year window of opportunity to pursue the low-cost provider strategy. For those health care systems that now enjoy significant cost advantages, this may be the time to establish clearly a reputation for cost-effective care. Once the differences in price and cost level out, in the longer term, a health care system may be able to retain its reputation as an efficient provider, especially with employers, health plans, and benefits consultants and brokers.

The low-cost provider strategy is something that most hospitals must attempt. But the idea that this strategy, by itself, will make it possible for hospitals to survive is probably not valid—especially in the long term, as increasingly sophisticated price and severity of illness measures are implemented, and as hospitals and their medical staffs modify their behavior in response to the publication of price data and increasing ADS and Medicare pressures.

14

Downsizing

Lest we seem overly critical of the health care industry for expanding its capacity beyond reasonable demand, we should note that we cannot identify a single major U.S. industry that has not done the same thing. The U.S. agricultural industry is capable of producing several times the country's needed food supply. The mining industry is operating at a fraction of its productive capacity. Most U.S. cities have a glut of office and retail space. Our automobile industry could produce several million more cars per year than we need. Colleges and universities need more students to fill empty classrooms. And we have too many lawyers, accountants, architects, and dentists—as well as too many physicians.

In our ongoing review of general business publications, we do not often read about the need for industries to reduce their productive capacity. We do read, however, about the need to run a tight ship, with close control of costs. Can the U.S. health care industry operate efficiently with the large overhang of excess bed and physician capacity? We believe it can. But as is the case in other industries, excess capacity breeds price cutting and other forms of stiff competition. Many health care systems and physician groups are truly in a fight for survival.

This chapter focuses on the economics of reducing capacity, of downsizing. No hospital would deliberately engage in a strategy of reducing its size unless it expected to gain economic advantage from such a move. As noted in "Downsizing Hospital Capacity," "The only purposes of downsizing are to render the hospital more efficient and maximize its competitive community position" (Doherty, O'Donovan, and O'Donovan, 1986, p. 5). We focus here on the positive aspects of downsizing and consider how it can be used as a strategy to gain competitive advantage. The key question addressed is this: is it possible to reduce the size of a health care organization and, at the same time, improve its bottom line and competitive position?

The health care literature on downsizing is meager, probably because many hospitals do not like to talk about it. Many of the articles on this general subject talk about the human side of handling layoffs or reductions in force. We are not focusing only on staff reductions, however—although it is obvious that such reductions are needed, and will continue to be needed as demand and utilization continue to drop. Instead, we are evaluating possible strategies for dropping product lines and services, closing parts of a hospital, and finding new uses for excess space, staff, and equipment.

An Overview of Downsizing. Mark Van Sumeren, a senior manager with Ernst & Whinney in Milwaukee who specializes in health care operations, provides a general definition of downsizing in the health care industry: "Organizational downsizing is a process where a hospital thoroughly and critically reviews its organizational structure and operating practices in response to a severe decline in occupany" (1986, p. 36). We might add that, in an ideal situation, a hospital would initiate this process in anticipation of a drop in census, not after the fact.

Although a detailed data base has not been developed, it is apparent that downsizing in the health care industry has been occurring for several years. The industry is moving toward "leaner and meaner" operations. In 1984, U.S. hospitals eliminated more than 10,000 staffed beds, or 1.1 percent of all beds (White, 1985, p. 66). In 1985, 75 hospitals throughout New York state decertified

2,000 beds ("New York Hospitals Decertify 2,000 Alternate Care Beds," 1986, p. 12). A survey of Wisconsin hospitals indicated that in 1984, 3,481 full-time-equivalent staff positions were eliminated in 105 hospitals, and 45 percent of these hospitals noted further reductions in 1985 (Wisconsin Hospital Association data summarized in Van Sumeren, 1986, p. 35).

The Downsizing Process. Downsizing can entail a variety of activities, which fall into one of four distinct classifications:

- *Staff reductions* (that is, layoffs, attrition, transfer of personnel). Downsizing-related staff reductions differ from other staff reductions in two important ways. First, downsizing-related staff reductions usually impact all levels of the organization (from management to nurses to technicians), whereas non-downsizing-related layoffs are often confined to a particular department or service. Second, downsizing-related staff reductions are usually accompanied by an organizational restructuring (that is, a combining of departments) and a reduction in capacity (fewer beds); layoffs not in the context of a downsizing effort are often implemented unilaterally, without corresponding changes in organizational structure. Third, downsizing-related staff reductions tend to be permanent, while traditional layoffs tend to be temporary, in response to a "short-term downturn" in patient volume.
- *Organizational restructuring,* usually consisting of departmental consolidation or elimination. It should be noted that organizational changes—for example, department consolidations—often occur on an interim basis. These short-term actions should not be confused with downsizing-related organizational changes, which are usually permanent.
- *Plant capacity reduction* (reduction of number of beds or operating rooms; closing a wing or floor; sale of excess equipment and supplies).
- *Conversion of use of facilities* (for example, an inpatient operating room to outpatient use, acute care beds into a skilled nursing unit) and sale of excess equipment.

Most downsizing efforts encompass more than one of these four elements. For example, organizational restructuring almost always results in staff reductions.

Five Case Studies

The application of downsizing concepts to real world situations is not always successful. At best, downsizing can result in a more efficiently run hospital with an enhanced market share and reputation. At worst, downsizing can backfire, resulting in work stoppages, poor morale, loss of market share, and poor community image.

In an example of an unsuccessful downsizing effort summarized in *Modern Healthcare* (White, 1985, p. 66), an unnamed midwestern teaching hospital closed an entire floor and laid off large numbers of employees. A patient overflow developed almost immediately, and operations were adversely affected. General medical patients had to be placed in rooms on surgery floors, while patients who had been stabilized in intensive care had to remain there because other beds were not available. Several key physicians severed ties with the hospital because they thought quality of care had been adversely affected. The hospital's image within the community suffered when rumors of bankruptcy and buyouts appeared in the press.

In the next few paragraphs we will summarize five *successful* downsizing efforts.

Griffin Community Hospital. Griffin Community Hospital (GCH) is a 261-bed hospital located in Derby, Connecticut. By 1985, its average daily census had dropped to 163 inpatient beds. Recognizing that several major change factors—DRGs, the wellness movement, greater use of outpatient services, and increased competition—meant that GCH would not be able to regain its former position of high occupancy, the management embarked on a five-part strategy:

1. *Organizational restructuring.* A parent company was created; the hospital was one of four subsidiary corporations.

2. *Closing a forty-four-bed nursing unit.* The section that was closed had been used for medical education; some functions were moved to other patient-care floors.
3. *Staff reductions.* Layoffs were not necessary; reductions were accomplished by increased use of flexible scheduling and an early retirement program.
4. *Increased emphasis on outpatient care.* Physical improvements and several administrative scheduling changes were made.
5. *Focusing inpatient services on community needs.* This included construction of a birthing center and consideration of a center for geriatric medicine.

The result of this downsizing strategy has been to stabilize the hospital's bottom line; earnings in 1986 are expected to exceed those of prior years (John Carlton, Griffin Community Hospital, Derby, Conn., telephone interview with the authors, May 1986).

Lincoln General Hospital. Lincoln General Hospital (LGH), a 286-bed facility in Lincoln, Nebraska, began planning for a major downsizing operation in September 1984. Admissions had dropped from 12,787 in 1980 to fewer than 10,000 in 1984 (White, 1985).

With the help of Ernst & Whinney, a Big 8 accounting firm, hospital management decided to close one surgery unit, eliminate sixty-five to seventy employees (including two top-level managers), and convert several beds into an outpatient youth behavioral medicine unit. Prior to the downsizing, LGH's occupancy rate was 50 percent; since the reductions it has averaged 65 percent. This has substantially improved the hospital's bottom line.

Ray Schweiger, an assistant administrator at LGH, said that the "medical staff is cooperating to modify their practices" to be more cost-effective and help bring actual hospital charges closer to the DRG levels (White, 1985, p. 71).

Lutheran Medical Center. The Lutheran Medical Center (LMC) in Cleveland, Ohio, is a 221-bed, inner-city acute care facility. Like many other hospitals, LMC was encountering the adverse impacts of declining utilization caused by an oversupply of beds and increased market control by third-party payers. Since it is an inner city hospital, administrators believed declining utilization problems would grow even more severe.

In mid-1985, LMC management initiated a downsizing program that entailed several major elements:

1. *Reducing work force.* About 100 full-time-equivalent employees were laid off. Layoffs were across the board; in other words, staff reductions were not confined to one department of the hospital. Many job categories (managers, nurses, technicians) were subjected to staff reductions. Longer, nine- to ten-hour shifts reduced the need for more workers.

2. *Combining key departments.* It was found that individuals previously managing a single department could manage one to two more units. Some "crossover" on the technician level was also introduced; for example, at LMC a respiratory therapist can now administer EKGs. Thus departmental consolidation resulted in management and staff savings.

   Business volume was a basic criterion used to determine which departments were likely candidates for consolidation. National and regional staffing standards per unit of service were applied. Once low-volume or overstaffed departments were identified, methods of lowering costs and increasing efficiency were analyzed; overhead expenses received special attention. LMC found that, for example, managerial costs for a department with only two or three people could be lowered through consolidation.

3. *Solicitation of physician-staff support.* A series of formal and informal meetings were held with all department heads and most affiliated physicians, at which the need for the downsizing effort was explained. The impact of DRGs and the increased control of patient referrals by third-party insurers and ADS received special emphasis. To lower overhead costs, physicians were encouraged to use the pharmaceuticals and supplies that the hospital purchased in quantity; however, doctors were not asked to change their practice patterns.

4.   *Process.* LMC management believes that downsizing is an ongoing process, not a one-time organizational change. Thus downsizing principles have been incorporated into its management systems. It is believed that this approach enables downsizing efforts to be fine-tuned to specific market changes and developments.

LMC's downsizing effort did not impact the census of the hospital; patient volume and patient mix did not change. However, due to lower overhead and direct costs, profitability (as a percent of revenues) improved by 3 to 4 percent.

George Washington University Hospital. In late 1983, George Washington University Hospital (GWUH) executives predicted that occupancy, which had been more than 90 percent, would decline. This prediction was based on a shift to ambulatory services and the planned implementation of Medicare's prospective pricing system (Sheila McCarthy, George Washington University Hospital, Washington, D.C., telephone interview with the authors, June 27, 1986).

Faced with a probable drop in revenues, hospital management adopted a long-term downsizing strategy. Major downsizing goals (in addition to cost reduction) included the following: "every effort would be made to accomplish downsizing without layoffs" (staffing reductions for specific departments would be achieved through attrition and the transfer of personnel to other areas in the hospital), and downsizing would be accomplished without decreasing care hours per patient or the percentage of registered nurses (McCarthy, 1986, p. 120).

The first phase of the downsizing process was implemented in early 1984, when the staff of the obstetric and newborn units was reduced. Guidelines were developed for conducting staff reductions, with major criteria including seniority and the need to retain the right staff mix (that is, an optimum ratio between registered nurses and patients). After receiving counseling and training, staff members needing to be reassigned to other departments were transferred to available positions. The obstetric department was reduced from forty-five to thirty beds.

A second downsizing effort was initiated in early 1985. First, the eighteen-bed ophthalmological surgical unit was consolidated with the general surgical unit. This was possible because the bulk of ophthalmological procedures was being performed on an outpatient basis, thereby reducing the need for inpatient beds. Second, the thirty-bed cardio-thoracic surgical unit was temporarily closed and later reopened in the old ophthalmological unit, resulting in a reduction of twelve beds.

Overall, the downsizing process of GWUH resulted in a net reduction of twenty-seven beds (the obstetric unit was reduced by fifteen beds and the cardio-thoracic unit by twelve beds). In addition, the ophthalmological unit was eliminated as a separate entity.

Fewer beds led to reductions in nursing and technical staff. The consolidation of the ophthalmological unit into the general surgical unit resulted in management as well as overhead reductions (housekeeping, administration, nursing, and so on).

GWUH was able to meet the goals of its downsizing effort; that is, an inpatient bed and work force reduction was accomplished without mandatory layoffs or a reduction in patient service levels. Management attributes the success of the effort to several factors:

1. *A high degree of management involvement.* The director of nursing, the hospital administrator, and the medical director were involved early in the process.
2. *Good communication.* Information was shared with middle-level managers.
3. *Fair treatment.* The consolidation of upper-management positions indicated to individuals on all levels of the organization that the hospital would implement staff reductions in an equitable fashion.

Highland Park Hospital. Highland Park Hospital (HPH) is a 321-bed acute care facility in Highland Park, Illinois. HPH initiated a downsizing program that resulted in the development of a new product line as well as cost reductions (Jay Goldstein,

Highland Park Hospital, Highland Park, Ill., telephone interview
with the authors, July 1, 1986). Major elements included:

1. *Market analysis.* The market was evaluated to identify
   potential health care needs in the marketplace that were not
   being adequately served; a number of potential services were
   considered (for example, outpatient surgery and a nursing
   home). A demographic analysis indicated that, while the
   average age of the market area population was thirty-five, by
   1990 the population sixty-five and over was expected to
   increase by almost one-third. It was decided that the market
   could support a conversion of forty acute care beds into a
   skilled nursing facility (White, 1985, p. 68).
2. *Certificate of need.* The conversion required the approval of
   state authorities. A certificate of need (CON) was applied for
   and granted.
3. *Management involvement.* The planned conversion was
   presented to most department heads. The planning committee
   of the board of directors was also directly involved. A level of
   support among physicians for a skilled nursing facility
   already existed.
4. *Staff reductions.* Staff reductions were accomplished through
   attrition and transferring some staff members to other units
   within the hospital; mandatory layoffs were not required.

The skilled nursing facility became operational in June
1986. In addition to providing long-term care to elderly patients, it
also enables stabilized hospital patients to recover in a less costly
environment. (The skilled nursing facility is lower in cost
primarily because of a lower nurse-to-patient ratio.)

HPH management is confident that the downsizing process
and resulting conversion will have several positive impacts on
hospital operations:

- Due to the lower staffing requirements of a skilled nursing
  facility, personnel costs will be reduced.
- Some elderly patients can be discharged from acute care beds
  earlier than normal, and readmitted into the skilled nursing

facility for convalescence. This results in cost savings and more profits from DRGs.

- The existence of a skilled nursing facility is expected to positively impact the marketability of the acute care component of the hospital, ultimately resulting in more favorable census levels.
- HPH will be better positioned to compete in the elderly care market.

Strategic Implications

The five successful downsizing efforts described in the previous case studies suggest the following conclusions:

- The ability of hospitals to implement downsizing efforts while improving financial performance suggests that downsizing can be accomplished without the loss of economies of scale. The loss of economies of scale would lead to higher per unit costs and, ultimately, to lower profit margins.
- Unless conversion is pursued, successful downsizing does not have to affect census levels or patient composition. Therefore, gross revenues may not be impacted; this was the experience at Lincoln General Hospital and Lutheran Medical Center. Financial rewards are reaped primarily through lower staffing levels and reduced costs, ultimately leading to higher profits.
- Hastily planned or poorly implemented downsizing efforts can decrease the confidence level of physicians and consumers, ultimately leading to lower census levels.
- Staff reductions without layoffs are possible. If the downsizing process is implemented at an early stage, adequate time exists to utilize other, less controversial strategies (attrition, early retirement, relocation). This may be increasingly difficult, however, since many hospitals have already trimmed much of the "fat" from their operations.
- In successful downsizing efforts, heavy emphasis is placed on communication with hospital employees and affiliated physicians. At the very least, a high level of interaction exists between department heads and the medical staff.

- Although downsizing efforts usually originate from management or an administrative department, a number of departments as well as the medical staff and board of trustees are usually involved in decisions leading to implementation of an appropriate downsizing strategy. This type of board involvement and support is critical to the success of downsizing efforts.

Downsizing is the last of the ten strategies described and analyzed in this book. As noted in the introduction to Part Two, these ten strategies are not mutually exclusive; most health care systems will employ several. The key strategic issues relate to the appropriateness of these strategies to various competitive situations (for example, a small hospital in a rural area, a university hospital, a suburban medical center in a large metropolitan area) and the level of resources (managerial and financial) to be applied to each.

Part Three

Charting the Best Course

In a recent study, over 700 hospital trustees were asked, "What is the top priority of your CEO?" We would be willing to bet that five years ago the answer would have been "financial management," "physician relations," or "cost containment." These goals are still important; indeed, they ranked two, three, and four in the recent survey. However, the number one priority today, by a wide margin, is strategic planning.

That finding is not surprising in light of the current health care environment. With all the changes, and with the tremendous number of options, the key issue for the typical CEO has to be strategy development. Meanwhile, based on the way health care systems operate now and on the future health care business environment, we suggest that a related issue will be the CEO's first concern of tomorrow: ongoing decision making and strategy implementation.

Part One focused on the changing characteristics of the health care marketplace. Part Two reported on the successes, failures, and future potential of ten generic strategies—potential building blocks for the local health care system's overall strategic plan for achieving competitive advantage. Part Three focuses on

213

what a local health care system has to do to chart the right course
and then carry it through to success.

Choosing the Right Mix of Strategies

The ten broad strategies discussed in Part Two are not
mutually exclusive; in many cases, they can complement one
another. However, the typical health care system or hospital is
likely to find that the appropriateness of a particular broad
strategy depends in part on the characteristics of the health care
system and the local marketplace. Some strategies apply more
readily to large, well-established systems in metropolitan areas, for
example, than to small, rural hospitals.

A second important consideration is that the strategies have
to work well together; they should reinforce one another. In
tomorrow's health care environment, few organizations will have
the luxury of attempting ten strategies with the hope that two or
three will succeed. Most health care systems will have to choose a
smaller number of strategic initiatives that can be integrated in
ways that reinforce one another—for example, choosing a diversification activity that uses space made possible by downsizing, or
building an aggressive marketing campaign around an existing
center of excellence. Chapter Fifteen addresses these and other
considerations involved in choosing among the ten broad types of
strategies and developing an integrated overall strategic plan.

Working out an overall strategy, and doing so in a way that
ensures it a chance of being implemented, requires an effective
strategic planning process. Whether the strategic planning process
is formal or informal, it must bring to bear the rigor of analysis
and speed in decision making that are needed in any changing,
market-driven industry, and include key decision-making constituencies—senior management, physicians, governing boards, middle
management—in a learning and adjustment process. Chapter
Sixteen discusses the key elements of strategic decision making for
tomorrow's successful health care system.

Carrying Through

In successful firms in other changing industries, strategic
and financial planning and ongoing management are so closely

coordinated that they virtually become one function; we believe this will also become the norm in health care.

Not-for-profit health care system trustees say that their biggest concern—after attracting patients and dealing with new forms of reimbursement (DRGs, HMOs, and PPOs)—is access to capital. Their concern may stem from an organization's already high level of debt, the volatility of tax-exempt bond markets, federal policies likely to reduce capital availability, and the need to compete against large investor-owned systems with access to equity capital.

Investor owned systems face many of the same challenges as not-for-profits, of course, and are also dealing with the emerging competitive environment. However, their ability to tap both the equity and debt markets and to offer greater incentives to top management (stock options, for example) affords investor-owned health care systems a different set of options when it comes to implementation of their chosen strategies. Chapter Seventeen addresses the access to capital issue and how it relates to bringing capital resources to bear on implementing strategic objectives.

The ability of not-for-profit hospitals and health care systems to make the hard choices relative to their future strategies is the subject of frequent criticism. Much of the skepticism relates to voluntary trustees and their ability to compete in the emerging health care environment. Chapter Eighteen discusses this important issue.

Facing the Future

This is, after all, only a midcourse correction. While we believe that the future will move toward stabilization, we have no choice but to continue to question our assumptions. Chapter Nineteen represents our attempt to look ahead and separate the real from the apparent; we present our candidates for ten myths and ten key realities concerning the future of health care delivery in the United States.

15

Choosing
and Integrating
Strategies

Decisions about the right broad strategies for a particular health care system must be based on several factors. What are the system's strengths and weaknesses? Does it have strengths in particular products and markets; is it a low-cost provider; is its location a strength or a weakness? What about local market conditions? How competitive are the local hospital, insurer, and physician markets? What are the opportunities to differentiate from the competition? What strategies can work together and complement one another in a specific marketplace? Finally, what strategies will sell to the health care system's several constituencies—trustees, physicians, employees, consumers, and financing sources? Choices among specific strategic initiatives, within the ten generic strategies, must be based on more detailed consideration of all these factors.

The purpose of this chapter is to demonstrate, through examples, how the ten types of health care strategies can be integrated to form the basis for an overall strategic plan, with emphasis on how they complement each other.

Three Health Care Systems and Their Opportunities Within the Ten Strategies

Exhibits 2, 3, and 4 summarize present and potential strategic initiatives, grouped within the ten broad strategies, for three different types of local health care systems. All three examples are based on actual cases. The characteristics of the three systems are listed below.

1. *Suburban health care system.* Includes 350-bed acute care hospital and 80-bed rehabilitation hospital; located in a metropolitan area with two million residents; 18 percent ADS penetration (Kaiser represents half of this amount); substantial excess bed capacity in market; physician surplus is large; three investor-owned chains are active.

2. *Teaching, tertiary care system.* Includes 1,000-bed hospital near center of growing metropolitan area of 800,000 and two small suburban hospitals; twenty-three HMOs and PPOs have 15 percent market penetration; substantial physician surplus; investor-owned chains are active; inpatient costs are above average for this marketplace.

3. *Rural hospital.* Includes 150 beds; no other hospital within 50 miles; dramatically declining census; $300,000 subsidy annually from county; difficult to attract and retain physicians; 30,000 people in service area; declining resource-based economy.

When the Ten Strategies Are Most Likely to Be Important

Table 14 shows the relevance of the ten strategies for each of the three types of local health care systems described above (suburban, teaching–tertiary care, and rural). This exhibit is intended to be illustrative; each health care system or hospital will need to assess the relative importance of each strategy in its own marketplace.

Exhibit 2. Ten Strategies Versus Present and Potential Initiatives: Suburban Health Care System.

Potential Strategies	Present Initiatives	Potential Longer-Range Initiatives
1. Differentiation on the basis of quality of care	Continue to emphasize quality with doctors and staff; patient feedback; risk management; perception of good quality image	Do more promotion of top areas such as women's health; expand OB; establish upscale services; standardize quality monitoring to show buyers what they are receiving for money
2. Alternative delivery systems (HMOs and PPOs)	Hospital-owned HMO; aggressive contracting with other ADS	Sell HMO; aggressively seek HMO contracts
3. Diversification (spreading risks)	Suburban health park; HMO; cooperative housing project; imaging joint ventures; wellness program	Strengthen long-term care; integrate rehabilitation hospital into system
4. Vertical integration	HMO; network with other acute care hospitals; urgent care centers	Develop network of primary care physicians; establish home health care
5. Aggressive marketing (market research, pricing, PR, advertising)	Developed pricing policy statement; have good market research base; extend market area boundaries to the south	Increase advertising and PR levels of effort; continue to tie in doctors; focus on employers; make better use of auxiliary; extend market areas to southeast and north; integrate marketing into product lines; refine pricing policies
6. Physician bonding (joint ventures, financial arrangements)	Medical office building; policy on financial arrangements; acquisition of new equipment/technology	Establish second medical office building; find new ways to enhance loyalty of medical staff; identify new financial sources to acquire technology
7. Centers of excellence (product lines)	Developing product line management in women's health, neuroscience, vascular, orthopedic specialties	Develop rehabilitation center of excellence with three other hospitals; add new product lines (pediatrics, others); recruit physicians in specialty areas
8. Networking	Regional system of alliance; informal network with two other acute care hospitals	Extend relationship with psychiatric hospital
9. Being a low-cost provider	Control costs; maintain prices that are competitive; not a price cutter	Put nurses and others on hourly basis (reduce fixed costs); reduce subsidies for several ventures; improve cost-accounting system to include product lines
10. Downsizing	None	Develop contingency plan for downsizing

Exhibit 3. Ten Strategies Versus Present and Potential Initiatives: Tertiary Health Care System.

Potential Strategies	Present Initiatives	Potential Longer-Range Initiatives
1. Differentiation on the basis of quality of care	Have quality image; strive to maintain quality of care	Develop better documentation of quality
2. Alternative delivery systems (HMOs and PPOs)	Participate in Partners National Health Plans; contracting with high percentage of local ADS	Sell value and maintain margins
3. Diversification (spreading risks)	Started suburban health park, including small hospital	Acquire other acute care hospitals in region
4. Vertical integration	Home health care; medical office building	Acquire nursing home; seek other new ventures
5. Aggressive marketing (market research, pricing, **PR**, advertising)	Close monitoring of consumers and physicians; active physician referral service; targeted marketing to doctor (nonstaff and newcomers); expanded **PR** department	Coordinate pricing strategies better; identify and serve upscale niche
6. Physician bonding (joint ventures, financial arrangements)	Have several joint ventures, including ambulatory care center	Continue to seek out joint venture opportunities
7. Centers of excellence (product lines)	Establishing strong children's and OB hospital on campus	Recruit physicians in specialty areas
8. Networking	VHA and VHA regional system	None
9. Being a low-cost provider	Costs are high relative to others in the area	Can reduce costs as marketplace accepts lower level of service, but can't become low-cost provider
10. Downsizing	Licensed for 1,000 beds, operating 700	Develop contingency plan for further downsizing

Exhibit 4. Ten Strategies Versus Present and Potential Initiatives: Rural Hospital.

Potential Strategies	Present Initiatives	Potential Longer-Range Initiatives
1. Differentiation on the basis of quality of care	Providing high quality for less complex cases; good reputation in market area	Emphasize personal care, convenience, and quality
2. Alternative delivery systems (HMOs and PPOs)	Contracting with HMOs & PPOs, a part of Intermountain	Negotiate better to hold prices
3. Diversification (spreading risks)	Rehabilitation hospital (30 beds)	
4. Vertical integration	Established urgent care center/clinic in neighboring community	Develop congregate housing, home health care; buy neighboring 200-bed nursing home
5. Aggressive marketing (market research, pricing, PR, advertising)	Advertising on billboards and in local newspaper; had community market survey	Develop program to keep patients from going to larger cities for medical care
6. Physician bonding (joint ventures, financial arrangements)	Actively recruiting physicians; no joint ventures	Continue to build medical staff
7. Centers of excellence (product lines)	None	None
8. Networking	Intermountain	Join regional system with other hospitals in area
9. Being a low-cost provider	Costs are average for rural hospitals in area	None
10. Downsizing	Closed 30-bed unit; operating 120 beds	Make contingency plan for closing additional beds

Table 14. Relevance of Health Care Strategies for Three Types of Hospitals.

Potential Strategies	Suburban Hospital in Large Metro Area Targeted by Major Chains	University Hospital, Tertiary Care	Small Hospital in Rural Area
1. Differentiation on the basis of quality of care	**	***	*
2. Alternative delivery systems	***	**	*
3. Diversification	***	**	*
4. Vertical integration	***	*	**
5. Aggressive marketing	***	**	***
6. Physician bonding	***	***	***
7. Centers of excellence (product lines)	***	***	—
8. Networking	***	**	***
9. Being a low-cost provider	***	—	*
10. Downsizing	**	**	***

*** Critically important; necessary for survival
 ** Important
  * Least important
  — Not relevant

Differentiation on the Basis of Quality of Care. Of the three, the teaching–tertiary care health system has the best chance of successfully implementing this strategy. It has a reputation for excellence in orthopedics and in the children's/OB area, and oncology is a major product line. Its affiliation with several medical schools brings it prestige in its market area.

The suburban health care system has a strong reputation within its market area for quality care, being the hospital of choice for 40 percent of the residents. However, the hospital continues to lose patients from its service area to other metropolitan hospitals, and it is not attracting as many patients from outside its service area as it would like. Several other metropolitan hospitals are marketing their centers of excellence, while the investor-owned chain hospitals in the area are relying on national brand-name identity. Although quality of care is important to the hospital's culture, it will be very difficult for this hospital to distinguish itself solely on the basis of this criterion.

The rural hospital can attempt to be known as a caring institution with an image of quality. However, dollars spent solely to improve the hospital's image are unlikely to pay off. Ensuring that the hospital receives positive word-of-mouth advertising is probably the most cost-effective outreach to persons living in this hospital's large, sparsely populated area.

Alternative Delivery Systems. The suburban health care system faces the biggest challenges in terms of developing an ADS strategy, and those challenges are numerous. In this market, having or not having ADS patients could play a key role in the hospital's occupancy rate. Should the suburban hospital agree to exclusive arrangements with selected ADS companies? Should it develop its own HMO? How can it network with other hospitals in the market area to provide adequate geographic coverage? How can this system motivate its medical staff to cooperate, when they can see big discounts, second opinions, and strong utilization review looming on the horizon? And how can the hospital resist the deep discounts requested by ADS firms?

The teaching hospital, meanwhile, has a different set of problems relative to ADS: maintaining margins and convincing employers of the value received from its more highly specialized services. ADS are not likely to present many issues to the rural hospital and its physicians, however, at least not for the next two to three years. As the sole provider in a large geographic service area, the rural hospital can be resistant to demands for discounting by ADS. It also gains no advantage by sponsoring ADS in its market.

Diversification. In health care there is a long list of diversification possibilities, but most represent relatively small ventures and are unlikely to affect the bottom line materially. Both the suburban and teaching hospitals described earlier are currently diversifying in terms of the proportion of their revenues coming from outpatient services and sources other than their inpatient business. But the "bed business" continues to provide all these two health care systems' profits, and it funds most of the new ventures; this is unlikely to change in the next two to three years (see Chapters Seven and Nineteen).

The typical rural hospital has only a limited number of diversification alternatives and cannot afford to take big risks in terms of committing funds to new ventures. This type of institution may be better off "sticking to its knitting."

Vertical Integration. Vertical integration is an interesting strategy, and one that was receiving considerable publicity at the time this manuscript was drafted. But can a local health care system or hospital realistically expect to be successful in vertical integration? In terms of backward integration (continuum of care), the answer is yes; but in terms of forward integration (a financially oriented strategy designed to control payers), our response is negative. Except under very unusual circumstances, few local systems can afford the forward integration strategy. It is costly, fraught with risks, and could actually result in fewer patients, especially if exclusivity arrangements are part of the strategy (see Chapter Eight).

If any of these hospitals has reason to try forward integration, it is the competitive suburban hospital. If it can aggressively start and control insurance programs, urgent care centers, primary care physician networks, and the like, it may be able to direct enough of the market to the hospital to increase dramatically its market share. We remain skeptical, however, that the potential benefits justify the commitment of capital, the long-term financial risk, or the possibilities of alienating a portion of the medical staff that accompany this strategy.

The teaching hospital should probably not invest in forward integration; it should concentrate on contracting with all possible ADS firms. It could, however, pursue backward integration—especially specialized services such as rehabilitation, alcohol and drug abuse treatment, and psychiatric care.

The rural hospital's best opportunities involve backward integration into services required by patients after they leave the hospital—rehabilitation and nursing homes, for example. The problem the rural hospital has is that its market may not be large enough to provide a consistent, high level of demand for either of these products.

Aggressive Marketing. We believe the secret to success in the marketing strategy lies in careful market segmentation (understanding the "pathways" used by various segments to get to the hospital or health care system), proper timing in terms of the product life cycle, and thorough research and analysis (both in anticipation of launching a major marketing effort and in monitoring the results). All three types of health care systems are capable of executing a successful marketing program in a cost-effective way.

It is clear that the teaching hospital should target physicians, both primary care and specialists, employers and their advisers (benefits consultants and brokers), and consumers. The thrust of marketing efforts to each of these segments and their numerous subgroups will vary, but will usually center on the theme of quality of care, high technology, and the attributes of the medical staff.

The suburban hospital's marketing program will be different. This hospital may be able successfully to communicate its warm, caring atmosphere, its location and convenience outlets, and one or two of its centers of excellence. It will often focus on primary care physicans and their referral network, consumers (especially women and the elderly), and employers via their health insurance sources (ADS and indemnity carriers).

As indicated earlier, the rural hospital's marketing can focus on enhancing work-of-mouth advertising and building the hospital's image in its community through public relations. Such a hospital may need little or no formal advertising but be able to generate substantial free publicity in local newspapers.

Despite the optimistic tone of these suggestions, we are not hopeful about most health care systems' ability to be successful in marketing—at least not to the extent that the funds invested in marketing will result in an equal or greater financial return to the system. For those health care systems that take the time to understand their markets, and the numerous market segments, the chances of success increase dramatically. For those who spend money on marketing, especially advertising, without clear-cut objectives, the marketing investment will often be wasted.

Physician Bonding. Nearly every health care system and hospital, regardless of the type of market it serves, must attempt physician bonding. This strategy includes joint ventures, special financial arrangements, use of doctors on governing boards, and making physicians part of the strategic planning process and partners in dealing with ADS. This strategy will complement all other competitive strategies and help to strengthen the identity of the hospital within the community.

The suburban hospital in particular has a great deal to gain from an aggressive approach to physician bonding. It should start by investing in its primary care physicians through referral services, medical office parks with attractive financial arrangements, and other initiatives. It should take the initiative in getting close to the early innovators among its medical staff. The very aggressive hospital under these circumstances will also find it worthwhile to get to know the early innovators on *competitors'* medical staffs, with the possibility that a significant group can be persuaded to change hospital affiliation.

Centers of Excellence. Although we have questions about the value of product line management and devoting resources to the development of centers of excellence, overall we believe that centers of excellence should be pursued by most suburban and urban health care systems and by all teaching and tertiary care hospitals. This strategy ties very strongly to the first strategy, differentiation on the basis of quality of care. Most hospitals have at least one product line they can build on to differentiate themselves from their competitors and use in resisting price-cutting efforts by ADS and others. This strategy may lend itself to focused marketing efforts that will likely have a more positive impact than programs that are less targeted.

The rural hospital has other ways to differentiate itself—location, convenience, a warm and caring atmosphere—and is likely to have more success emphasizing these attributes than attempting the center of excellence strategy.

Networking. As noted near the conclusion of Chapter Eight, networking is a low-risk strategy that should be seriously considered by nearly every type of health care system or hospital. It is especially important for rural hospitals, which stand to gain much from the benefits of large-scale purchasing of supplies (volume discounts) and access to capital, management expertise, and data on health care markets. It is also critical that suburban hospitals network to gain some of the advantages that are conferred to those competitors that are a part of a national chain, particularly the large investor-owned systems.

Being a Low-Cost Provider. A limited number of suburban and urban health care systems in each market area may be able to gain short-term advantage from being a low-cost provider, but most will not. Teaching hospitals, with their higher costs and more complex cases, will usually be above average in terms of their prices and costs. Rural hospitals do not often have the economies of scale needed to be low-cost providers; on the other hand, it is not as important for rural hospitals to pursue this strategy as it is for hospitals located in metropolitan areas, where the health care market is usually more competitive.

Figure 3. Establish Women's Health Program.

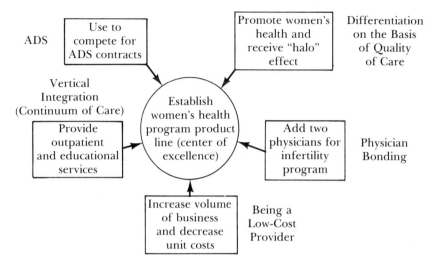

Downsizing. If the predictions of many health care industry observers are accurate, tremendous downsizing is in store for hospitals, yet very little has been reported about this strategy in terms of how to gain economic benefits. Downsizing is a strategy that nearly every hospital must consider, even if only to develop a contingency plan. Rural hospitals will experience the greatest difficulties in downsizing, since they tend to be small already, with few available options, yet even this group of hospitals will be under pressure to reduce the number of beds in use.

Complementary Strategies

Almost without exception, strategies that complement one another offer the best opportunities for local health care systems to gain competitive advantage. Based on the three case studies described earlier in this chapter, there are several examples of how a specific strategic initiative can interrelate within the overall context of the ten strategies.

Women's Health Center. Figure 3 shows how the establishment of a women's health program in one local health care system complements several other initiatives being considered. In this particular case, the women's health program would represent a new product line, with the potential of becoming a center of excellence within the market area. This would impact five other strategies of this system, as the figure shows.

Strategy	Impact of Women's Health Program Product Line
Differentiation on the basis of quality of care	Center of excellence can distinguish hospital on the basis of quality with women, one of the most influential market segments. There is potential for halo effect spilling over to other product lines. Hospital can become price leader rather than follower.
Physician bonding	By adding two OB/GYN doctors specializing in infertility, who received financial support to initiate the program, a hospital-based program is formed.
Being a low-cost provider	The primary objective of the women's health center is to attract patients to medical staff and hospital. Added volume improves efficiency and lowers costs; doctors become more proficient at managing care.
Vertical integration	Women's health program includes education, outpatient services, and counseling; hospital now offers a continuum of care, including primary care doctors.
ADS	The women's center is expected to appeal to employees and will help sell the local health care system to ADS firms, employers, and employees.

Establish HMO. IPA-model HMO described here was established by an acute care hospital and its medical staff. The primary reason, as far as the health care system was concerned, was

Figure 4. Establish HMO.

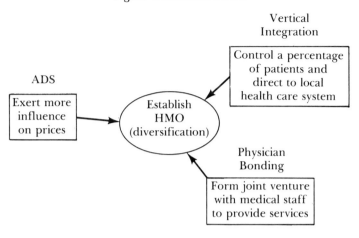

to diversify, to spread its risks. If the HMO does well in controlling utilization, the HMO investors will do well, but the doctors and hospitals will experience declines in business. Figure 4 shows how this initiative interrelates with three other strategies.

Strategy	Impact of HMO
ADS	By having some of its patients in its own HMO, hospital and medical staff can better maintain margins; they can negotiate with themselves.
Vertical integration	HMO fits into strategy of acquiring patients through ADS (forward integration).
Physician bonding	Perhaps the most important benefit is that medical staff members will retain and attract patients. Physicians will become joint venture partners.

Congregate Housing. In this example, a local health system established a 200-unit congregate housing facility (for seniors seventy-five and over) adjacent to the campus of its main hospital.

Figure 5. Establish Joint Venture.

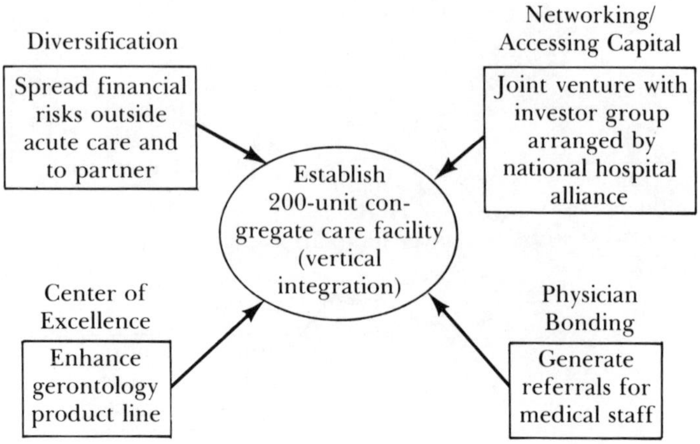

Most of the funds came from sources arranged by an alliance and included an investor group. Figure 5 shows how this vertical integration strategy (backward integration) relates to four other strategies.

Strategy	*Impact of Congregate Care Facility*
Diversification	It is hoped that the congregate care facility will be profitable and provide a financial return to the system. It spreads risks away from acute care.
Center of excellence	The hospital has a weak gerontology product line but intends to strengthen this area. Congregate care facility and programs for residents can be a building block toward creating a center of excellence in gerontology.
Physician bonding	The 200 units will generate patients for medical staff, thereby creating a larger user group.
Networking	The health care system has $3 million

at risk for this $18 million project; most of the dollars are from a mortgage arranged by a national alliance and private investors.

These are obviously only a small number of the possible combinations of strategies that can make sense at the local level. Choosing the right strategies for a particular health care system is the subject of the next chapter.

16

Strategic Planning

How, then, to chart the best course for a particular health care system? And how can strategic initiatives be designed in such a way that they really have a chance to be carried out? Charting a course, and then staying on it, is a challenging assignment in any fast-moving industry, and we expect it to continue to be particularly challenging in health care.

Charting a meaningful course of action means accomplishing the following:

1. Choosing and integrating the most appropriate of the ten health care strategies.
2. Developing the specific strategic initiatives most suitable to carry out the chosen broad strategies.
3. Communicating and implementing specific initiatives and the overall strategy.

As health care organizations adjust their decision-making styles toward a market orientation, they can benefit from what has worked in other rapidly changing industries, such as telecommunications, banking, and air travel. Still, health care is in some ways different than these other industries. First, the current decision-making environment in many health care systems makes it difficult to make decisions quickly. The decision-making structure is decentralized. CEOs, voluntary board members, physicians, and middle managers all have their own areas of decision-making responsibility—areas that evolved in a health care environment very different than that existing today.

To make matters worse, one side effect of destabilization is that there is often very little common ground in the perspectives of these different parties to the decision-making process. Many voluntary board members have yet to adjust to the emerging competitive environment. Some physicians are concerned that their health care system may be placing business ahead of service; yet other members of the medical staff are sizing up their hospitals as business competitors, partners, or sources of financing. Many health care system managers are worried that their physicians are insensitive to the pressures created by prospective payment; some managers express amazement when physicians accept economic incentives for referring their patients to another hospital.

This chapter discusses the strategic decision-making process within the health care system. How can lessons learned from other competitive industries and the realities of today's health care decision making be combined to arrive at a workable overall strategy? And what has to be done to ensure that the transition is made from an appropriate mix of strategies to successful implementation?

What to Expect from Strategic Planning

First, let us dispose of a few misconceptions about strategic planning. Strategic planning in a dynamic, competitive environment has almost nothing to do with traditional long-range planning or facilities planning. Many health care systems have long-range planning committees, and some of them believe that such groups are carrying out strategic planning. In reality, however, efforts to forecast and plan for future space and staffing needs represent only one small facet of strategic planning. This type of planning has only an indirect relationship to the development of a competitive strategy.

Just at the time health care systems are turning to strategic planning in droves, the concept of strategic planning is undergoing a long overdue reevaluation. Like many other management concepts, strategic planning has been highly touted, widely used, and often discarded. Corporations have enthusiastically installed planning departments that have created their own languages and bureaucracy. Consultants have made big fees from elaborate approaches based on "canned" matrices and flow charts. Thousands of bad decisions—for example, to limit achievement in an existing area of strength—have been made based on the "bigger picture." This is akin to a health care system neglecting its inpatient business because the experts and innovators say that the future of the industry is in outpatient services. The saddest part is that most of these abuses have been committed by aggressive organizations and smart people. Finally, however, a halt has been called. A wave of articles has recently appeared in *Fortune, Newsweek, Harvard Business Review,* and elsewhere critically reviewing current strategic planning practices and pointing up the differences between success and failure.

So what *is* good strategic planning? (Planning is challenging enough without repeating the mistakes of the past.) Eight characteristics of good planning are:

1. Strategic planning is participatory. The CEO plays a major role, but trustees, physicians, and managers are also involved throughout the process and in key decisions.
2. The planning process is market-driven. Data on market segments are developed up front, and market considerations are key throughout.
3. Middle managers are carefully prepared for strategic planning roles and included in the process from the beginning. Input from those closest to problems is sought out.
4. Qualitative information is given as much emphasis as quantitative data. Informed intuition of managers is drawn out and used.
5. Data and analyses emphasize the "nuts and bolts" of the business. Excessive reliance on abstract matrices is avoided.

6. There needs to be a "traffic cop," most often a consultant or key staff member, to force frank analysis of product lines or business ventures, avoid vague goals, reconcile data discrepancies, and keep the whole process moving.
7. Resulting strategies are aggressively "sold" to the organization.
8. Strategic planning is integrated with other management functions. Planning is never allowed to become a bureaucracy.

Each of these characteristics of good planning is discussed in greater detail below.

CEO Is Actively Involved. In our experience, a prerequisite of good strategic planning, as opposed to mediocre or even harmful planning, is the quantity and quality of CEO involvement. To begin with, the CEO has to be willing to take the risks associated with exposing internal weaknesses and external threats to trustees, physicians, and middle management. He or she has to be ready to contribute ideas and openly solicit opinions from others participating in the process. The CEO also has to devote considerable energy to pushing the process and then selling the results.

The CEO does not need to chair all meetings and be in total control of the process. This can be done by a chief operating officer, a director of planning, an up-and-coming assistant administrator, or a consultant. However, the CEO usually needs to participate actively in several of the task forces set up to support development of the plan.

Planning is Market-Driven. Competitive planning cannot begin with a financial or operations focus. It must start with a market focus—for example, the physician, employer, and consumer market segments we discussed in Chapters One, Two, and Three and elsewhere in this book. Detailed market segmentation, including a careful analysis and understanding of the ways in which customers come to the hospital or system, is a critically important element.

Middle Managers Are Involved Early. Many consultants believe that past managerial errors attributed to poor strategic planning often occurred either because those closest to the action and to creative solutions—the middle managers—were left out, or their innovative ideas were sacrificed to grandiose goal setting. We subscribe to this dual theory. So do, for example, Thomas Peters and Robert Waterman in *In Search of Excellence* (1982) and Robert Hayes in his *Harvard Business Review* article "Strategic Planning—Forward in Reverse?" (1985). One means of guarding against these pitfalls is early involvement of the up-and-coming creative thinkers in middle management. They need to be carefully coached in the role they should play (otherwise they will be frustrated and ineffectual) and given areas of responsibility. We make heavy use of task forces to get bottom-up input in our strategic planning efforts, and time and time again important contributions have come from middle management.

Subjective Information Is Valuable. It never ceases to amaze us that managers will ignore their hard-won "informed intuition" as to what is important in favor of critiquing and analyzing, in detail, those factors for which a larger data base is available or can be developed. In our experience, no industry is worse in this respect than health care. In general, the data available to health care managers are far more detailed and plentiful than those available in other industries. Nevertheless, there is a continuing obsession with getting still more data, and with deferring action until they are available (". . . but the product line categories aren't *right* yet"). Way down deep, most health care managers know the problems, whether they can quantify them or not.

Data Emphasizes the Nuts and Bolts of the Business. We spend a high proportion of our time in what some planners call internal assessment; we refer to this as *current business assessment.* Normally we assess all major hospital product lines and business ventures already under way. We have found that this type of analysis has double the value: it provides insights into the basic themes that characterize the organization and its goals, and it often leads to major changes in the ventures being examined. For example, in one strategic planning assignment we devoted substantial effort to analyzing a network of four minor emergency centers. No one in the health care system—staff or consultants—could figure out a way to reduce the losses from these centers. The nonfinancial contribution (number of referrals; community goodwill) made by two of the centers was also of questionable value. As a result, two of the centers were closed and the operations of the other two were modified to reduce their losses.

"Traffic Cop" Plays a Key Role. Coordinating planning efforts, deciding when to cut off the search for more data, ensuring that energy is not wasted on unproductive dreaming—these are the tasks of the facilitator. Facilitating strategic planning is part art, part science. Someone has to play this vital role. And this individual has to retain the respect and support of the CEO and the other participants throughout the strategy development process.

Strategies Are "Sold" to the Organization. There are a number of ways to "sell" strategies. For governing boards, retreats are an excellent approach. In our experience, governing boards are usually highly supportive of careful marketing and financially oriented planning, and they usually offer useful suggestions for fine-tuning the plan.

Physicians first need to be involved in one or more of the task forces or on a strategic planning executive committee. In addition, we use focus groups to seek physician input into the strategic planning process; all are invited to one of the sessions, although fewer than half will typically attend. Finally, dinner meetings with groups of forty to sixty physicians can be a useful mechanism to highlight major results of the plan, especially those portions of the plan that relate to doctors.

Employees can be briefed in a series of staff meetings. It is advisable that the CEO or a representative of top management attend these sessions to show support for the plan and to respond to questions.

Strategic Planning Is Integrated into the Management Process. If the previous seven steps have been carried out, this final step will usually follow quite naturally. It is often advisable to create a permanent strategic planning committee of the health system or hospital board, made up of a combination of trustees, physicians, and top-level managers. Periodic reviews of the capital budget, and its priorities, are a mechanism for continually evaluating the basic strategies agreed on as a part of the planning process. If a monitoring program has been established, this will continue to focus management attention on the implementation of the strategies. And, as discussed in Chapter Eighteen, tying the accomplishment of strategic objectives to an executive incentive compensation program is important.

Steps in Strategy Development

The strategic planning process can be formal or informal. Figure 6 illustrates the steps in such a process. The steps are generally the same in any competitive industry; they have been adjusted here to reflect the health care marketplace and the hospital's decision-making constituencies.

Current Business Assessment. The first step is an intensive self-examination. This is usually the most time-consuming part of the process. Internal marketing research is assembled—including current market shares and perceptions of quality by consumers, physicians, employers, and employees; current marketing efforts directed toward each major market (for example, consumers) and market segment (for example, seniors); and relationships between marketing and other activities within the health care system (product lines, new ventures). Medical staff internal trends often include age mix and geographic coverage by medical specialty; attitudes toward ADS, the hospital, and joint ventures; and capacity utilization within existing private practices. Physician concerns and attitudes are usually ascertained through interviews or focus groups. A comprehensive understanding of the past and current financial health of the organization is also developed.

Figure 6. Strategy Development Process.

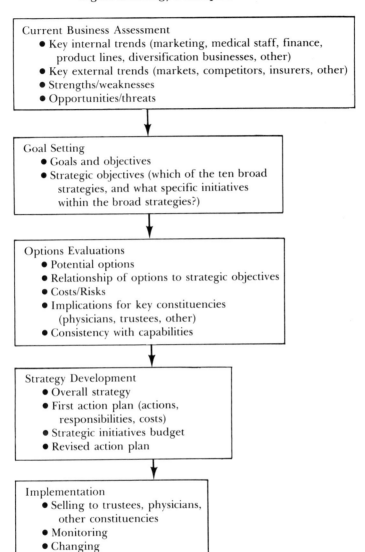

Current Business Assessment
- Key internal trends (marketing, medical staff, finance, product lines, diversification businesses, other)
- Key external trends (markets, competitors, insurers, other)
- Strengths/weaknesses
- Opportunities/threats

Goal Setting
- Goals and objectives
- Strategic objectives (which of the ten broad strategies, and what specific initiatives within the broad strategies?)

Options Evaluations
- Potential options
- Relationship of options to strategic objectives
- Costs/Risks
- Implications for key constituencies (physicians, trustees, other)
- Consistency with capabilities

Strategy Development
- Overall strategy
- First action plan (actions, responsibilities, costs)
- Strategic initiatives budget
- Revised action plan

Implementation
- Selling to trustees, physicians, other constituencies
- Monitoring
- Changing
- Reselling

Key external trends in marketing begin with anticipated actions by competitors, including ADS contracting and physician recruiting. Important external trends in the financial area include reimbursement trends, local employer conditions, the activities of health data commissions in publishing price information, and access to capital markets. Financial scenarios are often constructed based on alternative assumptions about future external conditions. The information is summarized in terms of strengths, weaknesses, threats, and opportunities.

Because decision making and implementation are shared, information must be shared. Physicians and middle managers participate in preparation of the current business assessment; trustees participate in its review. In our experience, a key to later success in strategy implementation is the degree of cross-communication of information at this point. For example, physicians and the chief financial officer, along with the marketing staff, must grapple with the marketing data.

We have been asked, "How can we involve our physicians in the details of our planning process? Once we let them in on what we're thinking, our competition will know our plans within twenty-four hours." Our response is "How can you afford *not* to involve them? How can you hope to get physicians to help carry out the strategic plan if they don't have a stake in it?" Admittedly, some information does have to be confined to those who can be trusted to maintain confidentiality, but as a general rule, the deeper the participation by physicians, the better the plan. This goes beyond the issue of buying in. It affects the quality of the plan and the chances for its successful implementation.

In formal strategic planning projects, the current business assessment is typically prepared by task forces that include physicians and often trustees. The task forces can be organized around those broad strategies that look most promising. For example, a strategic planning project might include four task forces: marketing, physician bonding, product lines/centers of excellence, and diversification.

Goal Setting. After the current business assessment is completed and task forces have identified strengths, weaknesses, threats, and opportunities, the goal-setting process can begin. At this stage of the strategic planning process, most health care systems and hospitals desire to have their trustees intimately involved.

Goals or mission statements should identify the "reasons for being" of the hospital or health system. Some trustees might argue that if the mission cannot be effectively met, the organization should no longer be in business. Statements of goals or mission are most useful in later phases of strategic planning, as a reference point. A trustee can challenge a strategy by asking, "Is this consistent with our mission?"

One pitfall in the goal-setting process is unrealistic statements of objectives. Our experience with trustees who have not grappled with the hard data in a current business assessment before setting goals is that they tend to be unrealistic. Without a firm grounding in the threats and constraints facing their institution, trustees tend to pontificate, to make expansive statements as to the lofty purpose of the health care system or hospital. In most cases, nothing of strategic importance is accomplished.

On the basis of the current business assessment and goals discussion, trustees and senior management will want to establish strategic objectives for the next several years. These objectives should respond to the threats and opportunities identified and be consistent with the mission. Objectives might be defensive ("protect market position," "clean up financial problems") or offensive ("establish certain product lines as regional centers of excellence").

Options Evaluation. The next stage of the process is to develop and evaluate alternatives for meeting the strategic objectives. Strategic planning should go beyond consideration of several options; it should establish an ongoing framework for evaluation. Our checklist of the factors to be considered in an evaluation of options follows.

1. *Does the option complement other strategic objectives?*
   • Complements more than one objective?

- Conceptual and future linkage, or tangible and immediate?

2. *Are the costs and risks acceptable?*
   - Pro forma projections reasonable?
   - Required capital available?

3. *What are the implications for key constituencies, such as physicians and trustees? Medical staff–board reactions?*
   - Acceptable to selective groups or all physicians?
   - Possible repercussions in terms of other actions?

4. *Is the option consistent with current or readily obtainable capabilities?*
   - Consistent with realistic appraisal of medical staff?
   - Skills and perspectives required for management available?

Strategy Development. Now is the time when priorities must be set. Trade-offs are often difficult. One simple technique that many health care systems find useful in categorizing the potential for existing or new product lines or businesses to contribute to an organization's financial situation is shown in Figure 7. This graphic display evaluates only two dimensions of the ranking process—potential revenues (volume) and profits. For example, those product lines or businesses in the upper left box have the least potential, while those on the lower right are the most promising.

A second tool that we find essential is the strategic initiatives budget. The strategic initiatives budget compares all of the most promising potential actions in terms of their costs and benefits. This approach is discussed in more detail at the end of this chapter.

Movement from strategy development to implementation begins with the development of the first action plan, which includes schedules, responsibilities, and budget. In our experience, the strategic initiatives budget is so useful in focusing priorities that the action plan often is revised after the budgeting step.

Implementation. As we have mentioned before, implementation begins with an aggressive selling of the plan within the

Figure 7. Ranking Options by Potential.

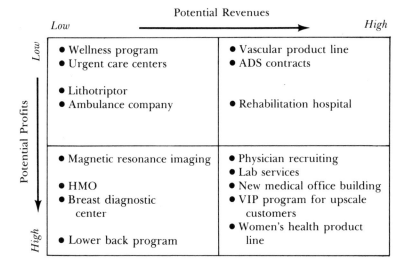

Potential Revenues

Low ————————————→ High

	Low	**High**
Potential Profits — Low	• Wellness program • Urgent care centers • Lithotriptor • Ambulance company	• Vascular product line • ADS contracts • Rehabilitation hospital
Potential Profits — High	• Magnetic resonance imaging • HMO • Breast diagnostic center • Lower back program	• Physician recruiting • Lab services • New medical office building • VIP program for upscale customers • Women's health product line

system. In a changing world, implementation also means monitoring progress, making adjustments to strategies, and reselling the adjustments.

There is no such thing as a *final* strategic plan. Implementation begins with a major campaign to sell the agreed-upon strategies. In this selling process, new ideas emerge and the strategies change. In monitoring implementation of the strategies, some will work and others will not. Again, adjustments are needed.

The Strategic Initiatives Budget

In discussing objectives to be met by a strategic planning effort about to be initiated, the chairman of the board of trustees said, "I want to be able to compare our investment alternatives. There are more needs and opportunities than we can possibly meet. Show us how we can compare various options and then make the best investment decisions." As a result of the chairman's demands, this particular health care system soon had its first long-term strategic initiatives budget, and it was a shocker. Realistic projections of needs and assumptions relative to potential liabilities incurred from ventures already entered into—a health park and a large senior housing cooperative—produced numbers far beyond the health care system's financial capabilities. This case is not unusual.

In our monitoring and review of health care industry publications, we have seen very little published on the subject of hospital capital budgeting. There are frequent articles and news stories about Medicare reimbursement of hospital capital costs but little on how hospitals plan their capital needs and select from among the many worthwhile projects usually available. In other industries, capital budgeting has been the subject of intense interest over the past twenty-five years, with a significant number of stories and articles appearing regularly in major business publications. The *Harvard Business Review,* for example, has provided numerous articles on how to compare alternative investment opportunities; this has been one of its most popular subjects.

In the competitive health care model, where it is necessary to make hard choices in the allocation of finite financial resources, the subject of budgeting for strategic initiatives will become increasingly important. Those organizations that begin the process soon, and continually update capital budgets as new data are available, will gain an important competitive advantage.

There are many variations on the strategic initiatives budget. Exhibit 5 is one example of how the ten-strategy analytical framework can be used to assess investment alternatives. The key to this type of approach is that it allows management and the governing board to assess whether or not the system's priorities are in balance, and it places capital expenditures, physician joint ventures, marketing dollars, and other forms of investment on an equal footing.

The size of the strategic initiatives budget depends on several issues—internally generated funds available, management's attitude toward taking risks, external networking and other financial alliances, and access to capital. How much can, or should, be borrowed? At what rates and under what conditions

Table. Comparison of Investment Alternatives, Next Three Years, Suburban Health Care System.

Potential Strategies	Specific Initiatives Proposed	Amount (Millions)	Potential Benefits
1. Differentiation on the basis of quality of care	• Buy new equipment/technology (3 years)	$4.0	Enhance image of quality with physicians and consumers
2. Alternative delivery systems (HMOs and PPOs)	• Invest in HMO to increase number of members	1.0	1,000 new members worth $300,000 to $600,000 in terms of value of HMO
3. Diversification (spreading risks)	• Add capital to wellness program	.5	Enhance image with community; no anticipated financial return
	• Establish new product lines for rehabilitation affiliate	1.0	Improve profitability of rehabilitation hospital by improving payer mix
4. Vertical integration	• Designate start-up funds for nursing home	4.0	Continuum of care; help "control" patients; respond to public need for nursing homes in area
	• Establish joint venture with psychiatric hospital	1.0	Continuum of care; also help develop a relationship with this organization
5. Aggressive marketing (market research, pricing, PR, advertising)	• Initiate 3-year, large-scale advertising and PR program	1.5	Increase patient-days by 2 percent (this will make a positive contribution to the bottom line)
6. Physician bonding (joint ventures, financial arrangements)	• Build new medical office building adjacent to main campus	7.0	Will add 40 new physicians to medical staff
	• Set up fund for buying/supporting PC practices	2.5	
7. Centers of excellence (product lines)	• Improve OB areas by adding 10 labor/delivery rooms	2.5	Enhance the opportunity to be the best with these improvements; attract younger obstetricians
8. Networking	• Invest in anticipated new venture through VHA	.5	Contingency fund assuming VHA comes up with new venture opportunities
9. Being a low-cost provider	• New computerized cost-accounting system	2.5	Know costs by product so can be more efficient and do better job in pricing, especially with ADS
10. Downsizing	• None	—	None

(restrictive covenants have turned out to be onerous for a number of hospitals)? What cash flow will be generated from operations? How much of this can be used for capital needs or debt service? These and other related questions are the subject of Chapter Seventeen.

17

Financing New
Strategic Directions

The chief financial officer of a 300-bed hospital shook us with his analysis of the hospital's financial prospects. "We're the equivalent of a 'mom and pop' operation," he said. "I don't think there's a place in the health care industry over the long haul for our kind of operation. We're either going to have to merge with another hospital to gain size, or consider selling out. We simply won't be able to go it alone."

Bernstein Research states it even more strongly, saying that the tax-exempt market will be in total chaos by 1988, and "virtually no free-standing not-for-profit hospital will be able to sell long-term bonds, unless the bonds are guaranteed by an insuring organization—and no insuring organization will be willing to guarantee any bonds, except perhaps those of the two major networks of hospitals, the Voluntary Hospitals of America and American Healthcare Systems (AHS). Even banks are likely to stop lending to hospitals. Hence, virtually all free-standing hospitals will have to sell out to for-profit hospitals, merge, or affiliate with a nonprofit system to avoid bankruptcy" (Abramowitz, 1985, p. 47).

Along with its strategic plan, every health care system, large or small, should have a comprehensive plan for generating the funds needed to meet its strategic objectives. The old days of simply floating another tax-exempt bond issue are fading fast; in the future there will be many more financing alternatives available, and a need to match more closely the type of financing with the strategic initiative (new product line, new business venture, equipment replacement, acquisition of a long-term care facility, and so on). The new era of health care financing will more closely correspond to the way other competitive industries raise money and avoid becoming too highly leveraged.

Of course, as in any other business, access to capital can evaporate or be blocked if the health care system or hospital begins to experience cash flow or earnings problems. Most lenders and bond rating agencies look at ability to repay a loan, not simply the size of an organization's net worth or financial reserves. Thus being able to access capital successfully depends on the hospital or health care system's financial performance, which in turn is dependent on keeping costs down, attracting patients, maintaining a favorable payer mix, achieving a reasonable spread between prices and costs, and enhancing its image for quality care.

Background on Health Care Industry Capital Needs

Since just after World War II, hospitals have relied on four major sources of capital: tax-exempt borrowing, direct grants from the federal government (as provided by the Hill-Burton Act), earnings and cash flow from depreciation, and philanthropy. The investor-owned systems also have access to equity capital.

Tax-Exempt Borrowing. Of the four major approaches to financing, borrowing on a tax-exempt basis has been by far the most important source of capital, representing 80 to 85 percent of the total. The dollar value of tax-exempt hospital bonds issued between 1975 and 1985 approached $80 billion (Cohodes and Kinkead, 1984, p. 114):

Year	Billions of Dollars
1976	$ 2.7
1977	4.7
1978	3.1
1979	3.2
1980	2.8
1981	4.6
1982	8.7
1983	9.1
1984	8.9
1985	30.5
Total	$78.3

The unusually high total for 1985—$30.5 billion—includes a substantial amount of advance refunding of existing debt.

By comparison, the Hill-Burton Act (formerly the Hospital Survey and Construction Act of 1946) provided $1.68 billion in matching funds for hospital construction projects between 1967 and 1972 and loan guarantees supporting another $1.45 billion in construction between 1972 and 1976 (Cohodes and Kinkead, 1984, p. 52). This program was discontinued in the late 1970s.

During this decade of relatively heavy borrowing by hospitals and health care systems, the ratio of long-term debt to equity increased from 55 percent to 64 percent (Healthcare Financial Management Association, 1977–1985).

Other Sources of Capital. It is estimated that over the past ten years, charitable contributions to hospitals ranged from $1 billion to $2 billion per year, or approximately $15 billion over the decade. Hospital earnings generated an estimated $50 billion over this same ten-year span.

Looking ahead, earnings in the hospital industry will probably flatten out or decline. Therefore, funds available from earnings will be in increasingly short supply; this will restrict the borrowing capacity of some health care systems. Philanthropy is not likely to increase for most hospitals; it has been a dependable source of funds, but future growth will be difficult. And, as noted above, direct grants from the federal government are no longer available.

Future Capital Needs. There are a variety of studies that have attempted to project the hospital industry's capital needs over the next decade; estimates range from $100 billion to $193 billion, with a best estimate of $100 billion to $120 billion by Cohodes and Kinkead.

Will this level of funding be available on either a taxable or tax-exempt basis? How can health care systems and hospitals improve their chances of attracting funding? Will other alternatives (for example, joint ventures with physicians, venture capital, leasing, real estate investment trusts) fill a meaningful part of the gap?

The Public Markets

Whatever we write about the status of tax-exempt financing for hospitals will be out of date by the time this book is published. For the past year, changes have taken place on a weekly, and sometimes on an hourly, basis.

Even though tax-exempt financing is still available to health care systems, there are no guarantees that it will remain in the good graces of Congress. Substantial sentiment remains, especially among congressional staff, to do away with this "subsidy" to the hospital industry.

In addition to the uncertainties surrounding future federal tax policies, there is a continuing policy debate about the appropriateness of not-for-profit hospitals, part of an industry with substantial excess bed capacity, having preferential treatment via tax-exempt financing. Herzlinger and Schwartz (1985), in a *Harvard Business Review* article, argued that ready access to tax-exempt financing has been a major contributing factor to high health care costs. Of course, the investor-owned chains argue that federal policy allowing not-for-profit hospitals to borrow on a tax-exempt basis puts tax-paying institutions at a competitive disadvantage.

There is also substantial evidence that hospitals and their capacity to service their debt are being judged by the same criteria as other industries (return on investment, debt leverage ratios, product line cost-accounting systems, and market-driven strategic plans). Ratings agencies and bond insurers are reevaluating their positions and becoming more selective. As a result, average bond ratings for hospitals are declining (American Hospital Association, 1986a).

Given the huge federal deficits of the 1980s, and the factors just discussed, it appears unlikely that not-for-profit hospitals will continue to have the same relatively free access to tax-exempt financing they enjoyed in the 1970s and through most of the 1980s. This does not mean that lending sources will not be available. In addition to the tax-exempt financing, many health care systems will be able to access the taxable bond market; however, borrowing will be more expensive and bonds will have shorter maturities. With interest expense likely to increase, a given level of earnings and cash flow will finance less debt. The overall result: less borrowing capacity for many not-for-profit hospitals.

Standard & Poor's Credit Week says that hospital use of the taxable market will not necessarily have an adverse impact on bond ratings. "Higher taxable interest rates and shorter maturities will reduce earnings and cash accumulation, resulting in retarded fund balance growth and increased leverage. Short maturities and balloon maturities will have a particularly negative impact. However, to the extent that the legal structure and maturity of taxable bonds resemble those of tax-exempts, impact on ratings will be minimal" ("Tax Reform Ails Not-for-Profit Hospitals," 1986, p. 15).

Characteristics of Losers. Cohodes and Kinkead have listed the characteristics of health care organizations that will fail in their efforts to tap external financing, and those that will succeed (1984, pp. 49 and 50). The "vulnerable" institutions will possess these characteristics:

- Poor payer mix and overdependence on cost or less-than-cost reimbursement
- Small size

- Bad debt ratio of more than 5 percent
- Location in an economically depressed area or an area where there is little or no population growth
- Inept management team
- Declining market share (low occupancy rate)
- Absence of internal cost control or of sophisticated management information system
- Inability to attract and retain new physicians and staff, resulting in an increasing average age of physicians and other staff members
- Large number of competitors in market area, some of them associated with sizable multihospital systems
- State and local government ownership
- Absence of thoughtful strategic planning and effective action to remedy identified problems

Winners. Conversely, the institutions that will be well situated to gain access to the capital markets will possess some or all of the following characteristics:

- Membership in an investor-owned or voluntary multihospital system
- Large size
- Location in a growing and attractive market area
- High occupancy rate
- Service predominantly to patients for whom third-party payers reimburse on the basis of charges
- Possession of a substantial endowment fund
- Ability to generate net revenues from operations
- Insulation from competitive pressures by serving as a teaching and referral center
- A competitive and far-sighted management team supported by a sophisticated information system and a directed strategic planning process
- Bad debt ratio of less than 5 percent
- Ability to generate substantial nonoperating revenues

The two major rating agencies, Moody's Investors Service and Standard & Poor's Corporation, apparently give as much or more weight to local market conditions and the strategic initiatives being employed by a local health care system as they do to financial measures. Robert Yagi, vice-president and manager of hospital ratings for Moody's, says that he gives serious consideration to marketplace factors (competition, economic trends), admission trends, and outpatient volume (presentation at Goldman, Sachs seminar on health care financing, Bretton Woods, N.H., Sept. 23, 1986). Along the same lines, Jan Weiss, vice-president of health care finance, Standard & Poor's, prefers to see a health care system with strategies designed to reach its local market area. These could include vertical integration, although ownership of large HMOs may add to the risk. Weiss also points out that while certain aggressive strategic initiatives may lead to a short-term reduction in bond ratings, the longer-range impacts may be positive (Goldman, Sachs seminar, Sept. 23, 1986). Both Yagi and Weiss agree that if the local health care market is thriving, and a health system's strategies are well-designed to serve the market, financial success will follow.

Importance of Size in Accessing Capital. Although we do not believe that a limited number of "supermeds" will dominate the health care industry, we feel confident that in the future, size will become a more important factor in accessing capital. Local health care systems built around a single small to midsized acute care hospital (500 beds or smaller) will simply not have the financing options that are available to larger organizations.

"Full-service, stand-alone hospitals are rapidly becoming a thing of the past—about as relevant to today's health care reality as Norman Rockwell's doctor paintings" (Mantel, 1986, p. 70). This assessment seems to us to overstate the problem, but it does focus on the issue of small to midsized health care systems' ability to access capital.

We sense increasing interest among local health care systems and hospitals in merging with other systems. There are many reasons for considering merger—to increase market coverage or market share, diversification, vertical integration, economies of scale—but one of the key factors is to increase access to capital.

Membership in one of the alliances may partially offset the negative aspects of being small. But in the new era (through the mid-1990s), larger organizations will have an advantage in that they are more likely to attract the appropriate kinds of capital needed to carry out their strategic objectives.

Teaching and Tertiary Care Hospitals. We are not as optimistic, in the short term, about the teaching and referral center hospitals' ability to attract financing. As noted in our discussion of the low-cost provider strategy (Chapter Thirteen), institutions will experience increased difficulty in signing contracts with price-sensitive HMOs and PPOs. Until the various prospective payment systems are revised to give weight to severity of illness, teaching hospitals will have an increasingly difficult time maintaining their earnings and cash flow.

The CEO of one large teaching hospital told us, "We have enough cash on hand or cash flow to get us through the next three years. Yes, I'm concerned about our long-term ability to access the capital markets, but I can't look that far ahead. Who knows what rules will be in place at that time? All I know is that if we can do a good job over the next two to three years, it will increase our chances of gaining access to the debt market."

Advantages of Networking. For those health care institutions most likely to gain access to the capital markets, Cohodes and Kinkead's first characteristic—membership in one of the large alliances, such as Voluntary Hospitals of America (VHA) or American Healthcare Systems (AHS)—is likely to be an advantage. VHA, through American Health Capital and VHA Enterprises, is exploring and implementing a number of options. For example, American Health Capital is attempting to find a major joint venture partner to work with the large number of VHA hospitals interested in long-term care. VHA Enterprises is joint venturing a variety of ambulatory ventures (outpatient surgery centers, mobile imaging, home health care) with member hospitals; this provides outside equity capital for not-for-profit hospitals. American

Health Capital also arranged a letter of credit from Mellon Bank in Pittsburgh for those member hospitals tapping the tax-exempt markets. Both of the biggest alliances say that finding new ways to make capital available to their members is a top priority.

In another example, SunHealth, a large, regional multihospital alliance located in Charlotte, North Carolina, has developed a pooling strategy in order to enhance its member hospitals' access to capital. "SunHealth in 1985 initiated for the network the strategy of pooling several hospital tax-exempt financings into one composite bond issue, thereby reducing issuance costs per participant and obtaining highly favorable terms. The initial composite bond issue in 1985 totaled $62.8 million and involved six hospital organizations in three states and six different issuing authorities" (SunHealth, 1986, p. 11).

Other, Nontraditional Approaches to Accessing Capital

We expect that, in the next three to five years, the health care industry will find a number of innovative ways to access capital from the private sector. In addition to the taxable markets, commercial paper, and private placements, these innovations include a wide variety of joint ventures between hospitals and their medical staffs, joint ventures between not-for-profit and for-profit systems, real estate investment trusts, and sale and lease-back of property and equipment. In certain cases, public funds may also be available through the conversion of not-for-profit hospitals to public status. This is most likely to happen in rural areas.

The *Wall Street Journal* reported that real estate investment trusts are flourishing in the health care industry, and cited Beverly Enterprises, Healthcare International, Meditrust, Inc., and National Medical Enterprises (NME) as the sponsors (Rundle, 1986a, p. 6). NME established Health Care Property Investors, Inc., a real estate investment trust (REIT), to acquire health care facilities. The new entity raised $77.2 million in equity capital in April 1985 ("NME-Established REIT Gets $77.2 Million in the Offering," 1986, p. 65). It is our understanding that this REIT will invest in the facilities of both not-for-profit and investor-owned hospitals.

In a similar vein, Abbott-Northwestern Hospital in Minneapolis has organized a REIT to provide alternative sources of financing for not-for-profit hospitals. It is reported that the REIT, which would attract its funds from private sources, was initially capitalized at $100 million.

We believe that sale and lease-back, or straight leasing arrangements, will become much more common as health care systems expand. The repeal of the investment tax credit, formerly available only for equipment leased to for-profit organizations, will make it more attractive for investors to lease equipment to not-for-profit hospitals (Traska, 1986, p. 56).

The product life cycle concept, discussed in Chapter Nine, is also useful in deciding what kind of capital is most appropriate. For example, in the start-up phase, the best sources of capital may be equity from joint venture partners (physicians, for example) or commercial bank loans with health care system guarantees. As the volume of sales increases and the new venture develops a track record, it may be possible to attract venture capital or to have a private placement. The key is to match the financing with the current positioning and prospects of the venture in the same way other industries have done.

Tapping Equity Capital

Edward Malstrom of Merrill Lynch believes that hospitals' entry into the equity market is inevitable. "The nonprofits cannot continue to rely entirely on the debt market," he asserts. "Those hospitals that have management and control of patient flow will potentially convert to a for-profit status and sell stock. Others will access the equity market through a for-profit subsidiary. It's just going to happen" (Sandrick, 1986, p. 20).

Merging or selling to an investor-owned chain is a more frequently discussed alternative for accessing capital, and it has been used by a number of hospitals in recent years (Wesley Medical Center in Wichita and Presbyterian–St. Lukes in Denver are two of the best-known examples).

In reviewing the four large investor-owned chains, the differing philosophies and strategies relative to interest in acquiring hospitals are marked:

- Humana's strategy is focused on its Humana Care Plus health plans and its network of physician-staffed centers, and their tie to Humana-owned hospitals. Humana is not involved in hospital management or other types of facilities (long-term care, rehabilitation, or psychiatric facilities). Nor does Humana appear to be interested in acquisition of hospitals.
- Hospital Corporation of America (HCA), the largest of the four, is oriented toward physicians, and is heavily involved in hospital management. It is also in the psychiatric hospital business. It continues to be interested in acquisition, but on a limited scale.
- National Medical Enterprises (NME) is more diversified and is heavily invested in long-term care facilities. NME does not appear to be placing as much emphasis on health insurance plans as the other three chains, nor does it have a strategy of aggressively acquiring acute care hospitals; in fact, NME recently sold several of its acute care hospitals.
- American Medical International (AMI) is stressing integrated health systems in selected markets and is acquiring hospitals, on a selective basis, in target markets.

A review of the annual reports of these four investor-owned systems shows that in 1985, equity capital was $4.9 billion, up $3.1 billion since 1981. Long-term debt was $6.6 billion in 1985, compared with $3.0 billion in 1981. Total financial resources generated between 1981 and 1985 from long-term debt and increased equity capital totaled $6.7 billion. At the same time, the four large chains improved their balance sheets by substantially reducing the ratio of long-term debt to equity; debt was 130 percent of capital in 1985 versus 170 percent of capital in 1981.

What is the capacity of these four investor-owned systems to acquire not-for-profit hospitals? A VHA task force studying this issue in early 1985 concluded that the four systems could devote $400 million to $500 million per year to the purchase of new facilities, and that each company could acquire at least one major hospital per year. If it fits their strategic objectives, however, the major investor-owned chains have the financial capacity to be more aggressive than VHA anticipates. The additional capital (long-term debt and equity) raised between 1981 and 1985—$6.7 billion—would finance sixty-seven acquisitions of $100 million each. By raising even more equity capital, potential funds available for acquisition could be increased even more.

Even though the financial capability exists for a significant number of acquisitions of midsized and large acute care hospitals, we believe the evidence supports the viewpoint that the investor-owned chains will be highly selective in the hospitals they acquire. They will attempt to dominate certain attractive markets, targeting their efforts. Hospitals finding themselves with low occupancy levels, poor earnings (or losses), or an unattractive market location will probably not have merger or acquisition by one of the large investor-owned systems as an option to fall back on.

John E. Curley, president of the Catholic Health Association, agrees that investor-owned chains are unlikely to acquire large numbers of not-for-profit hospitals. He noted that in the past five years, there have been fewer than five takeovers of Catholic institutions. "The so-called threat of the investor-owned chains that we've been hearing about for six or seven years is a myth," Curley said ("CHA President: The For-Profit Threat Is a Myth," 1986, p. 8). We agree; it appears that the investor-owned chains will be very selective in their acquisitions, making sure that any hospitals acquired fit into their integrated health care clusters.

An editorial in *Modern Healthcare* in late 1985 came to the same conclusion: the big investor-owned chains are virtually out of the acquisition market. "It may be too late for independent hospitals to sell to not-for-profit or investor-owned hospital chains. . . . To be a candidate for acquisition, a hospital has to be in a metropolitan area or region that a chain is trying to dominate. The chains are vertically integrating in growth markets, establishing clusters of hospitals, freestanding primary care and diagnostic facilities. Many are starting preferred provider organizations, health maintenance organizations or traditional health insurance companies" ("Alliances Need Members' Support," 1985, p. 5).

If the increasing financial resources of the investor-owned chains are not used to acquire large numbers of hospitals, what *will* these resources be used for? We agree with the editorial above; they are likely to be used to finance vertical integration as a part of an overall strategy designed to dominate targeted markets.

Accessing Capital: Implementation

Developing a long-term plan of action for accessing capital has to be a top priority for most if not all not-for-profit health care systems and hospitals. As is the case with cost reimbursement, the good old days of almost unlimited access to low-cost debt capital are gone. At the same time, financial needs for modernization, new equipment, and new ventures are reaching an all-time high. A very serious capital crunch is here for many organizations, and that crunch will be a primary factor if the oft-predicted shakeout in the hospital industry occurs.

In this chapter we have described several of the alternatives available, including continuing to use the tax-exempt financial markets; additional options will most certainly evolve as the tax laws change and as not-for-profit health care systems find creative ways to attract capital. Those hospitals or health care systems that are members of alliances such as VHA and AHS appear to have an advantage. These two alliances have the organizational structure (for-profit subsidiaries that can go public) and the expertise to make a significant contribution to the capital needs of member hospitals and health care systems.

In the short term, health care systems can greatly enhance their chances of success by developing, and continually updating, their systems for evaluating and choosing among various capital-intensive projects or new business opportunities. This is not the same as compiling a list of projects and comparing them against the system's debt limit or borrowing capacity. We are suggesting the need for rigorous analysis of the costs versus benefits and a ranking of the wide variety of options, ranging from a new addition to the physical plant to recruiting physicians to earmarking more money for marketing.

We do not view the investor-owned chains as a threat to the viability of the not-for-profit sector of the health care industry. Rather, we see them as a potential source of equity capital for a limited number of hospitals located in metropolitan areas targeted for expansion by the major proprietary systems. For the vast majority of not-for-profit hospitals, however, it is unlikely that this option will be available.

On the future of financial resources for health care systems, it should be noted that there is a large industry segment dedicated to maintaining the capital flow to health care organizations. This highly trained and motivated group includes investment bankers, accountants, attorneys, bond insurers, and others who have successfully combined their efforts in the past to raise huge sums of new money for the health care industry. This group will not stand still; it can be expected to continue to develop innovative approaches on behalf of client health care systems.

In summary, our primary concern over access to capital is not with the supply of funds; we believe that substantial financial resources will continue to be available to the health care industry. Availability of capital will be less democratic, however. The larger systems with a track record of success and well-developed strategic plans will be able to attract the capital to implement their plans. Smaller organizations located in weaker markets, and with declining earnings, will be virtually shut out of the capital markets. The result: more mergers and acquisitions, and some failures.

18

Making the Hard Choices: Top Decisions and Leadership

Gary Strack, president of the Orlando Regional Medical Center, likens a hospital to a university in terms of the need to deal with the medical staff (professors) and the governing board in the decision-making process. "It's organized anarchy," says Strack. "We have multiple objectives, often at cross-purposes. We have unclear technology; we can't predict where the next major breakthrough will occur. And we have different players (physicians and trustees) going in and out of the hospitals' decision-making process" (interview with the authors, Orlando, Fla., July 18, 1986). As a result, the job of the hospital or health system CEO is often precarious, especially if he or she gets caught between physicians and the governing board. Furthermore, the decision-making process is cumbersome.

Many industry observers believe that the present system of governance of not-for-profit health systems and hospitals is unworkable. The boards are too large and cumbersome in terms of their ability to respond to competition; the decision-making process takes too long; the role of the health system CEO is not strong enough vis-à-vis the board. The result: a significant competitive disadvantage for health care institutions structured along traditional lines (Johnson and Johnson, 1986).

Kenneth Abramowitz raises serious questions about hospital trustees; he says that "trustees leave their brains in the office" when they attend hospital committee and board meetings (presentation entitled "Future of Healthcare Delivery in America" made at Colorado Hospital Association seminar, Denver, Colo., Jan. 7, 1986). Abramowitz is not implying that trustees lack intelligence or commitment to their responsibilities but that they are uncertain about the appropriate value system for decision making at the hospital. What mission or goals does the hospital hope to achieve? Are trustees to make decisions from the viewpoint of what would be good for the community or purely on the basis of impacts on the health care system's bottom line? The competitive environment—with declining demand, the end of the cost-reimbursement payment system, and concerns over access to capital—has focused attention on the bottom line as a driving force in decision making.

This chapter deals with decision making in the board room of future health care systems. When the CEO and his or her staff have evaluated their strategic options and have a plan of action, will governing boards make the hard choices necessary to move ahead?

The Evolution of Health Care Management

As the health care environment has changed, so has the role of health care decision makers. Broadly stated, the role and mission of not-for-profit community hospitals has evolved in three phases: the era of charity, the era of expansion, and the era of competition. In the first phase, which lasted until the early 1950s, hospitals were mainly charitable institutions that attempted to provide care to individuals, most of whom did not have health insurance and lacked the ability to pay. Hospital managers were, first and foremost, social servants. Hospital trustees were effectively patrons of a charitable organization; they often underwrote capital improvements and the costs of operating the hospital.

The increase in health insurance coverage—along with the major social reforms of the 1960s, particularly Medicare and Medicaid—drastically changed hospital operations (Starr, 1982). From the mid-1960s through 1985 (the second phase in the evolution of not-for-profit hospitals), reimbursement from private and government sources greatly increased hospitals' access to capital for construction of new facilities. These changes resulted in a dramatic reduction in the relative importance of philanthropy to overall revenue for the vast majority of community hospitals.

The changes during this expansionary period also caused major shifts in the role of health care managers and board members. Health care management became a professional discipline. Hospital boards lost their earlier bottom-line focus and shifted to the cost-plus mentality common to so many federal programs (Ginzberg, 1986, p. 760). As hospitals grew in size and complexity, trustees were called upon to play a more active governance role, including the establishment of policies relating to quality of care, credentialing of the medical staff, and monitoring of financial performance.

In the late 1970s and early 1980s, toward the end of health care's expansionist period, diversification became the theme for many of the nation's best-regarded health care systems. Not-for-profit hospitals were now just one element of health systems, along with real estate and other for-profit subsidiaries and related enterprises. Health care system CEOs increasingly delegated the management of hospitals to subordinate administrators. Hospital boards often evolved into interlocking networks of boards for the various subsidiaries of the health care system.

Each of these first two phases in the evolution of not-for-profit hospitals has taken both managers and board members further away from health care's basic products and services, and further from the consumer. Each stage has created more and more decentralization of authority, leading to a more complex and interlocking decision-making process. These are not the characteristics of management and decision making in other rapidly changing industries, such as telecommunications, finance, and high-tech manufacturing.

But the expansionary period, based on cost-based reimbursement and nearly unlimited access to capital, has ended. The point of demarcation was 1984, although the shift began a year or two before that time when prospective payment for hospital services by Medicare was initiated. The competitive period—the third phase—can be expected to last well into the 1990s.

As the importance of the hospital in the delivery of health care has changed, so has the role of trustees. In their initial role, trustees were patrons of the institution and not actively involved in management. Within the past four years, however, health care system trustees have become increasingly involved in various aspects of complex decision making within the fast-changing environment.

The Job of Trustee

The chairman of the board of trustees of a midsized hospital was in our offices to discuss the characteristics of a CEO that his board was seeking to head the hospital's holding company. "I don't see how the voluntary governing board for nonprofit hospitals is going to survive," he said. "The job is just too time-consuming and demanding; the health care business has gotten too complex." He went on to say that, in its reorganization in 1980, the hospital had created eight new boards in addition to the hospital and holding company boards (for a total of ten separate entities, each with its own governance structure).

Governing boards of not-for-profit institutions are in a difficult and often complex position. Usually representing a broad spectrum of business and community leaders, trustees typically bring a variety of perspectives and expertise to the decision-making process. Such variance in knowledge may ultimately enhance the board's decisions. Often, however, voluntary hospital board decisions require a lengthy consensus-building process. Two factors often contribute to board delays: a mission statement and strategic plan that are not clearly understood, and limitations on board members' time.

Trustees of not-for-profit health care systems and hospitals are unique in the responsibilities they carry out on behalf of the institution and community. They have the power to sell or merge their system or hospital with an investor-owned chain or with another not-for-profit system. They can also close a hospital. They decide which physicians may practice at the hospital, and under what rules. They hire and fire the health care system CEO. They allocate capital resources and approve annual operating budgets. In many systems, they take the lead in efforts to increase philanthropy. They establish the hospital's pricing structure and determine its competitive posture. Ultimately, they are responsible for maintaining the high quality of medical care in their hospital.

So what is the trustee of today like? How is he or she handling the pressure of health care destabilization?

Reasons for Serving. According to our recent national survey of trustees, the two most common reasons for serving on a hospital governing board are a desire for community service and an interest in the hospital and health care industry. (This survey was carried out in conjunction with *Trustee* magazine in January 1986; statistics cited in the following pages are from this source.) Just over 25 percent of all trustees surveyed cited community service, and 21 percent indicated an interest in health care. Beyond these two reasons, responses were fragmented: 6 percent work in hospital administration and are on the board, 4 percent once worked in a hospital and developed an interest in the institution, 6 percent are interested in hospital survival, 6 percent are physicians selected as medical staff representatives, and 6 percent know a board member or hospital CEO and were invited to participate as a trustee.

Rewards. Once on a hospital board, nearly always as an unpaid volunteer, trustees find that their major rewards are helping the hospital succeed (18 percent), meeting community needs (15 percent), being part of a dynamic industry (14 percent), involvement in decision making (14 percent), participation with other professionals (8 percent), contributing to quality care (7 percent), and the personal challenge (7 percent). The following are typical of the comments we received from trustees: "I like having a part in keeping our hospital the best and most caring in town"; "the opportunity to be a part of an ever-growing, ever-changing, high-tech teaching hospital"; "an opportunity to be associated with a very important social institution in a time of great change socially, politically, and technologically."

Time Spent. The average trustee spends six to ten hours per month in board and committee meetings and in other hospital-related activities. Just over one-third of trustees, however, say that they spend the equivalent of two full days—or more—per month on hospital business. It is not surprising that the time commitment is viewed by trustees as the biggest negative factor in attracting new trustees and in retaining those already serving on governing boards.

Length of Service and Occupation. Most trustees have served their institution for three years or longer. The largest proportion (21 percent) are corporate executives. Also well represented on trustee boards are physicians (16 percent), independent business people (14 percent), bankers (11 percent), attorneys (6 percent), educators (5 percent), and clergy or others associated with religious organizations (5 percent). Nineteen percent of the trustees responding to the survey are retired.

The physician representation on hospital boards varies substantially from case to case. For example, the investor-owned chain National Medical Enterprises has a policy of 50 percent (or more) physician representation on its local boards.

Trustees' Willingness to Compete. As we view the health care industry, we have serious concerns for the future economic viability of health care systems whose trustees do not recognize the numerous change factors discussed earlier in this book and in the final chapter. Yet in the meetings we attend and in our discussions with trustees, CEOs, and physicians, we rarely detect a sense of urgency about the situation. There seems to be an attitude of "It can't happen to us," or business as usual.

Many health care system trustees are sitting by while members of their own medical staff establish new ventures designed to compete with some of the organization's most profitable activities (outpatient surgery, emergency services, various diagnostic services). We agree with the speaker at an American Hospital Association seminar who said, "If you don't want to fight for your hospital's business, resign from the board and let someone in who will do the job" (Rosenfield, 1986).

In general, however, we find that once trustees come to accept the changes in today's health care environment, they adjust relatively quickly. We see a remarkable change in many trustees' grasp of the industry, in their willingness to compete, and in their ability to integrate market-driven concerns into their policy analysis and decision making.

Inside the Board Room

When we were new board members, a thoughtful veteran took us aside to explain the realities of a board meeting. "You see," he said, "there are really two meetings going on at once. Down there with the CEO are the board members who understand what's going on, particularly with finances. At this end, we have the physicians, the fund raisers, and the religious representative."

Over the past six years, we have observed substantial change in the way voluntary hospital boards conduct their business. There are much greater expectations for market and economic analysis in support of funding requests for strategic initiatives such as new business ventures or capital improvements. Trustees are more inclined to put CEOs and senior health care system staff at financial risk through meaningful incentive compensation programs. And trustees are taking a tougher look at existing programs and services that fail to contribute to the bottom line.

Like any decision-making body, health care governing boards typically have a few very influential members. If these board members have done their homework, most of the initiatives they support will be funded. These influential board members tend to ask more questions and be more involved in discussions. On the other hand, many passive board members are silent on most issues.

With health care governing boards composed of members from diverse backgrounds, areas of expertise are acknowledged. For example, a home builder's opinions will count heavily in discussions of construction or real estate projects. The opinions of CPAs, bankers, attorneys, and other professionals will be heavily weighted on matters within their areas of expertise.

On an increasing number of boards, the physician voice is now being heard loud and clear. In both not-for-profit and investor-owned systems, the physician board member often plays a major role, expecially in issues related to the medical staff and physician bonding. Physician board members are being asked to take positions on physician joint ventures, act as liaison with key members of the medical staff, and serve as a sounding board for that increasingly rare commodity, "the collective opinion of the medical staff."

In the final analysis, we see the voluntary board system adjusting to change, not succumbing to it. A few members of most boards are responding to the challenge of keeping up with the changing health care business. Under the pressure of the increasing pace of complex decision making, we see fewer decisions made by broad consensus and more by specialization and delegation.

The CEO's task in working with the board is becoming more difficult. He or she must bridge the board members' specialties and help to sustain an appropriate policy balance. As a result, it is increasingly difficult for the CEO to stay in control. More and more frequently, specialist board members may be more up to date on a particular issue than is the CEO.

This change in the CEO's role can be healthy. Conceptually, today's CEOs have two choices for trying to instill market responsiveness and rapid decision making in their organization. They can generate and champion new ideas and take a strong role in leading the board to agreement on a coherent set of strategies. Or they can actively foster innovation by encouraging better communications among middle managers, who are close to the market, and the board. They can free up their daily schedule, do management in part by wandering around, and stimulate more and more regular contact between both physician and business board members and the CEO's staff.

As noted earlier, trustees of not-for-profit hospitals or health care systems experience problems with the changing value system in health care (with its increased emphasis on financial implications, decreased emphasis on community service). But this is changing, and we expect a continued shift in emphasis toward market and financial considerations.

In some organizations, trustees still see their primary responsibility as philanthropy. At a recent conference we heard a trustee (and chairman of the hospital's finance committee) say, "Our primary job as trustees is to raise money. We can do a lot better than we've been doing. Trustees should stay out of management; we don't know what we're doing." For most governing boards, we disagree; trustees' responsibilities go well beyond raising money to include credentialing the medical staff, reviewing the annual budget and strategic plan, and monitoring CEO performance.

A bank president we know has just completed his tour of duty as a board member. "I'd think twice about doing it again. Being on that hospital board is becoming too much like running this bank." He said this, however, with the touch of a grin. We know he would do it again.

Management in the 1990s

In order to compete effectively in the 1990s, health care systems and hospitals have to continue to adjust their management styles and recruit new talent. With respect to CEOs, we believe that the premium on good leadership will never be higher. We believe that all health care systems, including not-for-profits, will be well advised to develop competitive incentive structures—including performance-based incentives—to attract and retain the managerial talent this industry needs.

We believe that the typical health care system will have no choice but to recruit management selectively from market-driven businesses outside the health care industry. This, combined with a massive management training effort, will be required to translate strategic initiatives into market-driven business practices.

Recruitment of trustees will take on a new dimension. Persons with leadership potential already serving on trustee boards will need to be prepared for the assumption of greater responsibilities. The health care system that plans ahead in its trustee recruitment and education will gain a competitive advantage.

Here is our list of the personal characteristics of trustee leadership of the future:

• *Ability to think strategically.* Our experience is that not everyone, not even all successful business executives, are good at this kind of thinking. Being able to project ahead in terms of the competitive environment a health care system will have to face, and the multiplicity of options available, is a much-needed skill.

• *Objectivity.* We do not disagree that trustees need to be loyal to their institution, its management, and programs—but not to the extent of losing their objectivity. Evidence of objectivity can be seen in the types of questions trustees ask and the kinds of analysis they require of staff in support of the hospital's strategic planning and decision-making process.

• *Respect of medical staff and community.* Most trustees say they are becoming more and more involved in medical staff issues and physician-hospital joint ventures. Competition, increased market penetration by ADS, and the need for capital and risk-sharing partners will increase this part of a trustee's responsibilities. Credentialing issues are likely to become much more complex as well, with a large number of physicians and support personnel likely to seek admission to the medical staff. There may also be the need to dismiss some of the present physicians on the staff.

• *Health care industry understanding.* As we said, it appears to us that a large number of trustees grasp the fundamentals of the industry and enjoy the challenge. But as the industry becomes increasingly fragmented and complex, maintaining an adequate understanding will take more time. Therefore, a valuable trustee will spend more than the six to ten hours per month that is now the average.

• *Willingness to take risks.* John Horty, an attorney and frequent speaker at health care seminars, says, "The trustee of the past was a conservator of assets. Today, any trustee who is not willing to take risks stands to lose hospital assets. There are no guarantees of profitability, but trustees have to move ahead anyway" (1986, p. 103).

• *Proper balance between policy and day-to-day management.* Our experience is that many health care systems and hospital CEOs attempt to use their trustees (or at least those in board leadership positions) in areas that relate to day-to-day management. The proper balance, as frequently discussed in *Trustee* magazine, is critical; trustees have their hands full in staying knowledgeable about the local health care marketplace, ensuring that broad strategies and policies are developed and carried out, and reviewing overall performance.

These characteristics are not dissimilar from an ideal board member in any industry. A board comprised of individuals possessing these leadership characteristics is likely to have a productive and professional relationship with its CEO, and it should be able to adapt a style of operation that is appropriate for the institution within a competitive environment.

19

Future Prospects
for the Health Care
Industry

The CEO of a health care system who had just returned from an Estes Park Institute seminar in Sun Valley, Idaho, told us, "I've never seen so much uncertainty in the minds of seminar partici- pants as to where our industry is headed. Even the speakers, who normally agree on most health care matters, were divided on several issues. For example, will vertical integration be successful? Will ten or fifteen 'supermeds' dominate the industry? There was a lot of disagreement on these and other questions."

We believe that the period of destabilization in the health care industry is ending, and that the rapid changes of the past four years provide numerous clues about what the future will bring to the industry. In an attempt to describe the health care future as we see it emerging, we propose ten health care "myths" and ten "economic realities." We hope that our discussion will stimulate readers' thinking and lead to new discussions about what health care systems can do to position themselves for the future.

Ten Health Care Industry Myths

1. "Supermeds" Will Dominate the Health Care Market. It is popular, in looking ahead five to ten years, to predict a health care industry dominated by ten or fifteen very large, vertically integrated national firms, or "supermeds"—a situation that many physicians and hospitals see as threatening. Paul Ellwood predicts that this type of concentration will take place in the next decade ("Ellwood Says 'Supermed' Concept Gaining Ground . . . ," 1986). Some investment bankers, whose predictions of radical change in the health care industry appear to be widely accepted, also forecast an industry shakeout and the emergence of a limited number of supermeds. For example, Alex. Brown & Sons, Inc., predicts that health care will go from a "cottage industry" to "fewer than 15 major health care delivery systems" (Alex. Brown & Sons, Inc., 1986, p. 1). Todd Richter of Morgan Stanley says that by the mid-1990s, "an elite oligopoly consisting of seven to ten vertically-integrated managed-care systems will dominate the health care services field" (1986, p. 2).

We have heard the same kind of argument in banking—a few large national systems will swallow up smaller regional systems and independent banks. Yet in states such as California and Arizona that have a few very large banking systems, independent banks have continued to grow and prosper. Their secret? They are close to their customers, management and ownership are usually the same individuals, and they adapt quickly (in part because they are capable of fast decision making).

We agree that there will be a certain amount of health care industry consolidation but do not subscribe to the theory of a few large supermeds. The health care industry is dynamic, but there is also a tremendous amount of inertia in the system:

- Hospitals that are sole providers in rural areas and smaller communities will be slow to respond to the ADS trend, to vertical integration, and to other health care industry changes.
- Many community-owned, not-for-profit hospitals are in excellent financial condition, and their governing boards are

committed to local autonomy and control; they have the capacity to ride out many of the expected short-term pressures.

- There do not appear to be significant economies of scale in health care. Martin Feldstein concluded in 1981 that there were not significant economies of scale for very large hospitals (Feldstein, 1981, p. 60). Bigger is not necessarily better in the health care industry.

We contend that many hospitals and their medical staffs will adapt and survive. The health care industry will continue to become more efficient, with some of the less efficient, highly leveraged organizations dropping out. There will continue to be room for locally owned, community-oriented organizations and they will continue to provide the majority of health care services in their market areas. We just don't buy the supermed concept. Local health care systems, hospitals, and physician groups have a much greater ability to survive than many observers believe.

2. Physicians Will Become Employees of Hospitals. Many physicians are worried that they will become hospital employees, and several industry observers have predicted that they will. Quite frankly, it does not make economic sense for hospitals to hire doctors if they can possibly avoid it; variable costs would become fixed. In the professional services business—and hospitals are in that category—it is better to avoid fixed costs and allow costs to vary with volume. Most physicians have a desire to continue to be at risk, and that is where they are likely to stay.

3. Employers Are Actively Involved in Health Care Cost Containment. This cost-containment myth results from an overemphasis on survey results from large employers, many of which are unionized and very active in their efforts to contain health care costs. The vast majority of U.S. businesses are more concerned about attracting and retaining a quality work force, and health care benefits are an important component of that goal. Quality of care is important to employers, as is freedom of choice and accessibility to the system (good geographic coverage by physicians and hospitals). Employers want the most health care benefit for their dollars; but for the most part, they are not interested in sacrificing quality or dramatically changing employee access to health care services in order to save a few dollars. Employers and the health insurance industry are reluctant to alter benefits substantially; this reluctance will impede health care cost-containment efforts.

4. There Will Be Large Numbers of Hospital Bankruptcies and Closures. We believe that not-for-profit acute care hospitals have more staying power than is generally recognized. Most hospitals have constituencies of physicians, trustees, consumers, volunteers, and local business people who do not want them to fail; the emotional attachment to a community hospital is greater than to most other industries. In the case of rural hospitals— particularly sole-source providers—the public sector may assume responsibility, or increase subsidies for hospitals that are already publicly owned, rather than letting the hospitals close. There will also be a large number of mergers. We agree that there will be closures as well, but not on a massive scale. Many organizations will experience severe financial trials, but we expect a high proportion to adjust and survive.

5. Not-for-Profit Hospitals Are Less Efficient Than Investor-Owned Hospitals. There is ample evidence demonstrating that hospitals in the not-for-profit sector are controlling their costs just as well as their investor-owned counterparts. In Chapter Thirteen, where the low-cost provider strategy was discussed, we reviewed the results of several studies that compared costs for not-for-profit versus investor-owned hospitals; the results demonstrated that while for-profit hospitals charged more for their services and were staffed more leanly overall costs were comparable. We believe that both types of institutions will continue to improve in controlling costs, but we disagree with the assertion that not-for-profit organizations are inherently less efficient, and therefore less competitive.

6. Hospitals Will Price "at the Margin." Several industry observers have concluded that since hospitals have a high proportion of fixed costs, they will price just above their direct costs in order to attract additional business that will contribute toward overhead. The Twin Cities' experience has shown that hospitals are capable of shifting a high proportion of their fixed costs to a variable basis; with 60 percent of their costs in labor, hospitals are not, in the long term, high fixed-cost businesses. Pricing at the margin, assuming some poorly advised institutions attempt it, will not lead to the rock-bottom prices that many experts expect. As we have said many times in earlier chapters, we believe that price competition is a poor way to compete and recommend against it.

7. *The "Bed Business" Is Dead.* We have heard this myth many times, and totally disagree. There is no evidence that health care systems have made, or are capable of making, significant profits on outpatient services or other diversified businesses. At this time, the "bed business" is subsidizing many of these diversification activities. As discussed in Chapter Seven, there are several solid economic reasons why the inpatient business can continue to be profitable (it is capital intensive, there are significant barriers to entry, and so on). Health care systems that proceed on the basis of this myth will be in serious trouble within a short period of time.

8. *Consumers Cannot Judge Quality.* At the present time, about half of all U.S. consumers say they can differentiate among hospitals on the basis of quality. For those who claim to differentiate on quality, the reasons are often superficial. But this is going to change, and quickly. Advertising and public relations activities designed to communicate quality are increasing rapidly, and market research shows that the public is paying attention. The health care industry data base (both medical and financial) is increasing exponentially, and better measures of quality are sure to be available to the public in the next two to three years. Several states are requiring that hospital charges for various diagnoses (health care "products") be published; this will soon be followed by data that will allow consumers and employers to evaluate the other side of the coin—what they are receiving for their money.

9. Voluntary Governing Boards Cannot Successfully Compete. Voluntary boards of trustees have been confused about their own role and the mission of their institution, slow in making decisions, and unsupportive of CEOs in the face of physician pressure for change. But we do not accept the argument that such boards are incapable of responding to competitive pressures or that they are an albatross for health care systems needing to compete.

Our experience as trustees, and the results of the survey of 740 trustees described in the previous chapter, leads us to believe that governing boards are changing, and that many will adjust to the new health care industry realities. The potential exists for health care system and hospital governing boards to be just as effective as their counterparts in banking, manufacturing, and other competitive industries. There will be changes in the way they function—more authority granted to the CEO, greater attention paid to strategic issues, increased willingness to take risks, and a demand for more thorough staff work—and, as a result, the effectiveness of governing boards will improve.

10. Americans Are Unhappy with the Health Care System. It is common for consumers to express surprise and dismay at health care costs, especially hospital bills and surgeons' fees. Despite surveys that show that Americans are unimpressed with what they get for their health care dollars, we believe, based on our research, that there is substantial consumer satisfaction with the system. Consumers like having a choice of doctors and hospitals. There is a deep reservoir of loyalty toward certain physicians and hospitals. And the insurance system and employers have been generous—no complaints there! There is not, in our opinion, strong grass-roots interest in dramatically changing the U.S. health care system. We believe that change will come, but at a slower pace than many experts predict.

Ten Health Care Industry Realities

In sorting through the maze of conflicting opinions and projections, we believe there are a number of economic realities that health care industry governing boards, staffs, and physicians can generally rely on over the next three to five years.

1. Health Care Providers Will Concentrate on Local Markets or Regions. As a converse to Myth #1, which predicts supermeds, we believe there is increasing recognition among governing boards, CEOs, and sources of capital that health care is a locally oriented service business. There is increasing talk about trying to do a better job of meeting the needs of a health care system's "catchment" area, or local market. Even the large investor-owned chains are concentrating on a limited number of target markets. Many local systems and hospitals have strong name recognition and a reputation for quality in their area but are virtually unknown elsewhere in the country. There appears to be an increasing awareness of the dangers of becoming spread too thin. To be sure, national chains, networks, and insurers will continue to develop customized national coverage strategies for those employers who need them. But national coverage is not the issue for most health care decision makers. The trend of the future will be for health care systems to become more attuned to their own geographic areas and aggressively seek ways to better serve local needs.

2. ADS or Managed Care Will Dominate the Payer Market. Although we do not believe that changes in ADS market penetration will occur as rapidly as many industry experts do (see Chapter Six), it is evident that significant changes will occur by 1995; something on the order of 60 percent of all employees and their dependents will be enrolled in HMOs, PPOs, or some type of managed-care indemnity plan by that year. Therefore, there will be increasing pressure on hospital and physician profit margins, and an increasing proportion of patients will be directed to certain physician groups and hospitals.

The economic implications of this shift in the payer mix are immense, and many local health care systems and physician groups will face serious challenges in keeping their avenues open to patients and being able to charge a fair price for services rendered. A number of different approaches have been discussed—

more thoughtful pricing to different market segments (the upscale market, for example), better negotiating with ADS, networking with other providers to exert control over the delivery system, and acquiring a financial interest in certain ADS companies. The development of a well-conceived ADS strategy should be a top priority for every health care system and physician group.

3. *Teaching and Research Hospitals Will Survive.* In our review of the health care literature, we have found a wide divergence of opinion about how well research and teaching hospitals will perform, from a market and economic point of view, under the increasing pressures of ADS and DRGs. One school of thought is that since these types of institutions are normally high-cost providers, they will not be competitive in their efforts to attract ADS business and will not fare well under DRGs. Others believe that the growing recognition of distinction in severity of illness and variations in required intensity of care, and the reflection of those factors in the various payment mechanisms (especially DRGs), will allow research and teaching institutions to be reimbursed properly.

Bernstein Research maintains that most not-for-profit teaching and research hospitals are poorly positioned for the future. "These hospitals will be especially hurt if they try to maintain teaching and indigent care, since private buyers will not cross-subsidize these services" (Abramowitz, 1985, p. 47). In Minneapolis, a leading-edge market, HMOs have been reluctant to contract with the higher-priced University of Minnesota hospitals.

On the other hand, many university-related hospitals are tertiary care facilities, handling the most severe and complex cases. Early research into the various methodologies for reflecting severity of illness indexes in payment mechanisms such as DRGs is promising; it appears that severity of illness correlates with hospital and physician costs and charges.

Many metropolitan areas of the United States are also striving to develop themselves as high-tech research and development (R & D) educational and manufacturing centers. Boston, with its famous Route 128 R & D complex, combined with its outstanding educational institutions, is a prime example. The San

Francisco Bay Area, with Stanford University, the University of California/Berkeley, and Silicon Valley, is another example. In recent years, many states and metropolian areas striving to emulate these two areas have increasingly focused on biological or bio-tech R & D, and many of these efforts are built around large research and teaching hospitals. The R & D dollars brought in by medical researchers represent "basic income" to a community, thus stimulating additional economic development.

We have confidence in the future of most teaching and research hospitals; they have an important future role to play nationally and in their respective regions. They will come under increasingly intense economic pressure, especially in the short run, as their reimbursement problems are compounded by the normally high proportion of indigent care provided. But we believe that the states and communities where these centers are located will, in nearly every case, stand behind them. Finances will be tight, but most of these institutions will not be allowed to fail.

4. There Will Continue to Be Ample Financial Resources Available for the Health Care Industry. We do not accept the thesis that the health care industry is facing a capital shortage. As discussed in Chapter Seventeen, we see the issue as one of distribution among the "haves" and the "have nots." Health care systems with the size and market position to continue to operate profitably will be able to find capital to finance their strategic initiatives. Many poorly positioned and managed organizations, however, will not be successful in attracting external funds. On an overall basis, there is little or no evidence confirming a shrinkage of funds available to the health care industry; in fact, with the emergence of large Japanese banks and a greater focus on the taxable bond market, we believe the total supply of funds available to health care will become larger than in the heyday of the early 1980s. But these funding sources will also be more selective; this is the challenge facing nearly all health care systems.

5. Systems and Alliances Will Increase in Importance. As noted in our Chapter Twelve discussion of networking, there are reservations in the health care industry about the role of the big alliances, and whether or not they will be viable over the long term. We believe they will increase in their effectiveness and continue to bring benefits to their members. For example, both VHA and AHS are positioning themselves to play a much more important role in access to capital, both debt and equity, for their members.

We believe the larger regional systems and large national alliances are adaptive; they will be at the cutting edge of change in the health care industry, whether it be ADS, physician bonding, vertical integration, or accessing capital. As noted in Chapter Twelve, the alliances represent a low-risk, low-cost strategy for many local health care systems and hospitals. There will continue to be tensions between the alliances and their members, and occasional defections, but we look for the alliances to play an increasingly important role in the industry.

6. Significant Progress on Indigent Care and Malpractice Insurance Crises. We certainly hope we are correct in predicting some relief for hospitals and physicians on these two very important issues.

On the question of indigents, or uncompensated care, the health care industry cannot be truly competitive when certain institutions are saddled with a disproportionate share of these cases. Such hospitals will increasingly take a tougher stance on accepting indigents; they have to, as a matter of survival. State and local governments will be pressured into accepting more responsibility for indigent care. Given all the other budgetary pressures on state and local governments, it will not be an easy battle. But we predict that substantial progress will be make toward at least partially mitigating the indigent care problem over the next three to five years.

Progress is already coming on the malpractice insurance crisis. We are optimistic that in another year or two, most states will have taken steps to limit malpractice settlements, thus making the business more attractive to insurers. We expect strong public opinion, and the resulting pressure on legislators, to lead to major revisions in tort reform in favor of physicians and hospitals.

7. Better Definitions of the Health Care Product Will Emerge. Along with the indigent care issue, better definition of the health care product is a key element in creating a fairer competitive environment. As discussed in Chapter Thirteen, several research organizations are developing severity of illness indexes that may be combined with DRG definitions to provide more equitable payment; one such system, developed by Susan Horn and Johns Hopkins University, is on the market.

Tremendous pressure is building among payers—both employers and insurers—for hospitals and physicians to develop measures of outcome. Thus far providers have been slow to respond. However, as health care systems increasingly recognize that it is in their best interests to differentiate themselves from their competitors by showing evidence of their cost-effectiveness, such data will become available. We still hear the comment "Every case we handle is unique" as support for the conclusion that no health care industry standards are possible. We disagree: given the large number of cases processed each year, statistical measures of the effectiveness of various providers will be developed and used by health care purchasers as part of the physician and hospital selection process.

The Joint Commission on Accreditation of Hospitals (JCAH) has announced a new program to measure quality of care. Dennis O'Leary, president of JCAH, says, "We now have the fundamental knowledge and methodology necessary to begin to define and assure the quality of care you provide" ("New Bill May Give Hospitals Headaches," 1986, p. 7). O'Leary went on to say that measurement of clinical outcomes will be incorporated into the accreditation process.

8. Many Existing Health Care Ventures and Products Will Be Terminated. In the past, including the period from 1983 through 1987, many health care systems had the luxury of being able to establish and operate programs that were successful in terms of noneconomic criteria (for example, community service) but did not contribute to the bottom line. We sense an increased willingness on the part of health care system governing boards and CEOs to terminate those ventures and programs that are not justifiable on economic grounds. As new ventures are initiated, more thought will be given in the planning stages to what to do if performance criteria are not met. In other words, the more sophisticated health care systems will move quickly to minimize their financial losses. There will be less reluctance to recognize that a mistake has been made and to act on the harsh feedback of the marketplace.

This new reality is bound to be upsetting for many health care industry managers and trustees and to the various publics benefiting from service-oriented, but money-losing, programs. Nevertheless, we can see it coming, and coming fast. The need for health care systems to direct their financial resources to more economically promising areas will force the issue.

The ability to terminate financially marginal services is viewed by some industry observers as a major advantage for the health care industry, compared with other public service organizations such as municipalities or counties. In the case of local government entities, public pressure can often force the continuance of noneconomic services, and the result can be negative from a financial viability viewpoint. Most health care systems have much more flexibility.

9. Physicians Will Continue to Control a Major Proportion of the Market. With the rapid increase in ADS coverage, some health care systems are assuming that the role of the physician in directing patients to hospitals will substantially decrease in the next three to five years. We disagree. We believe that most physicians will contract with numerous HMOs and PPOs, and that they will have medical staff privileges at more than one hospital. This will allow physicians to continue to serve their patients.

As noted in Chapter Two, the evidence indicates that physicians are the most important health care market segment. We do not foresee much diminution in the role of physicians; therefore, the strategy of physician bonding is especially important for the future.

10. Many Health Care Systems Will Find Ways to Differentiate Themselves. As we discussed in Chapter Five and elsewhere, the ability to differentiate a health care system, hospital, or physician group from competitors is critically important. We have confidence that, over a period of time, most providers will make progress in accomplishing this important strategic initiative.

The need to differentiate intangible services is not unique to the health care industry; it is a problem facing nearly every U.S. business or professional group (CPAs, attorneys, engineers, even economists). And it is not likely to be a short-term effort; it requires careful (and objective) analysis of strengths and weaknesses by all organizations or individuals comparing themselves with competitors. Once marginal differences have been identified, a strategy for communicating these unique attributes can then be developed. Key questions are:

- What really makes our organization or medical practice stand out?
- What are our strengths and weaknesses vis-à-vis our competitors?
- Do our unique attributes matter to our customers? In what ways?
- What are the best ways to communicate or market these attributes?
- What are the costs versus benefits of various marketing or communications approaches?

In our research, especially with consumers and employers, we sense a real desire to be able to understand the differences among various health care providers. It is frustrating for buyers to be unable to tell the difference among alternative suppliers; they are afraid of being ripped off. With a few exceptions, we do not see evidence that American businesses are more interested in the cost of health care than in quality for their employees. But employers do want assurances that they are spending their health care dollars wisely.

Consumers will be faced with a bigger role in health care decision making. Most of the pressure is coming from HMOs and

PPOs, in which membership either excludes certain doctors or hospitals, or offers significant financial incentives to use specific providers. Hard choices will be made. Consumers are becoming increasingly sophisticated and active in health care decisions. The largest user group, persons sixty-five and over, will become more knowledgeable and develop strong preferences for certain health care providers. Consumer surveys of health care advertising awareness and its impact on physician and hospital selection clearly reflect the genesis of a significant long-term change toward more informed consumer decision making in health care.

If there is a single sentence summarizing this book, it is this: "Find a way to differentiate your organization, or face a future of competing as a generic health care provider (a commodity) on the basis of price." This is truly the bottom line for almost all health care systems, hospitals, health plans, and physicians. We are confident that most will be successful in meeting this challenge.

Appendixes

A.

Key Health Care
Industry Indicators,
1975 to 1985,
with Projections to
1990 and 1995

B.

Economic Analysis
and Modeling

Appendix A

Key Health Care Industry Indicators, 1975 to 1985, with Projections to 1990 and 1995

Tables A.1 through A.6 provide statistics on a number of health care industry indicators. Data for 1975 and 1980 were generally available from well-recognized sources, such as Health Care Financing Administration (HCFA) and the American Hospital Association (AHA). When data for 1985 were unavailable, we figured estimates based on 1983-1984 information. The projections to 1990 and 1995 are our own; in calculating them we assumed a 4 percent annual inflation rate.

As Table A.1 indicates, national health care expenditures are expected to continue to increase, but at a slower pace than in the recent past. The 70 pecent increase experienced between 1980 and 1985 is expected to drop to a 29 percent increase between 1985 and 1990 and a 22 percent increase between 1990 and 1995. The development and growth of alternative services—for example, outpatient and ambulatory services, home care, the expected proliferation of HMOs and PPOs, and the continuation of prospective payment systems—are key factors associated with this trend. Correspondingly, we expect the percentage of the GNP

289

Table A.1. U.S. Health Care Industry Indicators, 1975–1985, with Projections to 1990 and 1995.

Indicator	Historical			Projected	
	1975	1980	1985	1990	1995
1. Health care expenditures (billions):[a]					
a. Hospital care	$ 52.4	$101.3	$166.7	$217.0	$264.0
b. Physicians	24.9	46.8	82.8	110.0	135.0
c. All other (nursing homes, pharmaceuticals, dentists, etc.)	55.4	99.9	175.5	218.0	268.0
Total	$132.7	$248.0	$425.0	$545.0	$667.0
2. Health care expenditures ÷ Gross National Product[b]	8.6%	9.4%	10.7%	10.3%	10.0%
3. Payment for hospital care (billions):[c]					
a. Medicare	$ 11.5	$ 26.0	$ 48.5	$ 73.0	$ 94.0
b. Medicaid	NA	9.4	14.8	19.5	25.0
c. Other public sources (Department of Defense, Veterans Administration, other)	NA	18.8	26.5	37.5	45.0
Subtotal Public	NA	$ 54.2	$ 89.8	$130.0	$164.0
d. Health insurance (including ADS)	NA	$ 38.6	$ 59.3	$ 70.0	$ 85.0
e. Direct patient payments	NA	7.5	15.6	15.0	13.0
f. Philanthropy	NA	1.0	2.0	2.0	2.0
Subtotal Private	NA	$ 47.1	$ 76.9	$ 87.0	$100.0
Total	NA	$101.3	$166.7	$217.0	$264.0

a. Health Care Financing Administration, 1985, Table 12; Health Care Financing Administration, 1986, Tables 3 and 9; and "Health Care Spending's Share of GNP Reaches a New High," 1986.

b. Health Care Financing Administration, 1985, Table 6; and United States Department of Commerce, 1986, Table 11.

c. Abramowitz, 1985, Table 6; and Health Care Financing Administration, 1985, Table 9.

allocated to the health care industry to decrease somewhat from 10.7 percent in 1985 to 10.3 percent in 1990 and 10.0 percent in 1995.

Public funds will continue to be the major source of payment for hospital services. By 1995, it is estimated that 62 percent of all hospital services will be paid for by Medicare, Medicaid, and other public sources. The aging of the U.S. population, and the growing number of senior citizens utilizing disproportionate amounts of health care services, is a major contributing factor.

Table A.2 presents indicators for all U.S. hospitals. It is projected that between 1985 and 1995, over 700 U.S. hospitals will close. The majority of these will be smaller community hospitals, located primarily in rural areas. It is also projected that the hospital bed supply will decrease by nearly 180,000 beds between 1985 and 1995.

Table A.3 contains data and projections for community hospitals that are primarily acute care facilities. The total number of beds, admissions, and patient-days are all expected to decline significantly in the next ten years. Occupancy rates, which reached an all-time low of 64 percent in 1985, are projected to remain relatively stable through 1995. The average length of stay for all community hospitals dipped to 7.1 patient-days in 1985 and is projected to decrease to 6.5 in 1990 and 6.4 in 1995.

Hospitals will decrease staffing levels in response to the declining census, but full-time-equivalent employees per occupied bed are expected to remain near the 5.0 level.

Table A.4 focuses on physicians. The number of physicians in the United States is expected to total an estimated 675,000 by the year 1995. This represents a 25 percent increase from the 541,000 physicians in 1985. Correspondingly, the ratio of physicians per 100,000 persons is expected to reach a high of 261 per 100,000 in 1995, compared with 227 per 100,000 in 1985. Rural areas of the United States will benefit from the predicted physician surplus; by 1995, 20 percent of all physicians are expected to be practicing in rural areas.

Enrollment of students in U.S. medical schools is expected to decrease between 1985 and 1990, and then again by 1995.

Table A.2. U.S. Hospital Indicators, 1975–1985, with Projections to 1990 and 1995.

		Historical			Projected	
Indicator	1975	1980	1985	1990	1990	1995
1. Number of hospitals	7,156	6,965	6,872	6,500	6,100
2. Number of beds (thousands)	1,466.0	1,365.0	1,318.0	1,278.0	1,150.0
3. Hospital beds/1,000 U.S. residents	6.8	6.0	5.6	5.1	4.7
4. Occupancy rates (percentage of beds)	76.7%	77.7%	69.0%	66.0%	68.0%
5. Number of admissions (millions)	36.2	38.9	36.3	35.0	33.0
6. Average length of stay	11.3	9.9	9.2	8.8	8.7
7. Number of patient-days (millions)	409.1	387.1	331.9	308.0	287.0
8. Percentage of beds in investor-owned chains[a]	NA	9.2%	11.8%	15.0%	18.0%

Source: American Hospital Association, 1985, Tables 1, 2A, and 4A; and *Hospital Statistics*, 1986, Table 1.
a. Abramowitz, 1985, Table 10.

Table A.3. U.S. Community Hospital Indicators, 1975–1985, with Projections to 1990 and 1995.

Indicator	Historical			Projected	
	1975	1980	1985	1990	1995
1. Number of hospitals	5,875	5,830	5,732	5,550	5,050
2. Number of beds (thousands)[a]	942.0	988.4	1,001.0	934.2	849.3
3. Hospital beds/1,000 U.S. residents	4.4	4.4	4.2	3.8	3.4
4. Occupancy rates (percentage of beds)[a]	75.0%	75.6%	64.8%	63.0%	64.0%
5. Number of admissions (millions)[a]	33.4	36.1	33.4	33.0	31.0
6. Average length of stay[a]	7.7	7.5	7.1	6.5	6.4
7. Number of patient-days (millions)[a]	257.2	270.8	237.1	214.5	198.4
8. Number of full-time-equivalent employees (millions)	2.4	2.9	3.0	3.0	2.8
9. Number of full-time equivalent employees/occupied bed[a]	3.4	3.8	4.6	5.1	5.2

a. *Hospital Statistics*, 1986, Tables 1 and 5; Richter, 1986, pp. 11–21; U.S. Bureau of the Census, 1985b; U.S. Department of Commerce, 1986, p. 54.3; and U.S. Department of Health and Human Services, 1985, Tables 70 and 71.

Table A.4. U.S. Physicians, 1975–1985, with Projections to 1990 and 1995.

Indicator	Historical 1975	Historical 1980	1985[e]	Projected 1990	Projected 1995
1. Number of physicians by major specialties (thousands):[a]					
a. Primary care	130.6	159.9	182.0	206.0	228.0
b. OB/GYN	21.7	26.3	31.0	37.0	36.0
c. General surgery	31.6	34.0	38.0	43.0	45.0
d. All others	209.8	247.4	290.0	339.0	366.0
Total	393.7	467.7	541.0	625.0	675.0
2. Number of students in U.S. medical schools (thousands)[b]	56.2	65.5	67.1	65.0	62.0
3. Ratio of physicians/100,000 people[a]	180	202	227	251	261
4. Geographic distribution of physicians:[a]					
a. In metropolitan areas	87.1%	86.9%	85.0%	82.0%	80.0%
b. In rural areas	12.9	13.1	15.0	18.0	20.0
5. Percentage of physicians in ADS[c]					
a. Contracting with HMOs	5.0%	20.0%	40.0%	60.0%	85.0%
b. Contracting with PPOs	—	—	45.0	70.0	90.0
6. Percentage of physicians in group practice[d]	23.5%	26.2%	30.0%	40.0%	50.0%

a. American Medical Association, 1984, Tables A.1, A.2, A.6, and A.7; and U.S. Bureau of the Census, 1985b.
b. Crowley, Etzel, and Petersen, 1985, Table 1, p. 1565.
c. Authors' estimates.
d. American Medical Association, telephone interview, Penny Havlachek, Spring 1986.
e. Data for 1985 were estimated.

Table A.5. Trends in Medicare, 1975–1985, with Projections to 1990 and 1995.

		Historical		Projected	
Indicator	1975	1980	1985	1990	1995
1. Number of Medicare enrollees (hospitalization insurance and/or supplemental insurance) (in millions):	25.0	28.5	31.0[a]	34.0	37.0
2. Medicare reimbursement (billions):					
a. Hospital care	$11.5	$25.9	$48.5	$ 73.0	$ 94.0
b. Physician services	3.4	7.9	17.1	28.0	45.0
c. Nursing home care	.3	.4	.6	1.0	1.3
d. Other personal health care	.1	.5	1.1	2.0	2.5
e. Other services and appliances	.3	1.0	3.2	6.0	8.0
Total	$15.6	$35.7	$70.5	$110.0	$150.8

Source: Data extracted from Sawyer, Ruther, Pagan-Berlucchi, and Muse, 1983, Tables 2.1, 2.6, and 3.3, and Figure 2.3; *Health Care Financing Review,* 1985, Table 4; and Health Care Financing Administration, "Medicare Data," Oct. 2, 1985.
a. Figure for Medicare enrollees in 1985 is estimated.

Table A.6. Other Indicators for U.S. Health Care Industry, 1975–1985, with Projections to 1990 and 1995.

Indicator	1975	Historical 1980	1985	Projected 1990	1995
1. HMOs:[a]					
a. Number	178	236	393	600	800
b. Membership/enrollment (millions)	5.7	9.1	18.9	37.5	65.0
c. Percentage of population enrolled	2.6%	4.0%	8.0%	15.0%	25.0%
2. PPOs:[b]					
a. Enrollment (millions)	NA	NA	5.8	50.0	78.0
b. Percentage of population enrolled	NA	NA	2.5%	20.0%	30.0%
3. Number of urgent care centers[c]	NA	180	3,000	5,500	7,000
4. Outpatient surgery:[d]					
a. Number of freestanding centers	41	128	407	800	1,000
b. Percentage of all surgeries performed	NA	NA	28%	35%	40%

a. InterStudy, 1982; InterStudy, 1985b, Table 1; U.S. Department of Health and Human Services, 1980a, p. 1; and U.S. Department of Commerce, 1986, p. 54.4.

b. National Center for Health Services Research, 1985 (unpublished study).

c. Commerce International Inc., *FEC Factor II Study*, 1985; National Association for Ambulatory Care, telephone interviews, June 1986; and McNerney, W. J., 1986.

d. SMG Marketing Group, *Freestanding Outpatient Surgery Directory*, August, 1984, Table 5B; SMG Marketing Group, telephone interview, June 1986; and McNerney, W. J., 1986.

In an effort to establish and secure a position in the marketplace, physicians will be more likely to join group practices and contract with HMOs and PPOs. By 1995, it is expected that 85 percent of all physicians will have contracted with an HMO and 90 percent of all physicians will have contracted with a PPO.

Based on data and projections in Table A.5, Medicare will continue to increase in enrollment and reimbursement levels as the U.S. population ages and lives longer. The total number of Medicare enrollees is projected to reach 34 million in 1990 and 37 million by 1995 (nearly 15 percent of the total U.S. population).

Total Medicare expenditures, which more than doubled between 1980 and 1985, are expected to increase 56 percent by 1990 (to $110.0 billion) and an additional 36 percent by 1995 (to $150.8 billion).

Table A.6 summarizes our projections for HMO and PPO market penetration and for urgent care centers and outpatient surgery. HMOs numbered 178 in 1975 and increased to 393 by June 1985. It is projected that there will be 800 HMOs by 1995. HMO enrollment is expected to reach 65 million persons and cover 25 percent of the U.S. population by 1995. We expect PPOs to experience more growth than HMOs. PPO enrollment should reach 78 million people and account for 30 percent of the U.S. population by 1995.

Urgent care centers and outpatient or ambulatory surgery centers are increasingly popular alternative care settings. It is projected that the number of urgent care centers will increase from 3,000 in 1985 to 7,000 in 1995. The number of freestanding surgery centers is expected to grow from 407 in 1985 to 1,000 in 1995. By 1995, it is estimated that these freestanding centers will account for 40 percent of all surgeries performed.

Appendix B

Economic Analysis
and Modeling

Patient acquisition models. Box-Jenkins forecasts. Multiple regression analysis. If terms like these are not already familiar, they are likely to become so—and in a hurry, as health care systems face difficult resource allocation decisions.

The use of economic analysis and modeling is in its infancy in the health care industry. Nearly all of the strategies described in Chapters Five through Fourteen require in-depth market, economic, and financial analysis to weigh the costs (or capital investment) against the potential benefits. Increasing limitations on capital availability for certain hospitals and systems within the not-for-profit segment of the health care industry, described in Chapter Seventeen, place special emphasis on the need for careful economic analysis in order to allocate financial resources, and to identify potential returns and risk factors associated with investments supporting new strategic initiatives.

Two of the most useful modeling techniques are multiple regression analysis and Box-Jenkins time series forecasting. Multiple regression analysis is used to develop a formula which attempts to explain the relationship between a dependent variable and one or more independent (or predictor) variables. As a statistically based technique, significance levels can be associated with individual variables and the overall model to identify key variables or model formulations. Box-Jenkins can be considered a

298

special type of regression model where the dependent variable is a function of the same variable at earlier points in time (such as, hospital admissions at month t as a function of admissions at month t-1, t-2, etc.). This type of time series model is applicable to forecasting when seasonal trends and long-term trends need to be considered.

Working as consultants over the past sixteen years, we have applied these and other economic modeling techniques for clients in banking, telecommunications, energy, real estate, local government, and other industries. For example, in pricing radio advertising time, we developed a multiple regression model of the value of a thirty-second advertising spot. The final model was the result of the analysis of several thousand spots in different "day-parts" (drive time, weekend, and so forth) over a three-year period. This model is used by a major radio network to develop favorable pricing strategies. We also developed a Box-Jenkins statistical forecasting technique by which a regional transportation district could project month-to-month sales tax revenues derived from a half-cent sales tax.

In the health care industry, these and related economic analysis and modeling techniques are gradually coming into use. For example, some hospitals are now forecasting admissions, patient-days, and other key variables using the Box-Jenkins model. Various patient acquisition models are also in use, and in-depth economic feasibility analysis is becoming a more important part of the health care decision-making process.

Appendix B focuses on four of the most applicable general types of economic models for the health care industry.

1. *Demand (market/competition) models.* These are used to estimate demand for specific products or services in a complex market. Market research (surveys, focus group interviews) often provides input into these types of models.

2. *Economic feasibility models.* These compare anticipated revenues, operating costs, and cash flow with capital investment to determine payback period, return on investment (ROI), or other relevant factors. The role of economic feasibility analysis is especially important in an organization's

resource allocation decision-making process (see Chapter Sixteen).

3. *Economic impact models.* To date, these have had limited use in the health care industry, but they are used extensively in other areas of economic activity (for example, in assessing the impact of a decline in energy prices, evaluating the economic impact of an industry on a community or region). However, hospitals are finding it necessary to identify and assess their economic impact on the community, and this type of modeling is useful for that purpose.

4. *Econometric models.* These are used to explain and predict the behavior of market and economic factors, such as pricing a complex group of products or services or identifying the factors influencing length of stay in a hospital. Econometric modeling relies heavily on mathematical and statistical techniques and usually involves computer processing of large amounts of data. Multiple regression and Box-Jenkins are examples of econometric models.

Demand Models

Although the health care industry is now heavily involved in market research, primarily through surveys of consumers and employers, the modeling techniques used in other industries to estimate demand—the number of customers or purchases—have not been extensively applied. The factors influencing demand for health care services are often more complex than those in other industries. This complexity points out the need for sophisticated demand modeling within the health care industry; we believe that organizations successfully using demand modeling will gain a significant competitive advantage.

Examples from Other Industries. The cellular radio-telephone, a new type of mobile telephone, is a new growth industry in the United States. As part of the government application and licensing process, competing systems (as many as 100 applicants in some metropolitan areas) have had to demonstrate understanding of the market through market research and carefully designed demand estimates. Demand modeling for the cellular radio-telephone typically considers these variables:

- Price (installation cost, per-minute charges)
- Number and type of businesses in the metropolitan area
- Market area growth prospects (new business formation, jobs created)
- Population growth and income levels (especially the proportion of high-income households)
- Geographic configuration of the market area (highway system, location of major employment centers)
- Interest in subscribing to cellular service at different prices (usually based on a telephone survey of businesses)
- Rate of adoption (a model predicting how quickly the new technology would gain acceptance)
- Anticipated competition and competitors' pricing structures

The demand estimates developed using these variables could be prepared manually but most often are accomplished by computer spreadsheet.

In banking, a model designed to estimate deposits for each of the first three years considers these variables:

- Configuration of the primary service area
- Economic base of the service area (number of businesses, number of employees, number of households, age and income patterns of residents)
- Average deposit for each customer category (businesses, employees, households, and local government entities); business interviews and household surveys are often used to provide data
- Present banking patterns
- Competing financial institutions (banks, savings and loan associations, credit unions)
- Likely share of the market for the proposed bank (a function of location, access, type of facility planned, management, capital, and services to be provided)

The bank deposit model uses a combination of publicly available economic and demographic data (for example, income levels from U.S. Census reports), surveys, inventories of businesses, and past experience. Since many of these commercial banks *do* open for business, and their deposits are then reported quarterly, actual versus projected deposits can be compared, making it possible to fine-tune the model.

Examples in Health Care. We recently developed two different computerized ADS demand models. The "comprehensive" model considers these factors in arriving at a five-year ADS demand forecast:

- Population (size of the market area)
- Community growth prospects (employment, population)
- Consumer characteristics (age, income)
- Likely future competition (number and strength of competitors)
- Employer receptiveness to ADS
- Industrial mix (proportion of larger firms, types of industries)
- Present ADS penetration levels

The "employer-specific" model more closely resembles, in terms of output, the kinds of data required for federal HMO applications (enrollment by type of plan by specific employer, monthly, for a five-year period). This model uses a two-step approach, estimating first the share of the employer market and then the percentage of employees likely to enroll in the plan. Sources used for this model include an economic-demographic study, surveys, "shopping" of competitive health plans, and overall knowledge of the market area.

In order to estimate employee participation, the model considers comparative premium costs to the employee, geographic coverage of the provider network, quality of HMOs currently offered, benefits design, employee social and economic characteristics, and size of business (HMOs usually obtain a high percentage of employees in smaller businesses). The two parts of the model are combined, using a spreadsheet analysis, to estimate HMO demand by month and by type of plan.

Several firms have developed models to forecast hospital demand for inpatient and outpatient services by product line (women's health, orthopedics, pediatrics, and so forth). Input required to operate models of this type include:

- Market area definition
- Demographic forecasts (population by age group, sex, income)
- Admission forecasts by DRG (available from the STRAPCO model developed by American Hospital Supply)
- Product line definitions
- Payer-mix estimates: Medicare, indemnity insurance, ADS, and uncompensated care (developed from a number of national and local data sources)
- Average charge per discharge
- Other hospital performance data

Figure B.1 is a schematic illustration of a patient acquisition model. The model is used to project admissions, patient-days, and revenues by product line and by total market area and local health care system. It can also be used to assess the potential impact of competitors' actions (price cutting, new services or facilities) and the impact of increasing ADS penetration. Various strategies relating to physician recruiting can also be assessed in terms of their impact on inpatient-days and revenues.

Economic Feasibility Models

Economic feasibility models go beyond demand projections (although demand is a critically important variable), typically including estimates of capital investment, operating costs, profits, depreciation, and cash flow. The analytical part of these models involves projecting the various factors into the future in order to estimate return on investment (ROI), payback period, benefit-cost ratios, or some comparable measure of economic feasibility. Use of economic feasibility analysis is critically important in the strategic initiative budgeting process described in Chapter Sixteen.

Figure B.1. Patient Acquisition Model, Acute Care Example.

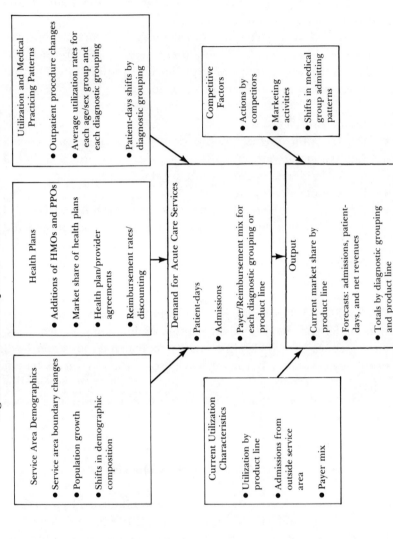

Utilization and Medical Practicing Patterns
● Outpatient procedure changes
● Average utilization rates for each age/sex group and each diagnostic grouping
● Patient-days shifts by diagnostic grouping

Competitive Factors
● Actions by competitors
● Marketing activities
● Shifts in medical group admitting patterns

Health Plans
● Additions of HMOs and PPOs
● Market share of health plans
● Health plan/provider agreements
● Reimbursement rates/ discounting

Service Area Demographics
● Service area boundary changes
● Population growth
● Shifts in demographic composition

Demand for Acute Care Services
● Patient-days
● Admissions
● Payer/Reimbursement mix for each diagnostic grouping or product line

Output
● Current market share by product line
● Forecasts: admissions, patient-days, and net revenues
● Totals by diagnostic grouping and product line

Current Utilization Characteristics
● Utilization by product line
● Admissions from outside service area
● Payer mix

Examples from Other Industries. In banking, demand for financial services is most often measured in terms of deposits; the theory is (and it usually works) that if a bank has the funds, it can lend them out in the form of consumer, agricultural, commercial, or real estate loans. Bank earnings come primarily from three sources—interest earned on loans, interest earned on investments, and service charges. Expenses result from labor (about one-third of total expenses), interest paid to depositors (another big expense item), and overhead (occupancy costs, utilities, marketing).

Most new banks are started with at least $1.5 to $2.0 million in capital. A successful bank will break even during its second year and earn a significant profit in its third year; regulators consider economically feasible a bank that looks likely to achieve this level of performance. Investors usually look at it differently; they expect a 15 to 20 percent after-tax return on their investment.

The cellular radio-telephone example cited previously is similar, in that demand estimates are the first element in developing an economic feasibility model. With cellular systems, operating costs include marketing and sales (major cost factors), service, staffing, and administration. Investment—usually $8 million to $20 million for a cellular system in a metropolitan area—goes to cover start-up costs, transmission and receiving equipment, computers, and related telecommunications requirements. The dollars associated with these items are modeled, and the FCC and potential investors can proceed with an adequate understanding of potential returns and risks.

Examples in Health Care. We were asked to evaluate the economic feasibility of a $28 million regional diagnostic center to be located in southeastern Denver. The proposed center was being sponsored by a major specialty hospital in combination with private investors, a real estate developer, and two large equipment suppliers, IBM and General Electric. In addition to imaging (CAT scan, MRI, and others), the center was to provide a wide range of outpatient services; it would have a medical staff in excess of 100 physicians.

On the demand side, the services fell into many categories, such as outpatient surgery, urgent care center, CAT scan, laboratory, and birthing center, each with different market areas. Potential demand and competition for each of these services was estimated, both currently and projected to 1990.

Operating costs were estimated, using data from a variety of sources including the developer (occupancy costs), hospital representatives (labor costs, supplies), and published sources. When these data were combined with revenue estimates, cash flow was found to be inadequate to service the anticipated $20 million debt. Pro forma projections five and ten years into the future indicated that the center would not achieve a break-even volume of business. The project was terminated.

In another example, the economic feasibility of a hospital investing $2.5 million in a magnetic resonator (MRI) was assessed. In terms of economic feasibility, the model projected a loss for the first four years (after interest on the debt and depreciation), with profitable operations beginning in the fifth year; by the tenth year, annual profits were projected to be $561,000. Based on these estimates, the return on investment was estimated at 12 percent.

In this case, however, the economic feasibility study represented only one consideration in the decision-making process. The likely impact on the medical staff represented an additional important concern. Furthermore, the potential for a large number of other MRIs in the state suggested that the project was high-risk. The potential 12 percent return looked small when weighed against the various risk factors.

In a third example, the economic feasibility of three different proposals for an outpatient surgery unit at a Catholic hospital were compared. One alternative was a freestanding unit; the other two proposals were for in-hospital units but involved different considerations (special ORs versus existing ORs, transportation of patients, patient convenience and access).

In this example, three focus group interviews with physicians in surgically oriented specialties led to the immediate disposition of the freestanding alternative. The doctors were strongly opposed to this concept because of inconvenience, concerns over quality of care, and excess OR capacity in the hospital.

Two economic feasibility models were used to analyze the remaining alternatives. The investment required for one alternative was estimated to be $700,000; the other required $900,000. As it turned out, the model showed that both alternatives would break even in five years and that both were marginally feasible. The recommendation, favoring the alternative using existing ORs, was strongly influenced by the physicians' preferences in the focus group discussions.

In summary, economic feasibility analysis is an important tool in nearly every U.S. industry and is now coming into more widespread use in health care. The keys to sophisticated analysis are realistic demand estimates and an analytical framework that considers a large number of variables in deciding whether or not the expected return on investment is adequate.

Economic Impact Models

Economic impact models have been refined and are heavily used in a number of industries; there have been only a limited number of applications in health care.

Examples from Other Industries. For an electric utility headquartered in Oregon, the social and economic impact of a large, coal-fired power plant on a small city in Wyoming were assessed. Factors considered were the number of construction and permanent employees, increases in the property tax base, additional housing and public services required (school classrooms, police officers, social workers), and related factors. The results indicated that, on balance and over the long term, the Wyoming community would benefit from this new source of industrial activity. The economic impact of a private university on the Denver area economy was calculated through an economic impact model. Economic factors included the number of full-time jobs, size of payroll, student expenditures, research contracts received, and local purchases. The university used the results to show potential donors the importance of the institution to the community.

Examples in Health Care. A university hospital gathered data on its 4,000 employees, their earnings, the $15 million in research grants funded by the federal government, the indigent care provided, local purchases of supplies and equipment, and other economic factors in order to demonstrate to the state legislature and to potential private donors its economic impact. The economic impact study also reflected the cumulative economic impact of a number of small businesses that were spinoffs from the hospital. We are aware of other hospitals that have engaged in this type of economic analysis, primarily to demonstrate their importance to the community in which they are located.

In 1986, VHA released a report assessing its value to its shareholders (Novak, 1986). The study on which the report was based found that shareholders had invested $6.2 million in VHA stock; another $51 million was raised by VHA Enterprises. The study also showed that shareholders have realized $230 million in savings, $23 million in additional patient revenues, and $20 million in stock appreciation, for a total of $273 million. We expect this sort of economic analysis to become increasingly common and more sophisticated in the health care industry.

Econometric Modeling

Econometrics is "the science of model building [that] consists of a set of tools, most of them quantitative, which are used to construct and then test mathematical representations of portions of the real world" (Pindyck and Rubinfeld, 1976, p. xi). The types of models the authors refer to include multiple regression and Box-Jenkins time series analysis. The authors go on to define three types of models: time series models, single equation regression models, and multiequation simulation models. These models, as esoteric as they sound, are being commonly applied to market and economic problems in a variety of industries, including health care; the results have been valuable.

Examples from Other Industries. Development of a regression model allowed a major sports league to predict attendance at specific games. Variables used in developing the model included day of the week, records of home and visiting teams, presence of a superstar, and whether the game was televised locally. (The initial purpose of the model was to help value television rights for home games.)

Development of a model allowed one metropolitan water system to predict future water consumption. Variables included rainfall, size of residential lots, proportion of multifamily housing, presence of water meters, price, and other factors. This model is being used for major public policy decision making involving capital expenditures in the hundreds of millions of dollars.

Examples in Health Care. It is possible to develop an econometric model that will more accurately predict length of stay for each DRG. Data available from medical records can identify the factors (for example, age, sex, severity of illness, prior medical history, day of week, and time of admission) that influence length of stay for each DRG. In this way, the performance of the medical staff can be more accurately monitored. The physician who tends to have patients with longer hospital stays will typically say, "I get sicker patients, more complex cases." Econometric modeling can help formulate an appropriate response.

The econometric model is also useful in in-depth analysis of market research results. A recent survey identified the percentage of consumers, physicians, and employers interested in a new type of health plan contemplated by a national health care system. Through use of discriminant analysis (another econometric technique), the system was able to identify characteristics of likely customers for this new plan. This information was used in developing a marketing strategy.

Box-Jenkins analysis, another econometric model, is being used by hospitals for monthly forecasting of key indicators. It is applied to variables such as hospital admissions, patient-days, and out-patient visits. This technique is especially applicable where there are significant long- and short-term trends, including seasonal variations, as there are in most health care markets. Figure B.2 shows actual admissions versus Box-Jenkins projections for a 320-bed acute care hospital.

Figure B.2. Actual Versus Projected Admissions for 1985,
Denver Area Acute Care Hospital

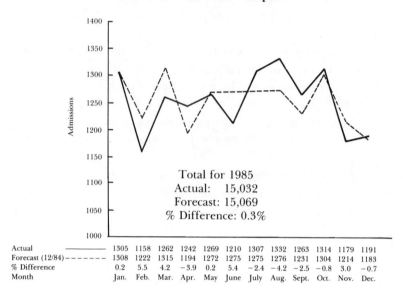

Total for 1985
Actual: 15,032
Forecast: 15,069
% Difference: 0.3%

	Jan.	Feb.	Mar.	Apr.	May	June	July	Aug.	Sept.	Oct.	Nov.	Dec.
Actual	1305	1158	1262	1242	1269	1210	1307	1332	1263	1314	1179	1191
Forecast (12/84)	1308	1222	1315	1194	1272	1275	1275	1276	1231	1304	1214	1183
% Difference	0.2	5.5	4.2	−3.9	0.2	5.4	−2.4	−4.2	−2.5	−0.8	3.0	−0.7
Month	Jan.	Feb.	Mar.	Apr.	May	June	July	Aug.	Sept.	Oct.	Nov.	Dec.

Other Box-Jenkins applications in the health care industry include:

- *Personnel scheduling.* Since the methodology produces extremely reliable results on a monthly basis, it can be used to plan staffing levels.
- *Budgeting.* The starting point for developing a hospital budget is a one-year projection of admissions, patient-days, and outpatient visits. Use of this technique provides an objective basis for realistic volume projections for the coming fiscal year.
- *Incentive compensation.* Some not-for-profit hospitals have incentive compensation (bonus) programs for management. One factor often considered in allocating bonuses is how well the hospital performed vis-à-vis the Box-Jenkins forecasts prepared at the beginning of the year.

Economic Modeling and Resource Allocation Decisions

Because of its size and complexity, the health care industry lends itself to economic and statistical modeling. In fact, several industry characteristics (for example, large numbers of transactions, predictable but difficult to identify usage patterns, a large epidemiological data base, huge capital requirements, a governance structure requiring careful, objective analysis in support of the decision-making process) suggest that economic and statistical modeling will be adopted at a very rapid rate over the next few years.

The costs of developing and using sophisticated modeling are small relative to the importance of the decisions being made. The advent of the personal computer, ready availability of software, and a pool of trained personnel from other industries all work in favor of rapid changes in this area of health care management and decision support.

The biggest barrier to widespread usage of these techniques is the lack of trained, experienced in-house staff. Most small to midsized hospitals do not have the staff necessary to perform economic and statistical analysis. Help is available, of course, from the numerous accounting and management consulting firms eagerly seeking to serve the health care industry. Larger hospitals and multihospital systems very often have this capability in-house.

Economic models are not a substitute for experienced decision making by health care professionals, hospital managers, and trustees. Such models do, however, represent a way of better understanding relevant economic forces and associated strategic implications. Those decision makers who combine economic and statistical analysis and modeling with their own experience and "feel" for the market will definitely gain a competitive advantage.

References

Abramowitz, K. S. *The Future of Health Care Delivery in America.* New York: Sanford C. Bernstein, 1985.

Alexander, J., and Brooks, D. C. "New Dimensions in Board-CEO Relations." *Trustee,* 1986, *39* (6), 24-27.

Alex. Brown & Sons, Inc. "HMOs, Insurance Companies and Hospitals: New Products and New Partners." Baltimore, Md.: Alex. Brown & Sons, 1986. (Duplicated.)

"Alliances Need Members' Support." *Modern Healthcare,* 1985, *15* (24), 5.

American Healthcare Systems. "The Positive Alternative for Not-for-Profit Hospitals." San Diego, Calif.: American Healthcare Systems, 1986. (Duplicated.)

American Hospital Association. *Directory of Multihospital Systems.* (4th ed.) Chicago: American Hospital Association, 1984.

American Hospital Association. *Data Book on Multihospital Systems 1980-1985.* Chicago: American Hospital Association, 1985.

American Hospital Association. "Credit Concerns in the Health Care Industry: Real and Perceived." *Hospital Capital Finance,* 1986a, *3* (2), 2-4.

American Hospital Association. "Growth of Convenience Clinics Questioned." *Outreach*, 1986b, *7* (1), 2.

American Medical Association. *Physician Characteristics and Distribution in the United States*. Chicago: American Medical Association, 1984.

American Medical International. "1985 Annual Report." Beverly Hills, Calif.: American Medical International, 1985. (Duplicated.)

Anderson, H. J. "19 Catholic Hospital Systems Form Alliance to Develop New Services." *Modern Healthcare*, 1985, *15* (17), 22.

Anderson, H. J. "Common Heritage Will Help Alliance Build Consensus, Avoid Conflicts." *Modern Healthcare*, 1986a, *16* (11), 42.

Anderson, H. J. "Largest Not-for-Profit System Forming." *Modern Healthcare*, 1986b, *16* (15), 22.

Arnett, R. H., Cowell, C. S., Davidoff, L. M., and Freeland, M. S. "Health Spending Trends in the 1980's: Adjusting to Financial Incentives." *Health Care Financing Review, 6* (3), 1–26.

Arthur Andersen & Co. and American College of Hospital Administrators. "Health Care in the 1990's: Trends and Strategies." Chicago: Arthur Andersen & Co., 1984. (Duplicated.)

Averill, R. A., and Kalison, M. J. "Present and Future: Predictions for the Healthcare Industry." *Healthcare Financial Management*, 1986, *40* (3), 50–54.

Barkholz, D. "VHA Hoping Deals Will Create Its 'Brand' of National Healthcare." *Modern Healthcare*, 1985, *15* (14), 82–86.

Bellhouse, D. E., and DeVries, R. A. "Four Approaches to Cost Consciousness-Raising." *Trustee*, 1986, *39* (4), 19–21.

Bhide, A. "Hustle as Strategy." *Harvard Business Review*, 1986, *64* (5), 59–65.

Boland, P. (ed.). *The New Healthcare Market: A Guide to PPOs for Purchasers, Payers and Providers*. Homewood, Ill.: Dow Jones-Irwin, 1985.

Booz-Allen & Hamilton Inc. "Comparative Economic Performance Among Tennessee's Proprietary and Not-for-Profit Hospital Sectors: Final Report." Atlanta, Ga.: Booz-Allen & Hamilton, 1984. (Duplicated.)

Brink, C. P. "Erisa vs. State Laws." *Minneapolis/St. Paul City Business,* May 28, 1986, pp. 28-30.

Buzzell, R. D. "Is Vertical Integration Profitable?" *Harvard Business Review,* 1983, *61* (1), 92-102.

Califano, J. *America's Healthcare Revolution: Who Lives? Who Dies? Who Pays?* New York: Random House, 1986.

Castro, J., Delaney, P., and Dolan, B. "Pinned Down by Medical Bills." *Time,* June 30, 1986, pp. 64-65.

Center for Health Management Research. "Forecast '87." Los Angeles: LHS Corp., 1986. (Duplicated.)

"CHA President: The For-Profit Threat Is a Myth." *Health Care Competition Week,* 1986, *3* (14), 7-8.

Coddington, D. C., Palmquist, L. E., and Trollinger, W. V. "Strategies for Survival in the Hospital Industry." *Harvard Business Review,* 1985, *63* (3), 129-138.

Coddington, D. C., and Pottle, J. T. "Hospital Diversification Strategies: Lessons from Other Industries." *Health Care Financial Management,* 1984, *14* (12), 18-24.

Coddington, D. C., and Steiker, A. B. "New Tools for Healthcare Decision-Making." *Healthcare Forum,* 1986, *29* (5), 25-27.

Coddington, D. C., and White, S. S. "What Physicians Expect from Their Hospitals." *Trustee,* 1986, *39* (7), 11-13.

Cohodes, D. R., and Kinkead, B. M. *Hospital Capital Formation in the 1980's.* Baltimore, Md.: Johns Hopkins University Press, 1984.

Coile, R. C., Jr. *The New Hospital: Future Strategies for a Changing Industry.* Rockville, Md.: Aspen, 1986.

Congressional Budget Office. *Physician Reimbursement Under Medicare: Options for Change.* Washington, D.C.: Government Printing Office, 1986.

Cooper, P. D. (ed.). *Health Care Marketing: Issues and Trends.* Rockville, Md.: Aspen, 1985.

Coopers & Lybrand. *1983 Group Medical Plan Cost Survey.* New York: Coopers & Lybrand, 1983.

Copeland, S. "Marketing: In Pursuit of Patients." *Ambulatory Care,* 1986, *6* (5), 8-15.

"The Corporate Transformation of Medicine in Minnesota: First of a Series: The Accelerating Industrialization of Health Care in the Twin Cities." *Minnesota Medicine*, 1983, pp. 667-676.

Council on Long-Range Planning and Development. *The Environment of Medicine.* Chicago: American Medical Association, 1985.

Crowley, A. E., Etzel, S. I., and Peterson, E. S. "Undergraduate Medical Education." *Journal of American Medical Association*, 1985, *254* (12), 1565-1572.

Deveny, K., and Power, C. "How Humana Got a Painful Black Eye." *Business Week*, July 21, 1986, p. 108.

Doherty, V., O'Donovan, T., and O'Donovan, P. "Downsizing Hospital Capacity." *Health Care Strategic Management*, 1986, *4* (4), 4-7.

Doody, M. F. *Fact Sheet.* Westchester, Ill.: Consolidated Catholic Health Care, 1986.

Dreuth, D. R. *The Corporation of Health Care Delivery: The Hospital-Physician Relationship.* Chicago: American Hospital Association, 1986.

Dychtwald, K. "The Senior Boom." *Hospital Forum*, 1985, *28* (3), 63-66.

Eisele, C. W., Fifer, W. R., and Wilson, T. C. *The Medical Staff and the Modern Hospital.* Englewood, Colo.: Estes Park Institute, 1985.

"Ellwood Says 'Supermed' Concept Gaining Ground, Expects Up to 10 Within a Decade." *Medical Benefits*, 1986, *3* (9), 9-11.

Fackelmann, K. A. "Nursing Home Crunch to Hit Hospitals Soon." *Modern Healthcare*, 1984, *14* (15), 42-46.

Feldstein, M. *Hospital Costs and Health Insurance.* Cambridge, Mass.: Harvard University Press, 1981.

Fine, M. "Bargaining for Health Benefits: Unions and Employers Can Cut Costs." In P. Boland (ed.), *The New Healthcare Market.* Homewood, Ill.: Dow Jones-Irwin, 1985.

Fink, R. "Is Working Nights Worth It?" *Medical Economics*, Mar. 18, 1985, p. 73.

Fox, P. D., and Anderson, M. D. "Hybrid HMOs, PPOs: The New Focus." *Business and Health*, 1986, *3* (4), 20-27.

Fox, P. D., Heihen, L., and Steele, R. J. "Determinants of HMO

Success." Washington, D.C.: Lewin and Associates, 1986. (Duplicated.)

Franz, J. "Peoria Hospital Cries 'Antitrust' as Rival Signs Preferred Provider Pact." *Modern Healthcare,* 1984, *14* (13), 94-95.

Fruen, M. A., and DiPrete, H. A. "Health Care in the Future." Boston: John Hancock Mutual Life Insurance Company, 1986.

Geisel, J. "Revenues Boom for 10 Largest Consultants." *Business Insurance,* 1985, *19* (51), 3.

Gertman, P., and Lowenstein, S. "A Research Paradigm for Severity of Illness: Issues for Diagnosis-Related Group System." *Healthcare Financing Review,* 1984 Annual Supplement, pp. 79-90.

Gilbert, R. N. "Hospital Revenue Diversification: A Case Study in Joint Venture Investing." *Healthcare Financial Management,* 1986, *40* (4), 46-52.

Ginzberg, E. "The Destabilization of Health Care." *The New England Journal of Medicine,* 1986, *315* (12), 757-761.

Goldsmith, J. C. "The Health Care Market: Can Hospitals Survive?" *Harvard Business Review,* 1980, *58* (5), 100-112.

Goldsmith, J. C. *Can Hospitals Survive? The New Competitive Health Care Market.* Homewood, Ill.: Dow Jones–Irwin, 1981.

Hall, J. B. "HMO Insurance Plans Face Some Threats to Own Good Health." *Wall Street Journal,* Jan. 16, 1986, pp. 1, 14.

Hayes, R. H. "Strategic Planning—Forward in Reverse?" *Harvard Business Review,* 1985, *63* (6), 111-119.

Health Care Financing Administration. *Medical Data.* Washington, D.C.: Government Printing Office, 1985.

"Health-Care Spending's Share of GNP Reaches a New High." *Medical Benefits,* 1986, *3* (16), 1-2.

Health Central System. *The Restructuring Health Industry: Progress Through Partnerships.* Minneapolis, Minn.: Health Central System, 1984.

HealthWest Foundation. "1985 Annual Report." Chatsworth, Calif.: HealthWest, 1985. (Duplicated.)

Herzlinger, R. E. "How Companies Tackle Healthcare Costs: Part II." *Harvard Business Review,* 1985, *63* (5), 108-120.

Herzlinger, R. E., and Calkins, D. "How Companies Tackle Health Care Costs: Part III." *Harvard Business Review*, 1986, *64* (1), 70–80.

Herzlinger, R. E., and Schwartz, J. "How Companies Tackle Health Care Costs: Part I." *Harvard Business Review*, 1985, *63* (4), 69–80.

Hillestad, S. G., and Berkowitz, E. N. *Health Care Marketing Plans: From Strategy to Action.* Homewood, Ill.: Dow Jones-Irwin, 1984.

"HMOs and Hospitals: An Update." Paper presented at Executive Forum 1986 by L. D. Schaeffer, sponsored by Witt Associates, Chicago, Feb. 13, 1986.

Hoart, H. "Survival of the Fittest: Hospitals Must Act Now." *Healthcare Competition Week*, 1986, *3* (14), 7–8.

Horn, S. D., Horn, A., and Sharkey, P. D. "The Severity of Illness Index as a Severity Adjustment to Diagnosis-Related Groups." *Health Care Financing Review*, 1984, pp. 33–45.

Horty, J. "Changing Hospital Law and the Future of the Medical Staff." Paper presented at Estes Park Institute seminar in Maui, Hawaii, Jan. 27, 1986.

Hospital Corporation of America. "1985 Annual Report." Nashville, Tenn.: Hospital Corporation of America, 1986. (Duplicated.)

Hospital Statistics. Chicago: American Hospital Association, 1986.

Hull, J. B. "Physicians Organize to Stop HMO's from Altering Practice of Medicine." *Wall Street Journal*, June 23, 1986, p. 25.

Humana, Inc. "1985 Annual Report." Louisville, Ky.: Humana, 1985. (Duplicated.)

Hunt, M. "Managed Care in the 1990s." *Health Care Strategic Management*, 1985, *3* (12), 20–24.

Ignagni, K. "Can Workers Afford PPOs?" In P. Boland (ed.), *The New Healthcare Market.* Homewood, Ill.: Dow Jones–Irwin, 1985.

Inglehart, J. K. "The Future Supply of Physicians." *The New England Journal of Medicine*, 1986a, *314* (13), 860–864.

Inglehart, J. K. "Canada's Health Care System." *The New England Journal of Medicine*, 1986b, *315* (12), 778–784.

Inguanzo, J. M., and Harju, M. "Are Consumers Sensitive to Hospital Costs?" *Hospitals*, 1985a, *59* (3), 68–69.

Inguanzo, J. M., and Harju, M. "What Makes a Consumer Select a Hospital?" *Hospitals*, 1985b, *59* (6), 90–94.

"Integrating Catholic Values and Business Survival Strategies." *Health Progress*, 1986, *67* (3), 18–22.

Intermountain Health Care, Inc. "1985 Annual Report." Salt Lake City, Utah: Intermountain Health Care, 1986. (Duplicated.)

InterStudy. *National HMO Census: June 30, 1981*. Excelsior, Minn.: InterStudy, 1982.

InterStudy. *National HMO Census: June 30, 1982*. Excelsior, Minn.: InterStudy, 1983.

InterStudy. *National HMO Census: June 30, 1983*. Excelsior, Minn.: InterStudy, 1984.

InterStudy. *National HMO Census 1984*. Excelsior, Minn.: InterStudy, 1985a.

InterStudy. *HMO Summary June 1985*. Excelsior, Minn.: Inter-Study, 1985b.

Jackson, B., and Jensen, J. "21 Percent Lack Regular Family Physician: More Men, Youth in Untapped Market." *Modern Healthcare*, 1984, *14* (10), 72–76.

Jackson, B., and Jensen, J. "Extended Hours for Physicians' Services Is at the Top of Consumers' Wish List." *Modern Healthcare*, 1985a, *15* (9), 84–86.

Jackson, B., and Jensen, J. "More Consumers Have Physicians, Few Say They Have Switched Doctors." *Modern Healthcare*, 1985b, *15* (12), 68–70.

Jackson, B., and Jensen, J. "Hospital Emergency Departments Are Attracting Fewer Patients." *Modern Healthcare*, 1985c, *15* (13), 46–50.

Jensen, J. "Advertising Helps More Consumers Select Hospitals." *Modern Healthcare*, 1985a, *15* (6), 58–60.

Jensen, J. "Ads Help Consumers Recall Hospital; Direct Mail Is Favored Ad Method." *Modern Healthcare*, 1985b, *15* (7), 96–98.

Jensen, J. "Consumers Want Hospitals to Include Price of Services in Advertisements." *Modern Healthcare*, 1985c, *15* (8), 48–50.

Jensen, J. "Women Pick the Provider Who Treats Their Illnesses, Those of Their Children." *Modern Healthcare*, 1986, *16* (10), 66–67.

Jensen, J., and Miklovic, N. "Consumer Satisfaction with Physicians Is High." *Modern Healthcare,* 1986, *16* (3), 60–63.

Johnson, E. A., and Johnson, R. L. *Hospitals Under Fire: Strategies for Survival.* Rockville, Md.: Aspen, 1986.

Kaiser, L. "Dramatic Changes to Impact Medical Practice in 5 Years." Paper presented at Estes Park Institute seminar in Maui, Hawaii, Jan. 27, 1986.

Laubach, P. B., Rand, R. L., and Laubach, C. L. *Survival Strategies for the 1990's.* Chicago: Foundation of the American College of Hospital Administrators, 1984.

Levitt, T. *The Marketing Imagination.* New York: Free Press, 1983.

Louis Harris and Associates, Inc. "American Attitudes Toward Health Maintenance Organizations." New York: Louis Harris and Associates, 1980. (Duplicated.)

Louis Harris and Associates, Inc. *A Report Card on HMOs: 1980– 1984 Summary Report.* New York: Louis Harris and Associates, 1984.

Louis Harris and Associates, Inc. "The Equitable Healthcare Survey: Options for Controlling Costs." New York: Louis Harris and Associates, 1985. (Duplicated.)

McCarthy, S. M. "The Nursing Challenge: Downsizing Without Layoffs." *Hospitals,* 1986, *60* (4), 120.

McMillian, N. H. *Marketing Your Hospital: A Strategy for Survival.* Chicago: American Hospital Association, 1981.

McNerney, W. J. (ed.). *For-Profit Enterprise in Health Care.* Washington, D.C.: National Academy Press, 1986.

Maddrell, P. D., and Rahn, G. J. *HMO/PPO Selective Contracting Issues for Hospitals.* Chicago: American Hospital Association, 1985.

Magill, J. R., and Scheuerman, J. L. " 'Baby Boomers' a Ripe Market for Healthcare Providers: A Study." *Modern Healthcare,* 1985, *15* (7), 128–132.

Mannisto, M. M. "Multis' Delicate Balancing Act: Corporate Goals and Local Board Autonomy." *Trustee,* 1984, *37* (11), 17– 22.

Mantel, B. "Increased Competition, Changing Demographics

Make Health Care Institutions Rethink Their Bottom Lines." *Journal of Accountancy,* 1986, *162* (3), 70–77.

MarketPULSE Measurement Systems. "Fortune 500 Healthcare Delivery." Indianapolis: Walker Research, 1985. (Duplicated.)

"Medical Benefits Costs and Their Management in Small to Mid-Sized Organizations." *Medical Benefits,* 1985, *2* (16), 10–11.

Medical Practice in the United States. Princeton, N.J.: Robert Wood Johnson Foundation, 1981.

Meighan, S. "Medical Staff, Board and Administration Relationships Must Change." *The Hospital Medical Staff,* 1984, 9–14.

Mercer-Meidinger. "Employer Attitudes Toward the Cost of Health." New York: Mercer-Meidinger, 1985. (Duplicated.)

Merrill Lynch Capital Markets. "Orange County Health Facilities Authority, Hospital Revenue Bonds, Series 1985, Orlando Regional Medical Center Project Official Statement." New York: Merrill Lynch Capital Markets, 1985. (Duplicated.)

Miller, I. *The Health Care Survival Curve: Competition and Cooperation in the Marketplace.* Homewood, Ill.: Dow Jones-Irwin, 1984.

Moore, M. "Blues Forming National Data Base." *Healthcare Competition Week,* 1985, *3* (14), 3.

Moore, M. "Silicon Valley Group Tries New Experiment." *Healthcare Competition Week,* 1986, *3* (20), 1–2.

Mott, B.J.F. "Four Critical Areas in Governance." *Trustee,* 1984, *37* (9), 41–47.

National Conference of State Legislatures. "What Legislators Need to Know About Health Data/Cost Information Programs." Denver, Colo.: National Conference of State Legislatures, 1986. (Duplicated.)

National Medical Enterprises, Inc. "1985 Annual Report." Los Angeles: National Medical Enterprises, 1985. (Duplicated.)

Needleman, J., and Derzon, R. A. "Milwaukee's Approach to Excess Hospital Capacity." *Business and Health,* 1986, *3* (9), 41–46.

Nelson, W. "Cost Not the Only Consideration in Health Care." *Minneapolis/St. Paul City Business,* May 28, 1986a, pp. 24–26.

Nelson, W. "Nurses' Strike Marked the End of an Era." *Minneapolis/St. Paul City Business,* May 28, 1986b, pp. 22–24.

"New Bill May Give Hospitals Headaches." *Health Care Competition Week,* 1986, *3* (36), 1–10.

"New Catholic Alliance Names CEO." *Modern Healthcare,* 1986, *16* (2), 20.

"New York Hospitals Decertify 2,000 Alternate Care Beds." *Modern Healthcare,* 1986, *16* (5), 12–14.

Nielsen, A. C. "1986 Nielsen Report." Northbrook, Ill.: A. C. Nielsen Company, 1986. (Duplicated.)

Nierenberg, G. I. *The Art of Creative Thinking.* New York: Simon & Schuster, 1982.

Nimer, D. A. "Nimer on Pricing: Meet the Competition? Why Should I?" *Healthcare Forum,* 1986, *29* (4), 23–24.

"NME-Established REIT Gets $77.2 Million in Offering." *Modern Healthcare,* 1986, *16* (9), 65.

Novak, D. *The Value of VHA.* Irving, Tex.: Voluntary Hospitals of America, 1986.

Office of Health Studies and Economic Review, Arizona Department of Health Services. *A Summary of a Study of the Impact of Deregulation on Health Facilities in Arizona.* Phoenix: Arizona Department of Health Services, 1985.

Office of Technology Assessment, U.S. Congress. *Compilation of Responses to 1984/1985 Survey on Future Health Technology.* Washington, D.C.: Government Printing Office, 1985.

Oncken, W., and Wass, D. L. "Management Time: Who's Got the Monkey?" *Harvard Business Review,* 1974, *54* (6), 80.

Orange County Health Planning Council. "A Hospital's IQ: Indicators of Quality, A Study." Tustin, Calif.: Orange County Health Planning Council, 1985. (Duplicated.)

Orlando Regional Medical Center. "1985 Annual Report." Orlando, Fla.: Orlando Regional Medical Center, 1985. (Duplicated.)

Peters, J. P., and Tseng, S. *Managing Strategic Change in Hospitals: Ten Success Stories.* Chicago: American Hospital Association, 1983.

Peters, T. J., and Austin, N. K. *A Passion for Excellence: The Leadership Difference.* New York: Random House. 1985.

Peters, T. J., and Waterman, R. H. *In Search of Excellence: Lessons from America's Best-Run Companies.* New York: Harper & Row, 1982.

Pindyck, R. S., and Rubinfeld, D. L. *Econometric Models and Economic Forecasts.* New York: McGraw-Hill, 1976.

Plant, J. "Who's on First? Making the Transition to a Multiple-Board Structure." *Trustee,* 1985, *38* (8), 19-22.

Porter, M. *Competitive Advantage: Creating and Sustaining Superior Performance.* New York: Free Press, 1985.

Powills, S. "Hospitals Call a Marketing Time-Out." *Hospitals,* 1986, *60* (11), 50-55.

Public Relations Division, Health Insurance Association of America. *Source Book of Health Insurance Data 1984-1985.* Washington, D.C.: Health Insurance Association of America, 1985.

Relman, A. "Dealing with Conflicts of Interest." *The New England Journal of Medicine,* 1985, *313* (12), 749-750.

Reynolds, R. A., Ohsfedt, R. L., and Pieniazek, D. *Socioeconomic Characteristics of Medical Practice.* Chicago: American Medical Association, 1985.

Riche, M. F. "The Nursing Home Dilemma." *American Demographics,* 1985, *7* (10), 34-39.

Richter, T. B. *Gone with the Wind: An Analysis of the Past, Present and Future of the U.S. Health-Care Delivery System.* New York: Morgan Stanley, 1986.

Ries, A., and Trout, J. *Positioning: The Battle for Your Mind.* New York: Warner Books, 1981.

Robson, B. "Is Competitive Medicine Good for Your Health?" *Minneapolis/St. Paul Magazine,* 1986, pp. 69-80, 102-109.

Rosenfield, R. H. "Legal Issues in Joing Venturing." Paper presented at American Hospital Association Conference, Hilton Head, S.C., May 15, 1986.

Rundle, R. L. "REITS Flourish in Health Care Industry: Changing Financial Picture Spurs Popularity." *Wall Street Journal,* Aug. 27, 1986a, p. 6.

Rundle, R. L. "Some Firms Force Employees into HMOs and So Far Workers Don't Seem to Mind." *Wall Street Journal,* October 2, 1986b, p. 29.

Russell, J. A., and Ebner, G. H. "Adapting to a 1980's Style of Governance." *Trustee,* 1985, *38* (11), 29-31.

Rynne, S. "On the Women's Health Care Market." Paper presented at the Western Conference of the Foundation of the American College of Healthcare Executives, Phoenix, Ariz., Nov. 19, 1985.

Sandrick, K. "Predictions About the Future of Capital Financing." *Trustee,* 1986, *39* (6), 19–23.

Sawyer, D., Ruther, M., Pagan-Berlucchi, A., and Muse, D. *The Medicare and Medicaid Data Book, 1983.* Washington, D.C.: Government Printing Office, 1983.

Schaeffer, L. D. *HMOs and Hospitals: An Update.* Oak Brook, Ill.: Witt Associates, 1986.

Schlesinger, E. S. "The Health Insurance Product of the 1990s." Boston: Boston Consulting Group, 1985.

Schutte, J. E. "Hell Will Freeze Before I Take a Medicare Assignment." *Medical Economics,* 1985, *62* (12), 68–71.

Shahoda, T. "Alliances Move Too Slowly on Insurance: Members." *Hospitals,* 1986, *60* (9), 57–60.

Sheldon, A., and Windham, S. *Competitive Strategy for Health Care Organizations: Techniques for Strategic Action.* Homewood, Ill.: Dow Jones–Irwin, 1984.

Shortell, S. M., Wickizer, T. M., and Wheeler, J. R. *Hospital-Physician Joint Ventures: Results and Lessons from a National Demonstration in Primary Care.* Ann Arbor, Mich.: Health Administration Press, 1984.

Smith, H. L., and Reid, R. A. *Competitive Hospitals: Management Strategies.* Rockville, Md.: Aspen, 1986.

Snowmass Institute. "Organizing a Women's Health Program Overview." Paper presented at a symposium, "Marketing Health Services to Women," Denver, Colo., Sept. 12–13, 1985.

Starr, P. *The Social Transformation of American Medicine.* New York: Basic Books, 1982.

Steinwachs, D. M., and others. "A Comparison of the Requirements for Primary Care Physicians in HMO's with Projections Made by the GMENAC." *New England Journal of Medicine,* 1986, *314* (4), 217-222.

SunHealth, Inc. "1985 Annual Report." Charlotte, N.C.: SunHealth, 1986. (Duplicated.)

Super, K. E. "Hospitals Build Medical Malls in Hopes 'One-Stop' Concept Will Draw Patients." *Modern Healthcare,* 1986, *16* (9), 58.

Tatge, M. "HMO Enrollment Up 26.7% to 1.68 Million." *Modern Healthcare,* 1985, *15* (12), 138–141.

"Tax Reform Ails Not-for-Profit Hospitals." *Standard & Poor's Credit Week,* May 5, 1986, p. 15.

Temple, Barker, & Sloane, Inc. *Third Party Administrators: An Industry in Transition.* Lexington, Mass.: Temple, Barker, & Sloane, 1985.

Tibbitts, S. J., and Manzano, A. J. *PPOs: An Executive's Guide.* Chicago: Pluribus Press, 1984.

Touche Ross & Co. *U.S. Hospitals: The Next Five Years.* New York: Touche Ross, 1986.

Traska, M. R. "Something Good About Tax Reform? Yes—For Leasing." *Hospitals,* 1986, *60* (8), 56.

Trout, J. "Positioning—The Battle for Your Mind." Paper presented at Estes Park Institute seminar in Kauai, Hawaii, 1981.

"Understanding the Hospital Market . . . and Making It Work." *Employer's Health Benefits Newsletter,* Mar. 1985, pp. 1–6.

U.S. Bureau of the Census. *County Business Patterns, 1983, United States.* Washington, D.C.: Government Printing Office, 1985a.

U.S. Bureau of the Census, *Statistical Abstract of the United States: 1986.* Washington, D.C.: Government Printing Office, 1985b.

U.S. Department of Commerce. *1986 U.S. Industrial Outlook.* Washington, D.C.: Government Printing Office, 1986.

U.S. Department of Health and Human Services. *National HMO Census of Prepaid Plans.* Washington, D.C.: Government Printing Office, 1980a.

U.S. Department of Health and Human Services. *The National Ambulatory Medical Care Survey, United States, 1979 Summary.* Washington, D.C.: Government Printing Office, 1980b.

U.S. Department of Health and Human Services. *Health United States, 1985.* Washington, D.C.: Government Printing Office, 1985.

Van Sumeren, M. A. "Organizational Downsizing: Streamlining

the Healthcare Organization." *Healthcare Financial Management,* 1986, *40* (1), 35-39.

"Video Conference on PPO's—Don't Count on Discounts." *Health Care Competition Week,* 1986, *3* (21), 3-4.

Vignola, M. L. *Hospital Management: The Acquisition and Use of Medical Technology.* New York: Rothschild, Unterberg, Towbin, 1984.

Voluntary Hospitals of America. *Report and Recommendations of the VHA Special Task Force on Implications of Investor-Owned Hospital Systems Acquisition Strategy.* Paper presented at VHA Board of Directors Meeting, Amelia Island Plantation, Fla., March 1985a.

Voluntary Hospitals of America. *Strength Built by Design.* Irving, Tex.: Voluntary Hospitals of America, 1985b.

Voluntary Hospitals of America. *Hospital's Guide to VHA Companies & Services.* Irving, Tex.: Voluntary Hospitals of America, 1986.

Wallace, C. "Hospitals Pondering Continuing Care Must Proceed with Caution—Experts." *Modern Healthcare,* 1985, *15* (14), 79.

Wallace, C. "Common Mistakes Doom Hospitals' Efforts to Start Their Own HMOs." *Modern Healthcare,* 1986, *16* (10), 52.

Watt, J. M., Derzon, R. A., and Hahn, J. S. "Investor-Owned and Not-for-Profit Hospitals: A Second Look at Economic Performance." Washington, D.C.: Lewin and Associates, 1984. (Duplicated.)

Watt, J. M., and others. "The Comparative Economic Performance of Investor-Owned Chain and Not-for-Profit Hospitals." *The New England Journal of Medicine,* 1986, *314* (2), 89–96.

Webber, J. B., and Peters, J. P. *Strategic Thinking: New Frontier for Hospital Management.* Chicago: American Hospital Association, 1983.

Welles, J. G., Mahar, J. F., and Coddington, D. C. *The Financial Gap—Real or Imaginary.* Denver, Colo.: Denver Research Institute, 1961.

Wennberg, J., and Caper, P. "Medical Practice: Why Does It Vary So Much?" *Hospitals,* 1985, *59* (5), 88-90.

White, E. C. "Administrators Shrink Their Hospitals to Withstand

Competitive Pressures." *Modern Healthcare,* 1985, *15* (23), 66–71.

Williams, A. P., Schwartz, W. B., Newhouse, J. P., and Bennett, B. W. "How Many Miles to the Doctor?" *The New England Journal of Medicine,* 1983, *311,* 958–963.

Wotruba, T. R., Haas, R. W., and Hartman, H. W. "Targeting a Hospital's Marketing Efforts to Physicians' Needs." *Journal of Healthcare Marketing,* 1982, *2* (3), 46–56.

Yanish, D. L. "Kaiser Shifts Strategy to Retain Position in Prepaid Market Plan." *Modern Healthcare,* 1986, *16* (10), 68–70.

Index